Summa Philosophica

Summa Philosophica

By Peter Kreeft

ST. AUGUSTINE'S PRESS
South Bend, Indiana

Manufactured in the United States of America

2 3 4 5 6   18 17 16 15 14 13 12

Library of Congress Cataloging in Publication Data
Kreeft, Peter.
Summa philosophica / by Peter Kreeft.
p. cm.
Includes bibliographical references and index.
ISBN 978-1-58731-825-2 (hardbound: alk. paper)
1. Philosophy – Miscellanea. I. Title.
BD21.K73 2011
100 – dc23   2011039528

∞ The paper used in this publication meets the minimum requirements of the American National Standard for Information Sciences – Permanence of Paper for Printed Materials, ANSI Z39.48-1984.

ST. AUGUSTINE'S PRESS
www.staugustine.net

For W. Norris Clark, S.J.

Philosopher for the 21st Century

Preliminary Note

Dear prospective reader,

If you're wondering whether this book is worth your time to read or your money to buy, don't read the long, dull Introduction first. Browse through the book itself.

Contents

(NB: the subcontents are in the 11 pages that follow.)

Question I: Logic and Methodology

(Note: this is *not* the most crucial and important division of philosophy, nor is it the most interesting, nor is it even the first psychologically, but it is the first logically.)

Question II: Metaphysics

(Note: metaphysics is not a subdivision of the occult but that most fundamental division of philosophy which explores the most universal truths about all being as such, or all reality. All other issues in philosophy depend, at least implicitly, on metaphysics because what man is, or what knowledge is, or what goodness is, depends on what *is*. Metaphysics has become unfashionable due to the excesses of epistemological rationalism, the skepticism of Humean empiricism, and the even deeper skepticism of Kantianism. Therefore the first five questions concern the nature and status and justification of metaphysics itself.)

Article 1: Whether metaphysics is something esoteric, arcane, or occult?

Article 2: Whether metaphysics originates in experience?

Article 3: Whether metaphysics is a legitimate science?

Article 4: Whether metaphysics is practical?

Article 5: Whether metaphysics is unavoidable?

Article 6: Whether universals are real?

Article 7: Whether both oneness and manyness are real?

Article 8: Whether time is real?

Article 9: Whether all that is real is material?

Article 10: Whether all that is, is intelligible?

Question III: Natural Theology

(Note: once metaphysics is admitted, its two basic subdivisions naturally emerge: natural theology, the philosophical science of infinite, divine, eternal, or supernatural being, and cosmology, the philosophical science of finite, created, temporal, natural being.)

Question IV: Cosmology

Question V: Philosophical Anthropology

Question VI: Epistemology

Article 1: Whether skepticism is refutable?

Article 2: Whether truth is objective?

Article 3: Whether we know things-in-themselves?

Article 4: Whether appearance coincides with reality?

Article 5: Whether all ordinary (natural) human knowledge begins with sense experience?

Article 6: Whether there is *a priori* knowledge?

Article 7: Whether ideas are the immediate objects of knowing?

Article 8: Whether certain knowledge is possible?

Article 9: Whether the essential questions of philosophy are "mysteries"?

Article 10: Whether we can have *knowledge* of mysteries such as God, freedom, immortality, morality, and the meaning (purpose) of human life?

Question VII: General Ethics

Question VIII: Applied Ethics

Article 1: Whether there is a moral obligation to worship God?

Article 2: Whether it is immoral to worship idols?

Article 3: Whether leisure is as necessary for man as work?

Article 4: Whether family and ancestors must be revered?

Article 5: Whether private property is a natural right?

Article 6: Whether it is ever right to kill?

Article 7: Whether it is ever right to lie?

Article 8: Whether sex is sacred and not to be adulterated?

Article 9: Whether lust is evil?

Article 10: Whether greed is evil?

(The reader will note that these 10 questions happen to be answered by 10 rather famous Commandments.)

Question IX: Political Philosophy

Article 1: Whether the state is natural to man?

Article 2: Whether a good state is "one that makes it easy to be good"?

Article 3: Whether the state should have a substantive philosophy of the good life?

Article 4: Whether democracy is the best form of government?

Article 5: Whether freedom is an intrinsic good?

Article 6: Whether there is a double standard for good for states and individuals?

Article 7: Whether wars are ever just?

Article 8: Whether human law should be superior to human wills?

Article 9: Whether the principle of subsidiarity is true?

Article 10: Whether there should be a world organization of states?

Question X: Aesthetics

Article 1: Whether beauty is an objective reality?

Article 2: Whether beauty consists in harmony?

Article 3: Whether beauty is the object of love?

Article 4: Whether beauty moves us more than truth?

Article 5: Whether beauty moves us more than goodness?

Article 6: Whether souls are more beautiful than bodies?

Article 7: Whether persons are the most beautiful things in the world?

Article 8: Whether all persons are beautiful?

Article 9: Whether God is beautiful?

Article 10: Whether music is the primal art and language?

Question XI: Sample Questions in Ten Extensions of Philosophy

1. Philosophy of religion: Whether organized religion has done more harm than good?

2. Philosophy of history: Whether history is a meaningful story rather than a series of accidents?

3. Philosophy of science: Whether science and technology do humanity more harm than good?

4. Philosophy of education: Whether virtue can be taught?

5. Philosophy of language: Whether there is an ideal language?

6. Philosophy of culture: Whether there is a "culture war"?

7. Philosophy of sexuality: Whether sexuality is spiritual?

8. Philosophy of death: Whether death is a friend?

9. Philosophy of law: Whether reform and deterrence should be the only motives for punishment?

10. Philosophy of humor: Whether human life is a great joke?

Introduction:
Why This Book?

"Of the making of many books there is no end, and much study is a weariness of the flesh." (*Ecclesiastes* 12:12)

Too many books! Why one more?

First of all, this one is for beginners—like Plato's dialogs, which are the very best way for beginners to begin in philosophy; and like St. Thomas Aquinas's *Summa Theologiae*, which is the best way to begin in theology, and which, according to the author's own very short preface, is explicitly designed "for beginners."

(By the way, I deliberately misspelled the title of this book as *Summa Philosophica* instead of *Summa Philosophiae* because the *Summa Theologiae* is usually misspelled *Summa Theologica*—by beginners.)

Second, it is for impatient people, like myself. I have A.D.D. (So do most academics, though they don't know it.) I rarely finish reading a book, especially a long book. Why are there so many long books? How vain and self-important their authors look! Most of the great classics of philosophy and religion are short. The Bible is not a long book, but a library of 66 or 72 short books.

Here is a library of 110 short books. Each of the "articles" in this book, like those in the *Summa Theologiae* after which its form is modeled, is a short summary of a long argument, controversy, or question. Thousands of books have been written about each of these questions, and most of them are over 200 pages long. Here, each one is about two pages long. A *Summa* is a summary.

A *Summa* article is a condensation of another great philosophical form, the Socratic dialog. The literary form of the Socratic dialog emerged, in Plato's hands, from the actual practice of Socrates in *lived* dialog. And the format of the medieval *Summa* article emerged, especially in the work of St. Thomas Aquinas, from actual debates or

1

"scholastic disputations," which were something like formalized, systematized Socratic dialogs. The format of this book, which is the same, also emerged from my actual classroom teaching, questioning, and debating, as summaries ("summas").

Once my beginning students are exposed to the figure of Socrates in action, they get "hooked" on his method, and (with my encouragement) start writing Socratic dialogs of their own very quickly and, often, surprisingly well. The format seems to carry the content along, like an electric wheelchair. Beginners are always surprised at how easy, enjoyable, and engaging it can be to philosophize this way. They wonder (and so do I) why contemporary philosophers don't write in dialogs any more, why Plato was not only the first but also the last great philosopher to master this format.

The only way I could answer that question, it seemed to me, was to try to do it myself, and fail, and learn from my failures. So I wrote and published some books of Socratic dialogs. There are 13 of them so far, and I'm still waiting for the answer. So are my students. If beginners and their non-scholarly, popularizing professor can do it, why can't great philosophers and scholars do it? I still don't know.

Exactly the same is true of the medieval *Summa* article, which is derivative from the Socratic dialog format. My students also do excellent jobs in using this format to address all kinds of serious philosophical questions, both traditional and modern. And once again, I ask myself why the format has become unfashionable, and I get no answer. Thus this book. I suspect my question will remain unanswered.

The main reason the *Summa* article is unpopular today, I think, is that it "feels" very different to modern man than it did to medieval man. I have described it, above, as a short, systematic summary of a Socratic dialog; but most moderns "feel" a very different spirit in it than they feel in Socrates: they feel an artificial, stuffy, self-satisfied "gotcha!" They feel it is really a monolog instead of a dialog, and they feel an arrogance rather than a humility.

If this is your feeling, my only answer is that that feeling is indeed telling—about you, but not about Aquinas or about his format. Why, one might as well accuse a physicist's equations of being "arrogant," or a detective's fingerprinting. It is, indeed, impersonal and scientific and objective. But surely that is part of *humility*, while the demand to "share your own feelings" all the time is part of pride and self-importance.

This book is a short, provisional, preliminary, incomplete "summa" or summary of one hundred important philosophical questions, ten each in ten basic divisions of philosophy, with ten more added, from ten secondary philosophical divisions or spinoffs. I deliberately confined myself to that arbitrary number to put a limiting frame around a work that could easily expand indefinitely, since every great answer in philosophy tends to produce at least one more great question, and usually many more, like parents producing children.

The need for such a book in philosophy seems obvious to me. It is the need to join two of the most essential ideals of philosophy that, ever since the end of the Middle Ages, have tended to separate and flow in opposite directions, like a river divided into two by a spit of land. The two ideals are clarity and profundity, logic and wisdom. They are the ideals of our two eyes, the eye of the head and the eye of the heart. Even though in the last few decades there has been much more effort to bridge the gap—the gap between the "analytic" and the "phenomenological" or "existential" or "cultural" methods of philosophizing—yet English-speaking philosophers still tend to sound like chirping sparrows or computers, and Continental European philosophers like growling locomotives or muttering witch doctors.

But this was not always so. The Scholastic philosophers of the Middle Ages dealt with the deep questions like God, freedom, and immortality, in clear, straightforward syllogisms. Too neat, perhaps, but you at least always knew exactly where you stood. And it is always easy to complexify what is too simple, while it is much harder to simplify what is too complex.

So I am hoping that these efforts to combine the two ideals of clarity and profundity by imitating the medieval format of the *Summa* article will prove to be only the first few small stones of a forthcoming avalanche of imitators.

What follows in the rest of this Introduction is just two points.

The first will be insultingly simple to those already familiar with the *Summa* article format. It is simply a summary of its structure and strategy by giving its four Aristotelian causes: (1) its structure, or formal cause; (2) its content, or material cause; (3) the mentality that made it, or its efficient cause; and (4) its purpose and proper use, or final cause. The second point will be a justification of this format by answering objections to it.

(1) The formal cause, or structure, of a *Summa* article can be summarized as follows. (I quote from the Introduction to my *Summa of the Summa*.)

The "Article" is the basic thought-unit of the *Summa*. These are grouped into more general "Questions." What we mean in modern English by an "article"—an essay—is what St. Thomas means by a "Question," and what we mean by a "question"—a specific, single interrogative sentence—is what he means by an "Article," e.g. "Whether God Exists?" or "Whether Sorrow Is the Same as Pain?"

Each Article begins by formulating in its title a single question in such a way that only two answers are possible: yes or no. St. Thomas does this, not because he thinks philosophy or theology is as simple as a true-false exam, but because he wants to make an issue finite and decidable, just as debaters do in formulating their "resolution." There are an indefinite number of possible answers to a question like "What Is God?" If he had formulated his questions that way, the *Summa* might have been three million pages long instead of three thousand. Instead, he asks, for example, "Whether God Is a Body?" It is possible to decide and demonstrate that one of the two possible answers (yes) is false and therefore that the other (no) is true.

Each Article has five structural parts. First, the question is formulated in a yes or no format, as explained above, beginning with the word "Whether" (*Utrum*).

Second, St. Thomas lists a number of Objections (usually at least three) to the answer he will give. The Objections are apparent proofs of the opposite answer, the other side to the debate. These objections begin with the formula "*It seems that*" (*Oportet*). These Objections must be *arguments*, not just *opinions*, for one of the basic principles of any intelligent debate, woefully neglected in all modern media, is that each debater *must* give relevant *reasons* for every controvertible opinion he expresses. The Objections are to be taken seriously as *apparent* truth. One who is seeking the strongest possible arguments against any idea of St. Thomas will rarely find any stronger ones, any more strongly argued, than those in St. Thomas himself. He is extremely fair to all his opponents. I think he descends to name-calling only once in the entire *Summa*, when he speaks of the "really stupid" idea of David of Dinant that God is indistinguishable from prime matter, or pure potentiality—an idea not far from that of Hegel! (See *ST* I,3,8.)

Third, St. Thomas indicates his own position with the formula "*On the contrary*" (*Sed contra*). This is not his strongest proof; in fact, sometimes it is not a proof at all, but only a reminder that authoritative sources teach his position. When it is an argument, it is single, brief, and an "argument from authority"; i.e. the premise is from Scripture, the Fathers of the Church, or recognized wise men. The medievals well knew their own maxim that "the argument from (merely human) authority is the weakest of all arguments" (see *ST* I,1,8, obj. 2). But they also believed in doing their homework and in learning from their ancestors—two habits we would do well to cultivate today.

The fourth part, "*I answer that*" (*Respondo dicens*), is the body of the Article. In it, St. Thomas proves his own position, often adding necessary background explanations and making needed definitions and distinctions along the way. The easiest (but not the most exciting) way to read a *Summa* Article is to read this part first.

Fifth and finally, each Objection must be addressed and answered—not merely by an argument to prove the opposite conclusion, for that has already been done in the body of the Article, but by explaining where and how the Objection went wrong, i.e. by distinguishing the truth from the falsity in the Objection, usually by distinguishing two means at one of the Obector's terms

No one of these five steps can be omitted if we want to have good grounds for settling a controverted question. (1) If our question is vaguely or confusedly formulated, our answer will be too. (2) If we do not consider opposing views, we spar without a partner, and paw the air. (3) If we do not do our homework, we only skim the shallows of ourselves. (4) If we do not prove our thesis, we are dogmatic, not critical. (5) And if we do not understand and refute our opponents, we are left with nagging uncertainty that we have missed something and not really ended the contest.

(2) The material cause, or content, can be anything under the sun or beyond it, from the existence of God to why you should buy a Volkswagen. All the creativity comes here, in the *matter*; the *form* is rigid, like the structure of a syllogism or the AEI or O logical forms of categorical propositions.

The confining form actually liberates the content. This is a universal principle in the human arts. The confining form of a haiku liberates and expresses *satori* or *kensho*. Within the Apollonian confines of the sacred dance, Dionysian energies can safely be released. Only because the children play inside the playground fence can they play wildly, safe from running into cars or over cliffs. (The Commandments are God's fence to protect our play.)

The original *Summa* (St. Thomas') included not only philosophical arguments, whose premises were taken from reason alone, but also theological arguments, some of whose premises were taken from divine revelation. I have done the same, for two reasons: (1) Although my readers include many more unbelievers than his, they also include many believers in the Christian revelation. (2) Philosophy and theology are quite naturally (though not necessarily) in bed with each other; they are not unable to mate, like dog and cat, but able, like man and woman. So I have *not* assumed that this mating is adulterous, as modern philosophers typically do, and have allowed it here. But I have tried to make it always clear (as St. Thomas did) which is which. Those who do not believe the theological premises can simply discount the theological arguments.

(3) The efficient cause, the mind that makes this product, must possess certain qualities. Not everyone can make a good *Summa* Article, just as not everyone can cook a delicious dinner, even though in both cases both the material ingredients and the formal steps can be set out in clear, objective order. These mental qualities include: (a) a firm belief in objective truth and in the ability of human reason to know it; (b) a love of form and order and structure (or at least not a rankling hatred of it); (c) a conviction that the question is important and therefore to be treated with great care and respect and accuracy; and (d) a conviction that logic is not merely a man-made method for winning arguments but the very structure of reality, and that therefore there is a real "line-up" between knower and known; that definitions, propositions,

and arguments can reveal real essences, existences, and causes; and that when an argument has no ambiguous terms, false premises, or logical fallacies, it really does prove its conclusion to be true. This is definitely *not* Deconstructionism.

(4) The final cause, or end, or good of the *Summa* Article is *understanding*: to help the reader better understand what things really are, whether they are, and why they are. It is a way of *showing* the landscape of being, as through a telescope.

The format is easily misused, since *corruptio optimi pessima* (the corruption of the best things are the worst things). Some of its tempting abuses are the following:

(a) It is not a private language to distinguish professionals from amateurs, or scholars from non-scholars, or the unusually bright from the ordinary. It is natural, simple, and commonsensical. It is addressed to ordinary people. Remember, Aquinas wrote the *Summa Theologiae* "for beginners."

(b) It is not simplistic, just summary. The topics typically dealt with demand, and reward, much longer, more complex, more detailed, and more nuanced treatment. For instance Aquinas himself used 21 paragraphs in the *Summa Contra Gentiles*, which did *not* use the "article" format, to treat the first of his famous "five ways" of demonstrating the existence of God, and took up only one paragraph in the *Summa Theologiae*, which did use this method.

(c) It is not a "handbook" of arguments to use as weapons to win debates with, like an outline of "proof texts" from the Bible for Fundamentalists to hit unbelievers on the head with. These rigid arguments are to be used flexibly, as a rigid sword is to be swung creatively.

(d) And the swordsman's enemies here are not debate opponents. Like a Socratic dialog, a *Summa* Article is not a civil war between two opponents but a joint raid against the common enemies of confusion, ignorance, and error, using the common weapons of the common master, Reason. ("Reason" means "the *three* Acts of the mind": (1) understanding clearly *what* a thing is, (2) knowing and judging truly *that* it is, and (3) reasoning rightly to prove *why* it is.)

(e) The rigidity of the form does not entail or condone mental rigidity or a dogmatic attitude. There is more than one way to skin a cat.

7

Since the reader may still have doubts and objections against the possibility of using the *Summa* Article format for philosophy today, some of these objections may be stated and answered as follows:

Objection 1: The Thomistic, Scholastic *format* implicitly presupposes a Thomistic, Scholastic *content*. This limits the book to use by Thomists.

Reply: Format is connected to content only accidentally and historically; it can easily be abstracted from content. For instance, one can write a Socratic dialog to argue for any philosophical position, including anti-Socratic, anti-Platonic positions.

Objection 2: The Scholastic format lends itself to misuse as a quasi-mathematical system, impersonal and automatic, like an encyclopedia, a handbook, or a self-playing "player piano" instead of an instrument played differently by different players.

Reply: This too is an accidental misuse. *Abusus non tollit usum* ("the abuse does not take away the use"). Because format can be abstracted from content (Reply to Objection 1), it can be employed rightly or wrongly, like any tool or power.

Objection 3: The format is appropriate to the Middle Ages but not to today. It is not a mere historical accident that this format has totally disappeared from serious philosophy today. "You can't turn back the clock."

Reply: Chesterton answers that cliché in three simple words: "Yes you can." A clock is a human invention, and when it keeps bad time, it can and should be turned back. It is not our master but our servant. The objection assumes that history is destiny. If the Socratic dialog format can be resuscitated, there is no reason why the *Summa* Article format cannot.

Objection 4: The search for a neat, closed system in philosophy is a wild goose chase. Knowledge is open and evolving, and so is wisdom. It is also always limited and perspectival.

Reply: This is true. But a Summa is *not* a system, certainly not a closed system. It is ordered but open, an incomplete summary of incomplete knowledge. Aquinas himself asserted that we can never have complete knowledge of the essence of anything, even a flea.

* * * * *

The questions in this book are a mere sample, and another author would inevitably have selected other questions. But not *wholly* other questions, for these 100 include many of the classical, recurring ones in the history of philosophy.

They do not pretend to constitute a logical outline, as those of Aquinas's *Summas* do. Though everything follows logically *within* each Article, the topic of one Article does not follow with logical necessity from the previous one.

Each one is a short, skeletal summary of a possible "article" in the modern sense, in a journal. Writers are invited to use any of them as such, adding pages of rhetorical flesh to their bones. There is no law against "plagiarizing" arguments, only plagiarizing words.

As to the answers given, they are simply my own (though I add some references for further reading, for the curious), and they do not claim any authority beyond that. They are eclectic, but almost always gravitate toward the most commonsensical and traditional position. This is why, if you had to classify them in terms of philosophical schools, they would be labeled more "Aristotelian" and "Thomistic" than anything else (though they also may include or imply some "Platonic," "Augustinian," "Kantian," "existential," or "personalist" themes). Readers are, of course, quite free to disagree with any of them. But the *rules* of disagreement are not free: if my conclusions are false, their arguments must contain undefined, wrongly defined, or ambiguous terms, or false premises, or logical fallacies. And correcting these false conclusions requires pointing out one of these three sources of error.

Some of these questions are treated at much greater length than others because their importance is much greater. The format (including length) should always serve and express the content.

Question I:
Logic and Methodology

Article 1: Whether philosophy is still rightly defined as the love of wisdom?

Objection 1: *It seems that* it is not, for: "The love (*philia*) of wisdom (*sophia*)" is merely a nominal definition, and stems from the historical accident of the etymology of the word as made famous by Pythagoras and Socrates. But nothing nominal and historically accidental can define a natural essence. Therefore "the love of wisdom" does not define philosophy's natural essence.

Objection 2: Those who teach philosophy today in the philosophy departments of universities do not usually conceive of or practice philosophy in this way, as Socrates did—a sign of which is the fact that they no longer use the Socratic dialog form to teach, as Socrates did, and to write, as Plato did.

Objection 3: We no longer live in a pre-scientific era, as Socrates did. Science has rendered "wisdom," and the love of it, a questionable concept. For wisdom is not publicly and universally verifiable or falsifiable, as is any scientific idea, since wisdom is neither empirical nor mathematical, nor is it a matter of mere formal logical correctness. Thus no idea can be proved to be "wise" or "unwise" by any possible empirical observation, mathematical calculation, or reduction to formal logical validity. The rise of the scientific method has shown "wisdom" (and "philosophy" as the pursuit of it) to be a private, subjective, and unverifiable enterprise, not a public, objective, and verifiable one.

Objection 4: "Wisdom" is too high an end to be attainable or, therefore, practical. "Clarification of language and concepts" is more realistic today as philosophy's task. If we court Lady Wisdom, we will be bachelors for life and likely eventually turn into disillusioned skeptics.

Objection 5: If philosophy is the love of wisdom, it is a form of love. But there is no science of love or proof of lovability. Love is personal, subjective, and unverifiable. Romeo never tried to *prove* that Juliet was truly lovable, and no philosopher can prove his or her "wisdom."

Objection 6: Philosophy has never resolved its most important questions because, as Gabriel Marcel says, they are "mysteries" rather than "problems," questions about the questioner, questions in which the questioner is necessarily involved, not detached. . Thus philosophy as traditionally conceived is a wild goose chase, a playing with concepts, an intellectual masturbation.

Objection 7: Defining philosophy as the love of wisdom confuses it with religion. This is wrong whether these two enterprises are legitimate or not. For (1) if both philosophy and religion are legitimate enterprises, this definition is a confusion between two legitimate but different things, reason and faith. (2) And if religion is illegitimate (e.g. if there is no God), then philosophy becomes illegitimate too when its goal is made identical, or almost identical, with that of religion. And (3) if religion alone is legitimate wisdom, then philosophy is not. For if God alone is wise, then no man is wise. As God said to Job, in effect, "Two points: I'm God, you're not." In those four words is all of religion.

On the contrary, all three of its first founders—Socrates, Plato, and Aristotle—who were also three of the greatest philosophers of all time, define philosophy as the love of wisdom. (See Article 2, *on the contrary*, p. 16.)

I answer that philosophy is either an objective and unchangeable essence which we *discover*, or a changing human invention which we *create*. If it is the former, then all the arguments in favor of a changed, modern, scientific concept of it fail. What Socrates discovered, Socrates discovered. If, on the other hand, philosophy is a human invention, then it should be defined according to the concept, plan, design, and intention of its inventor(s), like any other invention. But as we have seen above, its three primary inventors all defined it as the love of wisdom. Therefore philosophy should be defined as the love of wisdom.

There may be other legitimate and worthy enterprises that can aid philosophy and which philosophy can aid, such as logical analysis of language; or enterprises that emerge in history by being gradually distinguished more clearly from philosophy, like the sciences; or enterprises that resemble philosophy in some ways but not all, like the "wisdom" aspects of religions, whether based on faith in a supernatural divine revelation, as in the West, or on mystical experience, as in the East. But the worthiness of these enterprises does not justify confusing them with philosophy. On the contrary, it demands their unconfusion, to preserve their proper identities, as well as philosophy's.

Reply to Objection 1: Nothing prevents a nominal definition from coinciding with a real definition. For instance, "democracy" means, both nominally (by etymology) and really (in practice) "rule (*krasos*) by the many, or the people at large (*demos*)." Names, even names of universal and unchanging essences, always emerge at a particular, contingent time in history.

Philosophy did not change from being the love of wisdom to being the cultivation of cleverness when it moved from Athens to Oxford. It died in transit.

Reply to Objection 2: It is true that the word "philosophy" has been, and is, used to designate other things than the love of wisdom, e.g. sophistry, intimidation of non-specialists by technical terminology, "publish or perish" scholarship, or ideological indoctrination and propaganda. (A proper mate for a proper goose is a proper gander.) And it is true that these things have tended to displace the actual love of wisdom in many philosophy departments, as means have tended to displace ends throughout modern society. But this need not, and should not, be the case. *Abusus non tollit usum.* Thus the objection is only an adult version of the child's silly justification for any folly: that "everybody's doing it."

Philosophy was not a "department" to its founders. They would have regarded the expression "philosophy department" as absurd as a "love department."

The dialog format, whether Socratic or Scholastic, is not essential to teaching or writing philosophy, but it is natural, and effective, and interesting, and there is no good reason for it to have dropped out of favor, and no reason why it cannot be restored. Use of Platonic dialog does not make one a Platonist, and use of Thomas's "summa" format does not make one a Thomist.

Reply to Objection 3: The objection implicitly assumes that modern science pursues the same end as philosophy, with a better means and method. But this is not so. Scientific method is indeed a better method than any other for pursuing purely physical, empirical, quantifiable questions; and premodern philosophers often addressed these questions with inadequate, prescientific methods. They often substituted philosophy for science. But modern philosophers often make the same mistake in reverse—substituting science for philosophy—when they dismiss philosophical questions because they cannot be investigated by the scientific method.

The objection implicitly assumes that the scientific method is the only valid or legitimate method. But that very assumption is self-contradictory and self-eliminating because it cannot be proved by the scientific method. If the objection assumes that only verifiable or falsifiable ideas are legitimate, and that only empirically or mathematically verifiable or falsifiable ideas are verifiable or falsifiable, that very assumption is self-contradictory and self-eliminating because it is not empirically or mathematically verifiable or falsifiable. Thus the objection is essentially the position of the early Logical Positivism of A.J. Ayer's *Language, Truth and Logic*, which is clearly self-contradictory.

Even in the sciences, except for mathematics, most scientists believe that no idea is ever definitively or certainly, but only probably, verifiable or falsifiable; and only increasing degrees of probability, not absolute certainty, is attained.

Reply to Objection 4: Philosophy does indeed seek the high goal of wisdom, which is (1) not just any knowledge but knowledge of ultimate causes; and (2) knowledge not merely of facts but of values, virtues, goods, rights, or duties; and (3) knowledge of invisible, rather than merely visible, things such as God, freedom, immortality, and self. Such knowledge is wisdom, and wisdom is "too high a goal" only for a materialist or a cynic. The question of which ends are too high for us is itself a question for philosophy, for wisdom. Only wisdom can establish or dis-establish wisdom.

And it is simply not true that all lovers of wisdom have become disillusioned skeptics, just as not all men who have courted beautiful women have become disillusioned bachelors.

Reply to Objection 5: Indeed there is no science of love as an object. But philosophy is not a science *of* love. It is a *loving*.

Reply to Objection 6: It is true that wisdom is "personal" in the sense that unlike logic, it differs greatly from one person to another. This is why philosophers will always disagree more than scientists and mathematicians. But although my opinions about which ideas are wise may differ from yours, it does not follow that truth itself differs according to different opinions—unless it be *assumed* that truth is only a matter of personal opinion. And if that is so, then one can ask whether *that* opinion is really true or only your personal opinion.

True wisdom is not *easy* to attain, but it does not follow that it is not *possible*. It is possible to catch a wild goose.

Philosophy is not intellectual masturbation because it is essentially thinking about being, not thinking about thinking. It is the love of wisdom, not the love of the love of wisdom.

Reply to Objection 7: Religion, at least as defined in the West, is essentially a relationship or binding (*religio, religare*) with God. This includes a "wisdom" dimension (e.g. the "wisdom" books of the Old Testament). Religion is both more and less than that "wisdom" dimension. It is more because it is essentially personal, like love. And it is less because it sees "through a glass darkly"; it is dependent on faith, not reason and argument alone. If religion were dependent on reason alone, all rational persons would believe the same basic religious ideas, as all rational persons believe the same basic scientific ideas.

Religion asks many of the same *questions* as philosophy, but its *method of answering* them is different: faith, trust, scriptures, prophets, mystics, religious experience, tradition, and authority, not merely reason.

Article 2: Whether philosophy begins in wonder?

Objection 1: It seems that it does not, for wonder is typical of children, while philosophy is an adult enterprise.

Objection 2: As Aristotle says (*Metaphysics* 1, 2), philosophy ends not in wonder but in the abolition of wonder once its questions are answered and the answers are understood:

> But the attainment of this knowledge must somehow give rise to an outlook directly opposite to that with which we embarked on our inquiry. All begin, as I have said, by wondering that things should be as they are: puppets, for example, or the solstices, or the incommensurability of the diagonal of a square with the side. It must, indeed, be surprising to one as yet unacquainted with the cause to find something which is not measurable by the smallest unit of its own kind. We invariably finish, however, with the opposite and (according to the proverb) the better view, as men do even in the cases alleged when they understand them; for nothing would so astonish a geometrician as to find the diagonal commensurable with the side.

Objection 3: Wonder is personal and subjective. Not all people are "wonderers." But all people philosophize, either well or badly, whether they know it or not. (As Cicero says, if you say you will not philosophize, that is your philosophy.) Therefore not all philosophy includes wonder.

Objection 4: Wonder is an implicitly religious attitude. It is not rational. It is contemplative and passive, not demanding and active. Philosophy, in contrast, is rational, active questioning.

On the contrary, all three of philosophy's great founders, Socrates, Plato and Aristotle, say that philosophy begins in wonder. See Plato, *Republic* 5.475c ff.; *Theaetetus* 155d; Aristotle, *Metaphysics* A, 2.

I answer that there are three kinds of wonder: (1) emotional wonder, or the astonishment or stand-still shock at the unexpected or surprising; (2) questioning, or intellectual wonder, the desire to know and explain the unknown and unexplained; and (3) contemplative wonder, the appreciation and admiration of some truth, goodness, or beauty.

(1) Emotional wonder is the origin of all ordinary human knowing, beginning with a baby's first exposure to the world,;and this wonder develops eventually into, and is the origin of, religion, art, science, and philosophy, as well as common sense.

Emotional wonder naturally gives rise to (2) questioning wonder, because we investigate what we are surprised by, not what we already know or think we know and take for granted. We have an innate desire to know all that is knowable about all that there is, both the facts and the explanations or causes (in all four senses of the word "cause" that Aristotle distinguished). And this is the desire that carries philosophy forward.

And when we achieve the knowledge which is the goal of questioning wonder, this naturally produces, in sensitive souls, the appreciation, admiration, and even sometimes the awe of (3) contemplative wonder. And this is the highest end of philosophical understanding.

Reply to Objection 1: "What is great must begin great" (Heidegger, *Introduction to Metaphysics*, ch. 1). The mature, adult contemplative wonder (wonder #3) is the fruit of questioning wonder (wonder #2), which in turn is the fruit of the "primitive" or childlike wonder of astonishment (wonder #1). For "the child is the father of the man" (Alexander Pope, "Essay on Man"). We contemplatively appreciate what we have investigated, and we investigate what we have found surprising. We grow.

Reply to Objection 2: Aristotle speaks here only of questioning wonder, and points out, correctly, that it does not lead back to its origin, the wonder of surprise. However, Aristotle also speaks of contemplation as the ultimate end of questioning, of philosophy, and of human life itself (*Nicomachean Ethics* X)

Reply to Objection 3: All people are by nature capable of all three forms of wonder, as they are capable of knowledge. And all three forms of wonder may be suppressed, unnaturally. E.g. Aristotle says, in the very first line of his *Metaphysics*, that "all men by nature desire to know," even though he knew that there were many uncurious "couch potatoes" in ancient Greece just as there are today. Our "nature" is not simply our observed acts but our innate potentialities and teleologies (natural ends). We can act contrary to our nature. Humans can be inhuman.

Even Nominalists, who deny that things have natural ends or universal natures, speak the language of this commonsensical philosophy. They do not expect pigs to fly or men to be infallible. If they were right about "natures" being unreal or unknowable, it would not be natural for us to say "that's natural" or "that's not natural" about anything. (See Question II, Article 6.)

Reply to Objection 4: Both philosophy and religion grow by including all three forms of wonder. So does science. If philosophy is to be reduced to religion simply because it begins, proceeds, and ends in wonder, then science should be too.

Article 3: Whether philosophy should use the method of universal doubt?

Objection 1: It seems that it should, for this is the first and most essential step of the scientific method, which is the most successful method for resolving disputes in the history of human thought.

Objection 2: Furthermore, this method of doubt is not limited to modern science. It was also the method of Socrates. And, of course, of Descartes (*Discourse on Method*).

Objection 3: This method is also the answer to skepticism. For if we begin with doubt we may hope to end with certainty, but if we begin with certainty, we will, if we think honestly, end with doubt.

On the contrary, Kierkegaard says: "It is a positive starting point when Aristotle says that philosophy begins with wonder, not as in our day with doubt. Moreover, the world . . . has never seriously done what it said. Its doubt is mere child's play." (*Journals*, 1841)

I answer that one must first believe something in order to then doubt it. So doubt presupposes belief. For instance, if no one believed that there exists a God, no one would come to doubt this belief. And to resolve the doubt, to progress from doubt to knowledge, whether certain or probable, we must use either knowledge or belief to evaluate and judge. For instance, when belief in God is doubted, we try to resolve the doubt by giving good arguments for judging either theism or atheism to be true. But good arguments require premises, which must be known or believed, not doubted. (For no conclusion follows from doubtful premises.) So the proper place for doubt must be in passing from a prior belief to a subsequent, more reasoned, belief or disbelief, or to knowledge. Therefore doubt cannot be an absolute beginning.

And it should not be an absolute end point either, for as Aristotle said (in the very first line of his *Metaphysics*, quoted above), "all men by nature desire to *know* not to *doubt*." To attain happiness in satisfying this desire to know, we use doubt as a means, or as a way of transforming mere belief into knowledge by doubting and questioning the belief. This doubt may be either a whole-hearted, personal doubt (as with a person who previously believed in God and now actually doubts His existence—or who previously believed in His non-existence and now doubts that), or it may be a merely intellectual, experimental doubt (as with a person who doubts not God but the adequacy of his reasons for believing in God—or for not believing in God—and seeks better ones).

Furthermore, doubt cannot be universal, as Descartes calls for it to be, for the same reason it cannot be an absolute beginning. For if it is universal, it can never be resolved, since resolution of doubt is done by argument, and therefore by assuming rather than doubting the premises of that argument.

Descartes, who introduced the method of universal doubt, changed his earlier resolution of this doubt, "I think therefore I am," to "I think, *or*, I am;" that is, he abandoned the attempt to escape universal doubt by an *argument* and instead claimed that "I am, I exist" is logically self-evident (tautological) and its contradictory ("I do not exist") self-contradictory. But the proposition "I do not exist" is *not* objectively and logically self-contradictory, only subjectively and personally self-contradictory, i.e. it is self-contradictory only to the person who utters it and only at the moment of uttering it. If Descartes' "I" means only "Descartes," then "I do not exist" means only "Descartes does not exist," and that is not only not self-contradictory but it is not even *true* at all times except during the few years when Descartes was alive.

Reply to Objection 1: The scientific method assumes many things, for instance the existence of the cosmos and the mind, the uniformity of nature, and the validity of human reasoning. It practices doubt only of previous scientific beliefs, not of everything.

Reply to Objection 2: Socrates practiced not universal methodic doubt but universal methodic belief: he began by provisionally accepting his dialog partner's opinions, and then subjected them to a rational critique. And his critiques always involved the admission of premises both on his part and on the part of the dialog partner. If either of the two had practiced universal doubt, they could not have had a dialog.

Reply to Objection 3: Universal doubt (a) amounts to skepticism, (b) is impossible, as shown above in the *I answer that*, and (c) is self-contradictory (for it involves doubting that you are doubting, et cetera ad infinitum). Thus it leads nowhere, and certainly not to certainty, as merely practical doubt often does.

Article 4: Whether there is a place for philosophy in addition to common sense, science, and religion?

Objection 1: It seems that there is not, because philosophy is not essentially distinct from science. For philosophy seeks to prove, or demonstrate, by objective logical reasoning, that its conclusions are true. But the only method by which this can be successfully done is the scientific method. For legitimate logical, objective reasoning convinces all reasonable thinkers of the truth of what it demonstrates. But philosophy has never done that, since philosophers have always disagreed, and have never been able to come to universal agreement, as scientists have. Therefore the only legitimate kind of philosophy is the kind that is a part of, or an aid or adjunct to, science, by clarifying and justifying its definitions and presuppositions and by evaluating the meaningfulness of its language.

Objection 2: It seems that philosophy is not essentially distinct from religion. For the most important concepts philosophy deals with— God, freedom, immortality, spirit, the meaning of life, man's ultimate origin, essence, and destiny, and the existence of moral absolutes— are religious concepts.

Objection 3: Furthermore, religion has a greater authority than philosophy and is more effective in persuading most people. Therefore philosophy is superfluous, as a weaker tool is superfluous when a stronger on is available..

Objection 4: It seems that philosophy is not essentially distinct from common sense. For the great questions and answers of philosophy, unlike those of the special sciences and of religion, are those of common sense. Thus, science is addressed only to the scientifically educated, or to those who are practicing science, or to those who are studying it; and religion is addressed only to believers, or potential believers; but philosophy is addressed to all.

Also, philosophy's method and instrument is simply common rationality, not either the method special to science (the scientific method) or the method special to religion (faith). Therefore philosophy is merely a refinement of common sense.

This is also evident from the fact that the most popular philosophers are not specialists but thinkers who write books everyone can understand and enjoy, like Confucius, Lao Tzu, Plato, Aristotle, Augustine, Boethius, and Pascal.

On the contrary, for the past 2400 years philosophy has in fact existed as a distinct enterprise from science, from religion, and from common sense. Evidence of this fact lies in the survival of the distinct use of the word "philosophy." Words are used to designate realities, including human enterprises, and we need only as many words as there are known realities, including human enterprises. Therefore the persistence of four distinct words, no two of which are used synonymously, is a sign of the fact that there are four distinct human enterprises here: science, religion, common sense, *and* philosophy.

I answer that philosophy is the pursuit of wisdom by means of reason. Wisdom is knowledge of truth about the most important questions, the ultimate questions, especially questions about value, or the good. Science does not raise these questions, and religion addresses them by faith, not by reason purely or primarily. And common sense does not insist on critical logical criteria for proving its conclusions, as philosophy does. There is therefore a distinct place for philosophy as distinct from these three other enterprises.

Reply to Objection 1: It is not true that the only method for legitimately or reliably demonstrating truth is the scientific method. For if that were so, then nothing would ever have been demonstrated legitimately or reliably, anywhere, by any means, in any culture, by anyone, whether philosopher, sage, or ordinary person, in any era, before the rise of the scientific method in the West about 500 years ago— which is absurd. Socrates was not a Sophist and Aristotle was not a myth-maker.

Also, as mentioned before, the statement that only the scientific method is reliable is self-contradictory, since that statement is not provable by the scientific method. It is like "sola scriptura," which is not found in scripture and thus refutes itself.

Reply to Objection 2: Philosophy's ultimate appeal is to reason, religion's is to faith. Thus they are essentially distinct in method even though their subject matter may overlap. And even this overlap is only partial; for instance, religion does not deal with such issues as the principle of causality and philosophy does not deal with such issues as church discipline.

Furthermore, the two are different because religion does not justify itself, while philosophy does. One need not be religious: it is logically possible that all religions are essentially in error, so religion is intellectually escapable. But one must be philosophical. For philosophy is not escapable. For if you say that all philosophy is essentially in error, you are philosophizing. You can have a good philosophy or a bad philosophy but you cannot have no philosophy. Even skepticism of all philosophy is a philosophy. But skepticism of all religion is not a religion (though it may be held with the same psychological *passion* and adamant certitude as a religious faith), because it has no religious *object*.

Reply to Objection 3: Religion does not make philosophy superfluous because even though philosophy deals with many of the same questions that religion pronounces on, philosophy also deals with many others, as well as using different powers of the soul (reason vs. faith) and different methods. Religion also can use philosophy to confirm by reason many of its faith doctrines, and to explore them more clearly and carefully. The two "tools" are not comparable because they are tools for different tasks: making saints and making sages.

Reply to Objection 4: Philosophy is indeed continuous with common sense but it is a refinement of it, as sainthood is a refinement of ordinary religious piety and morality, or as great art is a refinement of the primitive artistic impulse in everyone. This is evident from our ordinary use of the term 'wisdom,' according to which even if all men have some of it, some have more of it than others. There is indeed no sharp, clear line where common sense ends and where philosophy begins; and in that sense philosophy is more reasonably conflated with common sense than with science or religion. Even the use of critical logical thinking does not sharply distinguish philosophy from common sense, for it if did, common sense would be totally uncritical and illogical.

Article 5: Whether philosophy should be a required subject in schools?

Objection 1: It seems that it should not, for 95% of American colleges and universities have decided this question in the negative. The audience has spoken and has disinvited the speaker. In our society, philosophy may be a good choice for a small, leisured elite or for certain professions, but not for the majority and surely not for everyone.

Objection 2: Respect for freedom and autonomy in a democracy should leave this choice, to take philosophy or not, up to the individual. "Different strokes for different folks." America is not Plato's Academy.

Objection 3: Most people are more practical than theoretical. What can you do with philosophy? "Philosophy bakes no bread." People go to school to learn to make a living and to live in this world, the real world, not in another world of ideas and ideals.

On the contrary, as Aquinas says, in *Summa Contra Gentiles* I,2,1:

Among all human pursuits, the pursuit of wisdom is more perfect, more noble, more useful, and more full of joy.

It is more perfect because, insofar as a man gives himself to the pursuit of wisdom, so far does he even now have some share in true beatitude. And so a wise man has said: "Blessed is the man that shall continue in wisdom" (*Ecclesiasticus* 14:22).

It is more noble because through this pursuit man especially approaches to a likeness to God Who "made all things in wisdom" (*Psalms* 103:24).

It is more useful because through wisdom we arrive at the kingdom of immortality. For "the desire of wisdom bringeth to the everlasting kingdom" (*Wisdom* 6:21).

It is more full of joy because "her conversation hath no bitterness, nor her company any tediousness, but joy and gladness" (*Wisdom* 7:16)

I answer that whatever is necessary to educate our essential humanity should be taught to all. But philosophy is necessary to educate our essential humanity, for both the questions of philosophy (such as "Why do I exist?" and "What is good?") and the instrument used by philosophy, reason, are essential to our humanity. Therefore philosophy should be taught to all. And since not all will take it voluntarily, it should be required, like "reading, writing, and arithmetic."

Reply to Objection 1: This issue depends on what one thinks philosophy is. In deciding not to require philosophy, modern colleges and universities may have chosen rightly if philosophy is conceived in a typically modern way. (See above, Question I, Article 1, Reply to Objection 2.) But if it is conceived as the love of wisdom, nothing is more necessary in education than philosophy. For no good society confines wisdom to a small elite, especially in a democracy.

The audience has indeed disinvited this speaker, but most unwisely. *Vox populi non est vox dei.*

Reply to Objection 2: "Different strokes" is true for accidentals, but not for essential aspects of humanity, like asking what living is *for* and *who* it is that is doing the living and the asking ("know thyself")—and this is what philosophy does.

Reply to Objection 3: True, there is not much you can "do" with philosophy. But there is much that it can do with you. It is like music in that way, or religion.

True, philosophy "bakes no bread," but it gives you reasons for baking bread. People go to bakers' school to learn to bake bread, and money-makers' schools (business schools) to learn how to make money; but a liberal education should teach you how to live, no matter what kind of a "living" you make, and this involves philosophy, which asks what living is *for*. We make money in order to buy bread, and we eat bread in order to live; but why do we live? If we have no light about *that*, we are surely living in "the dark ages."

Article 6: Whether logic should be a required subject in schools?

Objection 1: It seems that it should not be, for all the objections against studying philosophy apply also to studying logic, just as objections to studying astronomy apply also to studying telescopes. For logic is philosophy's instrument as telescopes are astronomy's.

Objection 2: Logic is very dull, and empty of content, like mathematics. Only "nerds" can be motivated to love it.

Objection 3: Logic should not be required for the Irish, for they have their own logic. As quoted in *Socratic Logic,* "I once asked my very Irish neighbor whether she believes in leprechauns and she answered, 'Of course not. But they exist all the same, mind you.'"

On the contrary, in *Socratic Logic* I offer thirteen reasons to study logic:

1. Logic builds the mental habit of thinking in an orderly way.
2. Logic has power: the power of proof and thus persuasion.
3. Logic will help you with all your other courses, for logic will help you to read any book more clearly and effectively.
4. Logic will also help you to write more clearly and effectively.
5. Logic can even help you attain happiness, for
   (a) When we attain what we desire, we are happy.
   (b) And whatever we desire, whether Heaven or a hamburger, it is more likely that we will attain it if we think more clearly.
   (c) And logic helps us to think more clearly.
   (d) Therefore logic helps us to be happy.
6. Logic can aid religious faith, in at least three ways:
   (a) Logic can often clarify what is believed, and define it.
   (b) Logic can deduce the necessary consequences of the belief, and apply it.
   (c) Even if logical arguments cannot prove all that faith believes, they can give firmer reasons for faith than feeling, desire, mood, fashion, family or social pressure, conformity, or inertia.
7. Although logic alone cannot make you wise, it can help. For logic is one of philosophy's main instruments, and philosophy is the love of wisdom.
8. "In a republican nation, whose citizens are to be led by reason and persuasion and not by force, the art of reasoning becomes of the first importance." (Thomas Jefferson)
9. Logic has limits, but we need logic to recognize and define logic's limits.
10. We need authority as well as logic, but we need logic to test our authorities.

11. Logic teaches us which ideas contradict each other and which do not.

12. Logic has outer limits, but it has no inner limits; like math, it never breaks down.

13. Logic helps us to find truth, and truth is its own end.

I answer that the thirteen reasons given above as just as true, just as relevant, and just as needed today as they ever were.

Reply to Objection 1: All the objections against requiring the study of philosophy have been refuted, and with them the objections against requiring the study of philosophy's instrument.

Furthermore, logic is useful not only for philosophy but for all thinking, as has been shown above.

Reply to Objection 2: Logic is indeed dull and empty of content, like mathematics. But the very fact that it is empty of content, or "formal," makes it universally applicable to any and all material content.

And one need not love a subject to profit from it. Few people love mathematics, but many profit from it.

Reply to Objection 3: It requires competence in logic to determine whether or not silly racial jokes have a place in philosophy texts. (They do, to relieve both tension and boredom and to counter over-seriousness and joylessness.)

Article 7: Whether all reality is logical?

Objection 1: It seems that it is not, for God transcends all that which is finite, and therefore transcends logic, which is the invention of finite human minds.

Objection 2: Furthermore, evil is not logical. It is contrary to reason. That's one of the things that makes it evil. Yet evil is real. Therefore not all that is real is logical.

Objection 3: Furthermore, love is real but love is not logical.

Objection 4: Furthermore, insanity exists, in many forms. But being insane, almost by definition, is the opposite of being logical.

Objection 5: Furthermore, having children is not logical. As Robert Farrar Capon says, "Having fits is more rational than having children." (*An Offering of Uncles*)

Objection 6: Jokes are also not logical. That's why they are funny. But there can be a certain truth to them.

Objection 7: We do not know all of reality. Therefore we do not know whether or not there is any unknown reality that is not logical. For if there were, it would not be knowable by us, since we must know a thing according to the laws of logic.

On the contrary, as *Socratic Logic* explains, "Just as 2 plus 2 are unfailingly 4, so if A is B and B is C, then A is unfailingly C. Logic is universal, timeless, unchangeable, and certain. It is not certain that the sun will rise tomorrow. (It is only very, very probable.) But it is certain that it either will or won't."

I answer that whatever is real is logical because whatever is real, is real and not not-real; and to say this is to assume the two basic principles of logic, the law of identity and the law of non-contradiction. To say that *not* all reality is logical is self-contradictory and self-refuting.

While it is quite possible for the human mind to conceive, and even to believe, things that contradict any other kind of laws—e.g. miracles, which at least seem to contradict the laws of physics–it is impossible for any human mind to conceive anything that contradicts the basic laws of logic, especially the law of non-contradiction. For instance, to say that a man walked through the wall may be to say that he performed a miracle; and that may be false, but it is *meaningful.* But to say that a man both walked through the wall and did not walk through the wall at the same time and in the same sense is not to say anything meaningful or comprehensible at all.

Reply to Objection 1: To say "God transcends logic" is to presuppose the principles of logic, such as the subject-predicate structure of a proposition and the law of non-contradiction ("God does transcend logic" must *not* mean "God does not transcend logic"). If God transcends logic, God transcends the law of non-contradiction, in which case "God transcends logic" can mean that "God does *not* transcend logic."

In fact, assuming the existence of God, God must be the ultimate ontological foundation for logic. That is why its supreme principles, identity and non-contradiction, are absolute, eternal, necessary, and known *a priori*, not dependent on the existence or knowledge of any other reality. X is X because God is God, because the divine nature is one and self-consistent; and X is not non-X because God is not non-God.

Logic is not a human invention. If it were, it could be changed. But its fundamental principles cannot be changed, but are necessarily true of all possible worlds.

Reply to Objection 2: When one chooses evil over good, one chooses contrary to reason (i.e. contrary to the right use of reason). But all statements about this irrational choice must conform to the laws of logic. For instance, if it is true that X is evil in a certain respect, it cannot at the same time be true that X is not evil in that respect. Evil choices are indeed irrational, but statements about them need not be.

Reply to Objection 3: The same distinction holds for love. Love may be irrational (in fact, some forms of it are, others are not), but statements about it need not be.

Reply to Objection 4: And the same is true for insanity. Also, as G.K. Chesterton says,

> The madman is not the man who has lost his reason. The madman is the man who has lost everything except his reason . . . if a man says that he is the rightful King of England, it is no complete answer to say that the existing authorities call him mad; for if he were the King of England that might be the wisest thing for the existing authorities to do . . . his mind moves in a perfect but narrow circle. A small circle is quite as infinite as a large circle; but, though it is quite as infinite, it is

not so large. In the same way the insane explanation is quite as complete as the sane one, but it is not so large. . . . Curing a madman is not arguing with a philosopher. It is casting out a devil. (*Orthodoxy*)

Reply to Objection 5: Not having children would be even less "rational" than having children. If universalized, it would end the human race.

Reply to Objection 6: If the laws of logic did not hold, jokes would not be funny. For even if a joke is funny because it seems to break a law of logic, a law must first exist in order to be broken.

Reply to Objection7: (1) If it were possible that any part of reality were truly illogical, not subject to the law of non-contradiction, we could not know which parts these were except by the law of non-contradiction. (2) If this were possible, then the reality that seems to us to be logical might in fact be illogical, and we could never know it was—which results in absolute skepticism, which is self-eliminating (Question VI, Article 1).

Article 8: Whether deductive arguments (e.g. syllogisms) really prove anything?

Objection 1: It seems that they do not, for as the ancient Greek skeptics pointed out, every syllogism depends on its premises, which it assumes rather than proves. In order to be certain of the syllogism's conclusion, these premises must be proved by other syllogisms, whose premises in turn depend on still other syllogisms and other premises, *et cetera ad infinitum*, so that nothing is ever proved with certainty.

Objection 2: As David Hume (implicitly) and John Stuart Mill (explicitly) point out, a syllogism cannot deliver the new knowledge it claims to deliver in its conclusion. For either the conclusion merely repeats in different words what has already been said in the premises—in which case there is no new knowledge, only new wording, and the syllogism is simply a complex tautology—or it adds to the knowledge that is already in the premises—in which case it commits the fallacy of *non sequitur*, for there is more in the conclusion than the premises warrant. So every syllogism is either a tautology or a *non sequitur*.

"All men are mortal and Socrates is a man, therefore Socrates is mortal" seems to prove that Socrates is mortal, but it does not; for we could never know that all men are mortal unless we already know that Socrates is mortal. So the conclusion, which seems to follow, or come after the premises, really must precede, or come before them.

Objection 3: People do not learn from syllogisms, nor are they convinced to change their minds by them, but by other factors, especially experience, intuition, and emotion. Syllogisms are therefore useful only for displaying the reasons one already has, not for changing others' minds. But education involves changing others' minds (i.e. students' minds, including your own, when you are self-educating). Therefore they are useless for education.

On the contrary, all the greatest philosophers, including those like Hume who wanted to persuade us of the uselessness of deductive reasoning, and especially syllogisms, have used deductive reasoning, and especially syllogisms, to persuade us.

I answer that "reasoning" means mentally moving from the judgment that some things are true (the premises) to the judgment that something else is true (the conclusion); and this is done in two ways: inductively, when the conclusion follows only with probability (usually because the reasoning proceeds from particular premises to a more universal or general conclusion) or deductively and with certainty (when the reasoning proceeds from a universal premise to a particular conclusion that logically comes under it). But all reasoning can be useful and persuasive. Therefore deductive reasoning, especially syllogisms, can be useful and persuasive.

Reply to Objection 1: Aristotle answered this objection very simply: the infinite regress of proving the premises of premises stops at two points: direct and indubitable sense experience and the direct and indubitable intellectual experience, so to speak, of logically self-evident first principles such as "Do good, not evil" in practical reasoning and the laws of identity, non-contradiction, and excluded middle (either p is true or not true) in theoretical reasoning. If any proposition can be shown to contradict either of these two starting points, that proposition is shown to be false. (See *Socratic Logic*, 3.1 edition, pp. 219–22)

Reply to Objection 2: The objection presupposes Nominalism (the denial of real universals) and empiricism (the denial of *a priori* knowledge). We can know that "all men are mortal" *before* we know that "Socrates is mortal" because we understand that mortality, unlike height or gender, is essential to all men because all men have animal bodies. We can and often do thus derive the knowledge of its properties from our understanding of a universal essence, *a priori*. (See *Socratic Logic*, 3.1 edition, pp. 222–30.)

The Nominalist and Empiricist objection to deduction is as fatal to science as it is to philosophy, for science too relies on deduction in predicting what the observed consequences of the truth of a hypothesis must be, before observing the presence or absence of these consequences. In fact, all applications of mathematics to nature are deductive and predictive: only if 2+2=4 universally can I be sure that 2 planets plus 2 more planets will = 4 planets tomorrow as well as today.

Reply to Objection 3: This very objection answers itself, for it seeks to change the mind of the defender of syllogisms—by a syllogism!

One may know both premises and not put them together in one's mind until someone does this in a syllogism. E.g. one may know (1) the general principle that animals that give live birth are mammals, and also (2) the particular fact that whales give live birth, and yet (3) not realize that whales are mammals, but believe that whales are fish. An important contemporary example of this principle is the following: according to the polls, each of the following propositions is believed by about two-thirds of Americans: (1) that an unborn human child is an innocent human being, and (2) that it is always morally wrong to deliberately kill an innocent human being, and

31

(3) that abortion, which is the deliberate killing of an unborn human child, is *not* always morally wrong. A syllogism may newly reveal to someone the inconsistency and logical impossibility of all these beliefs being true at the same time.

Article 9: Whether words intend real things?*

Objection 1: It seems that they do not, for one of the most popular and progressive philosophies today in Western civilization (Europe and North America) is Deconstructionism, whose central claim is that it is only a popular and traditional but mistaken myth that words ("text") have "intentionality," i.e. some fixed and objective meaning ("logos") as intending or pointing to or symbolizing things in the supposedly-objective and common "world." Deconstructionism denies this "intentionality" in words as well as in things. It maintains that not only are *things* not "words" (i.e. they are not signs, with fixed meanings or essences, as ancient man believed) but even *words* are not "words" (i.e. they do not "mean" or intend real things), but are simply opaque *things*. ("A poem should be palpable and mute/ Like globed fruit. /A poem should not mean but be" – Archibald MacLeish, "Ars Poetica.")

Objection 2: This philosophy (that words do not intend real things) is the third stage and culmination of critical thinking in the history of human thought. Ancient and medieval philosophy centered on

---

* NOTE: St. Thomas Aquinas abandoned his impersonal, objective, and scrupulously fair language and reverted to personal insults only for the most extreme and absurd of errors, such as that of David of Dinant, who identified God with prime matter, or Siger of Brabant, who maintained that the same proposition could be both true in theology and false in philosophy at the same time. To place my infant steps in those of the master, I therefore reserve my right to do some appropriate name-calling to point out the unparalleled absurdity of the philosophy that denies even this minimal truth, viz. Deconstructionism.

metaphysics, classical modern philosophy on epistemology, and contemporary philosophy on language. In each of these three stages, an initial naiveté (three forms of "logocentrism") was replaced by a more critical, skeptical, subjective, and relativistic outlook as a result of dialog among the great philosophers. The ancient Greek philosopher Gorgias could be seen as a prophet of the future history of philosophy when he summarized his philosophy in three theses, each of which denied one of the three fundamental meanings of "logos" or fixed, objective, natural essence: (1) in metaphysics, "nothing is real" (no "logos" in reality); (2) in epistemology, "if anything were real, it could not be known" (no "logos" in knowledge); and (3) in linguistics, "if anything could be known, it could not be said, or communicated" (no "logos" in speech).

Objection 3: Critical thinkers should use a "hermeneutic of suspicion." If they do, they will notice that opposition to Deconstructionism typically comes from bourgeois right-wing middle-class white male heterosexual conservative establishmentarians. This is evidence for the claim that behind all logocentric reasoning lies the "will to power" over non-bourgeois, non-white, non-male, non-heterosexual, non-conservative, "transgressive" anti-establishmentarians. When we hear them speak of "the truth" we should always ask "*Whose* truth?" For "truth" is a constructed mask on the face of the will to power. Truth is relative to race, class, gender, and sexual orientation.

On the contrary, every philosopher in the history of human thought who has ever intended to communicate his philosophy has broken with Deconstructionism's denial of intentionality in the very act of communicating. Even if the philosophy communicated was intended to be some form of skepticism, it was *intended* to communicate.

I answer that it is difficult to argue with a philosophy that does not argue or put any faith in argument, but merely dogmatically states its program of destruction. We will therefore instead give this philosophy its proper place in the history of human thought:

The first great philosopher to write, Plato, claimed that even *things* were "words" (*logoi*), i.e. signs or images of Platonic Forms. Christian philosophers like Augustine, Bonaventura, and Aquinas agreed with this, putting Platonic Ideas in the mind of God and concluding that the God who designed the universe could and did use things as signs (ontological words) of other things. (See *Summa Theologiae* I,1,10.) For instance, a lion could be a sign or icon of God through its royal quality (the "King of Beasts"). Not only did the word "lion" signify a lion, but a lion also signified the leonine aspects of God.

This Platonism was abandoned by atheistic, agnostic, materialistic, or resolutely secular thinkers, for whom only words were "words" (*logoi*) and things were only things. For instance, a lion was only a lion and meant nothing beyond itself, although the *word* "lion" meant something beyond itself: a real lion.

Finally, Deconstructionism claims that even words are not "words" (*logoi*) but only things. This is like a lion looking at a book about lions and concluding that it is only a toy to be chewed up. There is no need for serious philosophers to take this chewing seriously. I have already used far too many words to dismiss this philosophy which dismisses words.

The denial of the intentionality of concepts and words is the denial of either the distinction or the correspondence between language ("text") and reality ("world"). This is the most radical and indefensible form of skepticism in the entire history of human thought. For even total, simple, and unqualified skepticism, though immediately self-contradictory, must assume that its words are meaningful, and true. The denial of the very concept of truth, in Deconstructionism, is even more radical and more unjustifiable, more immediately self-contradictory, than the denial of our ability to find it (Skepticism).

If words are not signs, then neither are the words in the Deconstructionist claim that words are not signs. Thus the very statements of Deconstructionism destroy themselves; this philosophy is intellectual suicide. Or, even worse, it is not serious; it is a sneer rather than an argument, an "inside joke" against "naïve" traditionalists who take words and thought seriously—in other words all the human beings, of every philosophical persuasion, who have ever lived, in the entire history of the world, except the "in the know" Deconstructionists.

Reply to Objection 1: The fact that a philosophy is "popular" among philosophers is no argument for it, unless truth is told by polls. And Deconstructionism itself assumes this principle when it criticizes the more popular (outside the ranks of avant-garde philosophers) view that words mean real things.

And if we try to tell the truth with clocks instead of arguments, as we do when we say a philosophy is true because it is "progressive," we find that that itself is an argument, in fact a syllogism.

The rest of the "objection" is mere dogmatic assertion, not argument. It is the dogma that there can be no dogmas.

Reply to Objection 2: Gorgias was not a philosopher but a Sophist and a triple Nihilist: metaphysically, epistemologically, and linguistically. Deconstructionism is simply the third and final nihilism; and since nihilism is decadence, it is the final stage in intellectual decadence.

Reply to Objection 3: Traditional and commonsensical "logocentrism" is indeed a form of antidisestablishmentarianism. We are grateful to our opponents for one thing only: the opportunity to write the longest word in the English language.

Those who speak of the "hermeneutic of suspicion" and the "will to power" make one exception to that suspicion and that will: themselves. For if they did not, they would not only contradict themselves, putting themselves and their own theory under the same disqualifying suspicion, but also disqualify themselves from debate as terrorist bombers disqualify themselves from debate. Bombs are powers not arguments, whether they are physical or intellectual.

Truth can no more be reduced to power than light can be reduced to heat; this entire philosophy is based on an arbitrary and unjustifiable confusion of categories.

To say that "truth is relative to race, class, gender, or sexual orientation" is similar to saying that it is relative to height or weight or hair color. It is also self-refuting. This philosophy is a form of intellectual suicide—or pretended suicide, which is in a way worse because it is hypocritical. It lacks seriousness and honesty. It deserves as much attention as a sneer.

Article 10: Whether symbolic logic is superior to Aristotelian logic for philosophizing?

Objection 1: *It seems that* it is, for it is a modern development, and would not have become popular if it were not superior. In fact, 99% of all formal logic textbooks in print today use symbolic rather than Aristotelian logic.

Objection 2: It is as superior in efficiency to Aristotelian logic as Arabic numerals to Roman numerals, or a computer to an abacus.

Objection 3: Aristotelian logic presupposes metaphysical and epistemological realism, which are no longer universally accepted. Symbolic logic is ideologically neutral. It is like mathematics not only in efficiency but also in that it carries less "philosophical baggage."

On the contrary, the authority of common sense is still on the side of Aristotelian rather than symbolic logic. But common sense is the origin, basis, and foundation of all further refinements of reason, including symbolic logic; and a branch should not contradict its trunk, an upper story should not contradict its foundation. All philosophical systems, including symbolic logic, since they are refinements of, begin with, and depend on the validity of common sense, even while they greatly refine and expand this foundation, should not contradict it, as symbolic logic does. (See below.)

I answer that at least two essential principles of symbolic logic contradict common sense: (1) the counter-intuitive "paradox of material implication," according to which a false proposition materially implies any proposition, false as well as true, including contradictories (see *Socratic Logic*, pp. 266–369); and (2) the assumption that a particular proposition (like "some elves are evil") claims more, not

36

less, than a universal proposition (like "all elves are evil"), since it is assumed to have "existential import" while a universal proposition is assumed to lack it, since symbolic logic assumes the metaphysical position (or "metaphysical baggage") of Nominalism. See *Socratic Logic*, pp. 179–81, 262–63 and *The Two Logics* by Henry Veatch. Furthermore, no one ever actually argues in symbolic logic except professional philosophers. Its use coincides with the sudden decline of interest in philosophy among students. If you believe that is a coincidence, I have a nice timeshare in Florida that I would like to sell to you.

Reply to Objection 1: Popularity is no index of truth. If it were, truth would change, and contradict itself, as popularity changed—including the truth of that statement. And thus it is self-contradictory.

Reply to Objection 2: It is *not* more efficient in dealing with ordinary language. We never hear people actually argue any of the great philosophical questions in symbolic logic, but we hear a syllogism every few sentences.

Reply to Objection 3: Symbolic logic is not philosophically neutral but presupposes Nominalism, as shown by the references in the "*I answer that*" above.

Question II:
Metaphysics

(Note: half of these ten questions concern not issues *within* metaphysics but the status and legitimacy of metaphysics itself, because the entire science of metaphysics has been under suspicion among philosophers ever since Hume and Kant. [See my *Socrates Meets Hume* and *Socrates Meets Kant*.])

Article 1: Whether metaphysics is something esoteric, arcane, or occult?

Objection 1: It seems that it does, for this is how it is classified in bookstores in California. It is "under the sheets" with witchcraft.

Objection 2: Furthermore, most ordinary human beings view it this way. For as its very name indicates, it goes beyond (*meta*) ordinary human knowledge, as the physical sciences do not.

Objection 3: There is good reason for this classification, for metaphysics is supremely abstract and thus supremely removed from and irrelevant to the life of ordinary people.

On the contrary, the word "metaphysics" means simply "beyond physics." But most of the questions that people naturally ask (e.g. "Who am I?" "What is the highest value?" or even "Does he love me?") go beyond physics and beyond the competency of physics to answer. But these questions are not regarded as esoteric, arcane, or occult, except perhaps by the most adamant materialists.

A. 1: *Whether metaphysics is something esoteric, arcane, or occult?*

I answer that metaphysics goes "beyond physics" not by dealing only with *non-physical* realities but by dealing with more *universal* questions, questions about all of reality, or "being *qua* being": questions such as: (1) "Is causality a real relation?" (2) "Is time objectively or only subjectively real?" and (3) "Is there any reality that is intrinsically unintelligible?" These questions are (1) not esoteric, for everyone knows what "causality" means and everyone deals with causes and effects constantly; in fact, the very asking of this question is an attempt to mentally cause, or bring about, an answer. (2) Nor are they arcane, for "time" is not an arcane concept but very present and up-to-date! (3) Nor are they occult, for "intelligibility" is not only not an occult concept but its very opposite.

Reply to Objection 1: If we let California bookstores define our philosophy for us, we would all be "creating our own reality," naming and taming "our" angels, and taking out-of-body trips to Jupiter by channeling planetary spirits.

Reply to Objection 2: Every science in some way goes beyond ordinary knowledge, including philosophical sciences, which are "sciences" in a broader and looser sense than the physical sciences, but still a meaningful sense (for instance "the ordered, rational knowledge of reality through causal explanations").

Reply to Objection 3: As will be shown in question 5 below, metaphysics explores the necessary foundations of all human knowledge and the truths or principles that hold true for all objects of human knowledge. Thus the most fundamental differences of opinion in all the other divisions of philosophy, including the most relevant and practical questions of ethics and politics, are always based on differences of opinion in metaphysics. These differences have emerged even in logic, apparently the most metaphysically neutral division of philosophy. (See the last four Articles of question 1 above.) Thus nothing is more universally "relevant" than metaphysics.

Article 2: Whether metaphysics originates in experience?

Objection 1: It seems that it does not, for metaphysics, in order to transcend physics, must seek *a priori* knowledge, not *a posteriori* knowledge. But a priori knowledge by definition is prior to experience and does not originate in experience.

Objection 2: If metaphysics, like the special sciences, originated in experience, then its questions would be resolvable by experience, as the questions of the special sciences are, in which experienced data constitute the standard which verifies or falsifies hypotheses. But the questions of metaphysics are not resolvable by experience, for if they were, they would have been resolved by now, and the same universal or nearly-universal agreement would have been reached there as has been reached in the special sciences. These questions have *not* been resolved. And the reason is that metaphysical statements are not in principle verifiable or falsifiable by experience.

Objection 3: If metaphysics originated in experience, as both common sense and the special sciences do, its conclusions would reveal new facts of experience, as both common sense and the special sciences do. But it does not.

On the contrary, all human knowledge (as Aristotle says) begins in experience, though (as Kant says) it does not necessarily follow that it also ends in experience. Since metaphysics is part of human knowledge, it too must in some way begin in experience.

I answer that all of philosophy is an attempt by reason to understand and illumine our human experience in depth, rather than an attempt to expand it in width, so to speak, i.e. to add data or detail as the particular sciences do. And to understand experience, it is necessary to begin with experience. Therefore all of philosophy begins with experience. And metaphysics is part of philosophy. Therefore metaphysics begins with experience.

Everything we experience has one thing in common: it is real, it is some kind of being. Metaphysics explores this fact, and seeks the common laws and principles of all being.

"Being" is not a *contrast* or an *alternative* to experience; it is the *object* of all experience. As Marcel shows, it is also the subject of all experience, for my being is equally in question when I question being as such. (See II, 2.) For this reason, metaphysics, the study of being as being, does not ignore or fly from experience, as a rocket escapes the earth into the vacuum of outer space. Rather, it digs into the ground of experience, as an engineer builds a foundation under a building.

Reply to Objection 1: The objective truths sought by metaphysics are indeed *a priori*, for they are true universally, true of all possible experience. But the psychological *process of arriving at* these truths begins with experience.

Reply to Objection 2: Not only the questions of metaphysics, but also many other meaningful and important questions, in fact all or nearly all philosophical questions, in all the other divisions of philosophy, have not been "resolved" if "resolved" means "universal agreement."

An argument which resolves an issue or answers a question in an objectively valid way does not depend on everyone's subjective agreement for its validity. If it did, then "A=B and B=C, therefore A=C" would be made invalid if just one stubborn-willed or feeble-minded person denied it.

Actually, experience *is* the test of truth in metaphysics, just as it is in common sense or the sciences, though in a less direct or empirical way. For instance, the metaphysical positions of radical monism (the denial of real plurality) or pluralism (the denial of real unity) are both refutable because they fail to explain our *experience* of real differences or real unities. In metaphysics, as in the other sciences, a theory or hypothesis is judged by its adequacy in explaining the data of experience. The difference is that in metaphysics we explain a more total range of experience. In that sense, metaphysics relies on the *most* experience.

Reply to Objection 3: Metaphysics seeks not new experiential data but an illumination and explanation of experience. It seeks the ultimate grounds of, or conditions of possibility for, what we experience. It is like a patient's X-ray rather than an additional patient. It is like spelunking rather than engineering.

Article 3: Whether metaphysics is a legitimate science?

Objection 1: It seems that it is not, for every legitimate science has some distinctive subject matter by which it is distinguished and defined. But metaphysics has no distinctive subject matter, since it studies all of being *qua* being. Therefore metaphysics is not a legitimate science.

Objection 2: Metaphysics is an attempt to understand all of being, or being as a whole. But we are only parts of being, and the part cannot comprehend the whole. Only God could be a metaphysician.

Objection 3: To comprehend X, one must transcend X. For instance, the soul can comprehend the body, man can comprehend animals, adults can comprehend infants, and the wise can comprehend the foolish, but not vice versa. The reason for this is that *the understanding of X cannot be a part of X*. For the act of understanding X is an addition to X, as taking a picture of a person with a camera is an addition to that person and is not any part of that person. For the camera does not take a picture of itself. Thus only a being that transcends all being could understand all being. But "a *being* that transcends all *being*" is a contradiction in terms. Therefore metaphysics is impossible.

Objection 4: Human knowledge is always perspectival. It cannot know the universal laws of being, for it is limited to what fits into its human perspective, and is so conditioned by the knowing apparatus that it is impossible to know things as they are in themselves outside that perspective as conditioned by that apparatus.

On the contrary, "all men by nature desire to know," as Aristotle says. They desire to know all that is knowable. Bernard Lonergan in

Insight calls this "the unrestricted drive of the mind to know all that there is to know about all that there is." But no natural desire is in vain. For nature never produces a desire that corresponds to no real object, or one that is in principle unattainable. Therefore this knowledge is possible.

I answer that metaphysics is a legitimate science because philosophy is a legitimate science (see above, Question 1, Article 4), and metaphysics is a necessary part of philosophy. In fact, all the rest of philosophy depends on metaphysics. For instance, what knowing is (which is the question of epistemology) and what the human knower is (which is the question of philosophical anthropology) depends on what *is*. For instance, if all non-material reality is not real, then all non-material, non-empirical knowledge and powers of knowing in the human knower must also be unreal.

Reply to Objection 1: Although metaphysics does not have a specific and limited subject matter, it has a distinctive point of view (it studies being *qua* being), and this is how it distinguishes itself from all other sciences. As Heidegger says, metaphysics explores not only *what* things are but the fact *that* they are. (*Introduction to Metaphysics*, ch. 1)

Reply to Objection 2: Man can be observed to have a God-like power of transcendence over the whole from the mere fact that he raises questions about the whole. This is a fact whether or not one grounds this fact in the belief that man is made in God's image.

Reply to Objection 3: It would be a contradiction if man transcended all being in his *being*, but it is not a contradiction if man transcends all being in his *knowing* of all being. Thus, unlike a stone, a knower of a stone transcends the being of the stone in knowing the stone. This is the distinctive and remarkable thing about knowledge: that a knower can give another being a second being, another life, so to speak, in consciousness. An ephemeral rainbow can be eternalized in memory.

Reply to Objection 4: This Kantian principle, that things-in-themselves are unknowable, would indeed make "transcendent" metaphysics impossible, and has in fact made it questionable and unpopular among many modern philosophers. But the principle is false, for it is self-contradictory. It asserts *as a thing-in-itself* that things-in-themselves cannot be asserted. Or, if this assertion is not a thing-in-itself but only an appearance, which may not correspond to things-in-themselves, then it asserts nothing *and denies nothing* about things-in-themselves, or real being. And if it denies nothing about real being, it cannot deny the reality of traditional metaphysics.

Kant tried to draw a limit to all possible thought, but (as Wittgenstein pointed out) this is self-contradictory because "to draw a limit to thought, thought must think both sides of that limit."

This is not to deny that our knowledge of being itself is perspectival, and limited by our perspective. To know a mountain from below, or from above, or from halfway up, is indeed to know it from three different perspectives. But it is to know the real mountain!

Article 4: Whether metaphysics is practical?

Objection 1: It seems that it is not, for it seeks knowledge for its own sake rather than for action or practice.

Objection 2: The popular opinion of the "absent-minded professor" contains at least a basic truth: that philosophers in general, and metaphysicians in particular, are the least practical of human beings.

Objection 3: Action is always concerned with particular persons, situations, and choices. But metaphysics abstracts from everything particular in seeking the most universal principles of all being. Thus, in abstracting from the particular, it abstracts from the practical.

On the contrary, G.K. Chesterton says, "It is a practical thing for a landlady to know her tenant's income, but it is even more practical and necessary that she should know his philosophy." And Samuel Johnson says, "If your guest professes seriously to be a materialist, then when he leaves you should be careful to count your spoons."

I answer that how one lives is a most practical issue. But one lives according to one's philosophy, whether or not one adverts to it consciously. But all the other divisions of philosophy depend on metaphysics. Since metaphysics is the heart of philosophy, and one's philosophy is the heart of one's life, and life is most practical, it follows that metaphysics is most practical. Not to know or even inquire about the most basic laws and principles of the country one lives in is certainly not practical. But we all live in the country of being, unless we and/or the world we live in are only illusions.

The close connection between metaphysics and practice can be seen in studying any major philosophy. Four examples are Platonism, Aristotelianism, Hinduism, and Marxism.

Plato's ultimate metaphysical principle that unifies and explains all that is, the "Form" or "Idea" of the Good, is also the ultimate practical principle, since all practice aims at some good.

For Aristotle, all explanation is through causes; and of the four causes, the final cause, or the good (the essential meaning of "the practical"), is "the cause of causes" since only because any act is directed to an end or final cause, does the efficient cause impose the formal cause upon the material cause.

For Hinduism, the supreme good of human life is the realization of one's true identity or divine being, in a metaphysical insight or enlightenment.

For Marxism, because of its metaphysical materialism (that all reality is matter), and because matter is essentially competitive, all of history is competition (class conflict); and because economy regulates all material goods, economics is the key to all of human life and history.

Reply to Objection 1: Theoretical sciences, which seek knowledge for its own sake rather than for the sake of practice, typically yield the most practical and life-changing knowledge of all. For instance, Einstein's theoretical physics and mathematics produced the nuclear age.

Reply to Objection 2: Popular stereotypes, like analogies, may be good clues but they are bad arguments. Furthermore, it is "absent-minded professors" like Aristotle, Newton, and Einstein, who have in fact changed the world of human practice the most, however indirectly.

Reply to Objection 3: Abstraction leaves the realm of the particular, the immediately experienced, and the practical, only to return to it again with greater understanding (and thus greater freedom and power). Metaphysical knowledge moves in a great circle, from immediate experience, through questioning of its ultimate foundations, to understanding its ultimate principles, and finally back again, applying these principles to the world of experience.

Metaphysics is indeed the most abstract of sciences. But nothing is more practical than abstraction. It raises man above the animal and is the source of all science and technology as well as philosophy. Only when primitive man abstracted "sharpness" from "this sharp stone" did he conceive the technology of changing dull stones into sharp ones and thus invented knives.

All the valid objections against "abstractions" on the part of Existentialist and Personalist philosophers like Kierkegaard, Bergson, Marcel, and Buber are objections against the *reification of* abstractions, Whitehead's "fallacy of misplaced concreteness"—e.g. Descartes' two-substance anthropology ("the ghost in the machine"), or Locke's definition of ideas as objects of knowledge, or Aristotle's famous critique of Plato's Forms. But Aristotle used abstractions expertly.

Article 5: Whether metaphysics is unavoidable?

Objection 1: It seems that it is not, for most people do in fact avoid it. There are far more physicians than metaphysicians. Thus the signature protest of "Bones" McCoy to Captain Kirk from "Star Trek," "Dammit, Jim, I'm a doctor, not a philosopher!" (i.e. a physician, not a metaphysician).

Objection 2: It depends on a man's will whether he will inquire into any question. Thus, just as questions of economics are avoidable for those not interested in money, such as monks who take a vow of poverty, questions of metaphysics are avoidable for those who choose to avoid them. And most people do choose to avoid them, for they require the supreme degree of abstraction, which most people are neither capable of nor interested in.

Objection 3: Whatever is controversial is avoidable. For if an idea is controversial, only some, but not all, people embrace it; and those who do not, avoid it. But metaphysics is controversial, for the majority of philosophers today are skeptical of its possibility. Therefore, it is avoidable.

Objection 4: No single concrete example can be shown of a single practical, crucial issue that necessarily depends on metaphysics.

Objection 5: Persons are more important than abstractions like being. And the more important cannot depend on the less important. Therefore philosophical anthropology cannot depend on metaphysics.

On the contrary, no Israelite who heard (through Moses) the word from God in the burning bush, "I AM," could fail to understand it. But this was a metaphysical statement. (In fact, it was *the* metaphysical statement.)

I answer that there are three ways, at least, in which metaphysics is unavoidable: (1) by reduction; (2) by analysis of meaning; and (3) by an immediate and intuitive experience.

(1) Reduction is a kind of obverse of deduction, which is reasoning to a particular conclusion from a universal premise. When a conclusion is challenged, it is reduced to its premise in a *reductio ad absurdum*. For example, if Socrates is not mortal, then it is not true that all men are mortal; and if events, such as the Big Bang, can come into existence without being caused by any "Big Banger," then anything can happen for no reason at all, such as a large blue rabbit appearing on your head.

(2) It can be shown that the meaning of a statement that is not explicitly metaphysical nevertheless is so implicitly (such as "God exists," That's true for you but not for me," or "If I can kick it, it's real.")

(3) Finally, there are experiences that are common to all mankind that raise metaphysical questions, such as Heidegger's "fundamental question of metaphyiscs," "Why is there anything at all rather than nothing?", which he says is present in three common metaphysical moods:

> Why is there anything rather than nothing? . . . each of us is grazed at least once, perhaps more than once, by the hidden power of this question, even if he is not aware of what is happening to him. The question looms in moments of great despair, when things tend to lose all their weight and all meaning becomes obscured. Perhaps it will strike but once like a muffled bell that rings into our life and gradually dies away. It is present in moments of rejoicing, when all the things around us are transfigured and seem to be there for the first time, as if it might be easier to think they are not than to understand that they are and are as they are. The question is upon us in boredom, when we are equally removed from despair and joy, and everything about us seems so hopelessly commonplace that we no longer care whether anything is or is not—and with this the question "Why is there anything rather than nothing?" is evoked in a particular form.
> – (*Introduction to Metaphysics*, ch. 1, "The Fundamental Question")

Reply to Objection 1: There are more metaphysicians than physicians, for not everyone is a physician but everyone is a metaphysician, since everyone makes claims about being. "Bones" McCoy may avoid being a starship captain, since that is as much a special choice as being a doctor, but he cannot avoid philosophizing, and therefore metaphysicizing, even in the very protest against it, for he says that he *is* a doctor, not a philosopher.

Reply to Objection 2: What depends on our will includes our own subjective attention and interest. What does not depend on our will includes the nature of objective reality and the essential structure of thought and language. Thus we can choose to avoid turning our attention to being, but we cannot avoid being, unless we cease to be. As Kierkegaard says in *Concluding Unscientific Postscript*, "existence has the remarkable trait of compelling an existing individual to exist whether he wills it or not."

We *can* avoid abstracting from the particular to the supremely universal and thus we can avoid consciously entering the realm of metaphysical questions; but we cannot avoid existing and living in that realm, for there is no other. For outside being there is only non-being.

But though we can avoid making abstractions, we cannot avoid our inherent *capacity* to make them. Everyone, by having a human mind rather than merely an animal mind, is capable of metaphysical abstractions, such as: "If I can kick it, it's real"—which is a statement of metaphysical materialism.

Reply to Objection 3: Those who intend to avoid metaphysics do not really do so. For any indicative sentence, that is, any assertion that something *is* (an existential judgment), or that something is what it is (a copulative judgment about *what it is*, thus about both essence ["what"] and existence ["is"]), is by its nature a metaphysical statement, a statement about what *is*, even if the one who utters it does not attend to that fact. Thus one can avoid metaphysics only as one can avoid ethics: one can fail to attend to ends, goods, goals, and values, but one cannot fail to choose to act in one way or another because he desires to attain some end or good. As the choice to deny ethics is an ethical choice (e.g. Nietzsche's judgment that "beyond good and evil" is *better* than its opposite), so the choice to deny metaphysics is a metaphysical choice. It argues that reality, and/or reason, and/or the relation between reality and reason, *really is* such that metaphysics is impossible. E.g. Kant's claim that we cannot know things-in-themselves is a statement about things-in-themselves.

Reply to Objection 4: Whether or not it can be morally good, or permissible, to abort one's unborn child is certainly a crucial and practical issue. But this issue depends on metaphysics. For if universal essences such as human nature are in fact real (which is a metaphysical issue), and if all human beings possess this essence (which is an issue of philosophical anthropology dependent on the prior metaphysical issue), and if human knowledge is capable of knowing such universals (which is an issue of epistemology dependent on both the prior metaphysical and anthropological issues), and if there are universal moral rights possessed by human beings based on their possession of this universal human nature (and this ethical assumption is dependent on all the previous assumptions), then the "right to life" must be the first of these rights, and the foundation of all others; and abortion violates the essential rights of a human being, however small and undeveloped.

Another metaphysical dimension of this same practical issue of abortion is the ontological status of potentiality. If all individual human beings possess universal human nature, they also possess, as soon as they possess human nature, a real potentiality to exercise in the future distinctively human acts such as reasoning, even though some of them are not capable of exercising such powers at the moment, by reason of paralysis, or sleep, or coma, or by reason of being not yet fully developed, being unborn or newborn. And this assumption of real potentialities, like the assumption of real essences, is also a metaphysical assumption. If there are no real universal natures and no real potentialities inherent in them, it follows that we do not have the capacity to know them epistemologically, nor do we therefore have the moral obligation to recognize them and respect them.

A similar logical structure can be shown regarding slavery or racism. Metaphysical Nominalism, which denies the reality of universal essences or natures, and the consequent epistemological skepticism regarding our knowledge of such universal natures, would allow us to believe in a plurality of human species rather than just one—e.g. slaves vs. masters, or "last men" vs. "Übermenschen," as in Nietzsche, or blacks vs. whites—and this would allow radically different treatment of these different species, as we treat plants and animals in radically different ways (we do not break limbs off dogs as we break limbs off trees), or different species of animals (we do not crush cats as we crush ants), or animals and humans (we do not eat humans as we eat cows).

Objection 5: (1) Being is not the supreme abstraction, for if we abstract from everything we are left with nothing, not with being. Being (existence) is positive reality; it is essence that is negative in relation to existence, limiting existence to only a specific kind of existence.

(2) Personhood is not an accidental addition to being, but the fullness of being, the ultimate meaning of being, as Aquinas says: "The person is that which is most perfect in all of being." (ST I, 29, 3) See Norris Clarke, *Person and Being.*

Article 6: Whether universals are real?

Objection 1: It seems that they are not, for only individuals exist. If there are two horses in a stable, Tammy and Sammy, there is not a third horse there called Horseness, or the nature of horses.

Objection 2: Universals, or universal natures or essences, are potential, not actual. For instance, the nature of horse and the nature of unicorn are both universals, but only horses actually exist, not unicorns. Universals are existentially neutral. They do not *exist.*

Objection 3: No one tries to find horseness, or blueness. Common sense recognizes only individuals.

Objection 4: Whatever has actuality has activity. As Aquinas puts it, "first act" (actual being) always manifests itself in "second act" (activity) of some kind. But universal forms or essences do not and cannot act; only individuals do. Therefore they lack actuality. They are either mere potentialities or mere ideas.

Objection 5: Belief in universals leads to stereotyping, for instance: "You can't do that; that's not feminine, and you're a woman." Or: "Oh, you're Irish? Here's a drink. Tell me a story."

Objection 6: Universals are formulable in laws or rules. But "there's an exception to every rule," as is shown by the falseness of stereotypes.

On the contrary, Nominalism (the denial of universals) is self-contradictory, for it is a universal statement ("all universals are unreal"). As G.K. Chesterton says, "If [as Nominalism says] 'all chairs are different,' how can we call them all 'chairs'?" (*Orthodoxy*). (The "on the contrary" argument is typically an argument from authority, and the authority here is that of language, its inherent [universal!] structure.)

I answer that the reality of universals can be shown in three ways. (All of them can be found in Plato.)

The first way is epistemological. Universals are needed to account for the facts of human knowing. For intellectual knowledge, as distinct from sensation, is always of unchanging universals, such as triangularity, redness, or mass, not changing particulars, such as the Great Pyramid, a rose, or a ten-ton truck. If universals are unreal, then intellectual knowledge has no object.

The second way concerns values. Values are universals. If universals are unreal, so are values. Values, or goods, are objects of human willing. Human action and desire is a striving for not-yet-realized goals. These goals are not sensory particulars, for everything in the sensory world is already realized, or actual. Nor are they merely subjective; they are the *objects* of subjective striving. What we strive for is not our *desire for* happiness, or virtue, or money, or power, nor our *knowledge of* such things, but the things themselves.

The third way is metaphysical. All particular realities change, as Heraclitus rightly taught ("You can never step into the same river twice"). But the universal nature of being cannot change, as Parmenides rightly taught. Therefore the universal nature of being transcends particulars, as Plato taught.

To say that universals are real does not, however, necessarily entail the Platonic position that they are *separately* real, or existing substances. It may well be, as Aristotle held, that horseness is real only in horses and in the minds of those who know horses—i.e. that universals are not substances but the (real) forms of individual substances, and that they are real as separate abstract universals only in the human minds that abstract them. This (Aristotelian) position is called (by Aristotelians and Thomists) Moderate Realism as distinct from Platonic Extreme Realism.

Reply to Objection 1: Horseness is indeed not a third horse but is the nature of the two horses that are there. If there were no horseness, we could not truly call Tammy and Sammy two *horses.*

Reply to Objection 2: The nature of a unicorn is only potential, since unicorns do not actually exist, but the nature of a horse is actual because horses do actually exist. Since "universals are existentially neutral," they are not necessarily only potential but can also be in actual existence.

Reply to Objection 3: Common sense recognizes universals by using common nouns (like "horse") as well as proper nouns (like "Tammy" and "Sammy").

Reply to Objection 4: If universal forms are not real because they do not act, then matter (the co-principle with form) is not real either for the same reason. That which acts, the agent of activity, is the whole substance, not its universal form alone or its individuating matter alone.

Reply to Objection 5: "Abusus non tollit usum" (the abuse does not take away the use). Belief in universals does not necessitate stereotyping; it merely allows it. Similarly, belief in God does not necessitate blasphemy, but allows for it, and free will does not necessitate moral evil, but allows it.

Reply to Objection 6: Laws, rules, or generalizations which concern accidents do indeed have exceptions, but those concerning essences do not. For instance, using lethal violence, if necessary, to protect the innocent against a lethal aggressor is an exception to "thou shalt not kill," but no triangle has more or fewer sides than three.

"There's an exception to every rule" is a self-contradictory proposition. For either there is an exception to *that* rule, or not. If there is, then there's *not* an exception to *every* rule, and that proposition is false. If there isn't, then that proposition is also false, because that proposition says that there is.

Article 7: Whether both oneness and manyness are real?

Objection 1: It seems that oneness is not real, for existing things are many, and nothing can be both one and many, therefore existing things are not one.

Objection 2: Oneness is not real, for the universe is the sum total of all the many existing things, but the universe is not another existing thing. The universe itself is the only unity among its diverse entities.

Objection 3: Manyness is not real, for the authority of the great religious mystics uniformly testifies that ultimate reality is one, not many.

Objection 4: Manyness is not real, for, as Parmenides argued, manyness is the opposite of oneness; but being is one, for being is only being and not also nonbeing, by the law of non-contradiction. If being is one, it is not many, since many is the opposite of one, and nothing is the opposite of itself.

On the contrary, common sense always accepts both oneness and manyness, as can be seen in the very structure of language (e.g. the difference between common and proper nouns, and between the singular and the plural.).

I answer that the onus of proof is not on the one who would affirm the reality of both oneness and manyness, but on the one who would deny either one. But all the arguments for these two denials are refutable. We experience both oneness and manyness, and metaphysics should explain our experience, not explain it away.

Reply to Objection 1: Things can be both one and many in different respects. Thus some existing things—members of the same species—are many substances sharing one essential form.

Reply to Objection 2: (1) The very term "universe" implies both unity and diversity.

(2) If anything else exists besides the universe (e.g. God), then the universe is *not* the sum total of all the many existing things, so the premise is questionable.

(3) There are other unities, other than membership in the one universe, that are found among the diverse entities in the universe. For instance, there is also the unity of a species.

Reply to Objection 3: (1) It is improper when doing philosophy to settle a philosophical issue by religious authority, whether mystical or scriptural. (2) Not all mystics agree that the many is an illusion, even among Hindus (e.g. Ramanuja vs. Shankara), and much less among Christians, for whom the Trinitarian God is both one God and many (three) Persons.

Reply to Objection 4: Being can be both one and many in different respects. It is self-contradictory for the same proposition to be both true and false, and two contradictory propositions cannot both be true. But two contrary concepts or predicates or essences can be possessed by the same subject. E.g. I can be both visible (in body) and invisible (in soul), and both good (ontologically) and evil (morally).

Article 8: Whether time is real?

Objection 1: It seems that time is not real, for time is correlative to change, but change is logically impossible. For "X changes" is a self-contradictory proposition. For in order for X to change, it must become non-X. If X does not become non-X, then X does not change. If, on the other hand, X does become non-X, then X is no more, and ceases. But if a thing ceases, it cannot do anything, including change.

Objection 2: Time involves past, present, and future. But the past is unreal, because it is dead, and the future is unreal, for it is unborn, and the present does not move, but simply is. Therefore nothing that is moves and changes. But time involves change. Therefore there is no time.

On the contrary, everyone implicitly admits that time is real in every action they perform, whether mental or physical, for every human action takes time to perform.

I answer that to say or think that time is unreal takes time. So if time is unreal, we cannot say or think that time is unreal. But if we cannot say or think that time is unreal, we cannot argue for that proposition, for we cannot argue for what we cannot say or think.

Reply to Objection 1: In ordinary change, X changes in its accidents but not in its essence, which "stands under" (*sub-stans*) those accidents as a bridge stands under the cars that move over it. The objection fails to distinguish these two different aspects or dimensions of X.

Reply to Objection 2: It is not time that exists, but beings. And beings change—e.g. your mind while you read this sentence. Time measures change. The three dimensions of time are not three possible *beings*. The objection concretizes abstractions.

Article 9: Whether all that is real is material?

Objection 1: It seems that it is, for common sense always turns to material examples such as humans, animals, plants, minerals, or stars when thinking of examples of real beings.

Objection 2: No one has ever seen the invisible. But all knowledge begins with and depends on sense observation of the visible, or the object of one of the other senses. Therefore the existence of invisible, immaterial beings cannot be known, only believed.

Objection 3: The "principle of parsimony," or "Ockham's Razor," tells us to avoid needlessly complex explanations. But explaining the visible and tangible by supposing the existence of invisible and intangible beings (such as God, angels, or souls) is a needlessly complex explanation. For modern science can explain everything without recourse to immaterial beings. For instance, the most commonly believed example of an immaterial being is the human soul or mind, but there is no example of a mental act or activity or event that cannot be explained scientifically by a material event in the brain.

On the contrary, as C.S. Lewis says (in *Miracles*, ch. 3), "the knowledge of a thing is not one of that thing's parts." Therefore the knowledge of matter is not just a part of matter but transcends matter.

I answer that (1) the knowledge of any object cannot be a part (or

56

dimension) of that object. For if it were—if the-fact-that-I-knew-X (let us call that Y) was one of the parts of X—then the X that existed independently of my knowing it would not be the same as, but would be less than, the X that I knew, since it would lack one part: namely, Y, or the-fact-that-I-knew-X. But in that case my knowledge of X would not be a true knowledge of X, for true knowledge is the identity of knowing subject and known object.

(2) But I can know material things. Materialism could not be true if I did not know material things.

(3) Therefore my knowledge of material things must be not merely a part of the material things I know.

In fact, I can know, by science, some truths about the entire universe, about all of matter, about matter as such (e.g. that F=MA, or that E=MC^2). Therefore my knowing act must transcend the entire universe. But the universe is the sum total of all matter. Therefore my act of knowing transcends matter.

Reply to Objection 1: (1) Common sense is *not* materialistic. Most materialists are either philosophers or scientists, not ordinary people. (2) Common sense is not infallible. (3) It is more reasonable to take common sense seriously as a negative criterion than as a positive one; that is, what common sense strongly contradicts (e.g. materialism) is for that reason probably false, but what common sense does not claim to know (e.g. angels, or Black Holes) is not for that reason unreal.

Reply to Objection 2: From our experience of knowing the visible (e.g. a platypus) we can reason to the existence of the invisible (e.g. the mind that knows the platypus, or perhaps even the strange Mind that designed it).

Reply to Objection 3: (1) Ockham's Razor is a useful methodological principle for science, but this does not make it a true ontological principle for philosophy.

(2) We find many real beings that are superfluous and need not exist (e.g. the platypus). But explanations should conform to the nature of experienced reality, not to an *a priori* abstract methodological principle. The materialist's supposed empiricism is really anti-empirical.

(3) The material sciences have *not* explained all that exists, for they have not explained their own existence. Mere matter cannot think about matter, explain matter, or be either true or false about matter. For mere matter is not *about* anything; it just is. *Ideas* are "about" things. Materialism, which entails the denial of the existence of ideas, is an idea. Materialism is an "ism." Thus it refutes itself.

(4) Cybernetics has indeed shown a corresponding material event in the brain for every supposedly immaterial event in consciousness. But this no more disproves the existence of immaterial consciousness than the fact that every material event we can point to must be an event in consciousness by the very fact that we point to it disproves the existence of matter. An immaterialist (Buddhist, Hindu, or Christian Scientist) could use the same argument, with the same premise of Ockham's Razor, to eliminate all *material* reality and leave only thought, because any example of matter that anyone can ever think of is also an example of thinking.

Article 10: Whether all that is, is intelligible?

Objection 1: It seems that it is not, for if it were, we would all be intellectually satisfied. But we are not. If we are wise, like Socrates, we know that we are ignorant and therefore we ask questions, as he did. Asking questions stems not from our intellectual experience of and satisfaction with intelligibility, but our experience of and dissatisfaction with unintelligibility.

Objection 2: Not everything is intelligible, for God is not intelligible to finite minds, since He is infinite.

Objection 3: No one can experience all things. Therefore no one can know whether or not some of the things he has not yet experienced may be unintelligible, even if all the things he has so far experienced have been intelligible.

Objection 4: Mere formal logic reveals something that is unintelligible: *Unintelligibility* is unintelligible—by the law of non-contradiction.

Objection 5: It is impossible to prove that all reality is intelligible without begging the question, for all proof presupposes intelligibility.

On the contrary, Parmenides says, "It is the same thing that can be thought and that can be." And Hegel says, "The real is the rational and the rational is the real." Even if all the rest of what these two philosophers said is rejected, these two statements stand.

I answer that no natural desire is in vain. But we have a natural desire to know everything. If some of reality is not intelligible, our natural and innate desire to know everything, which defines us as human, is a meaningless and self-frustrating desire, a radical failure built into the very nature of things, human nature, and their relationship.

If reality as such were not intelligible, then our demand to explain what we experience and observe would be futile. For the fundamental principle of all explanation is the principle of intelligibility. All explanation is reduced to this formula: "If this hypothesis were not true, then the real data we experience or observe would not be intelligible." Thus all explanation and all search for explanation would cease if all reality were not intelligible or if we ceased to believe that it was.

Reply to Objection 1: There is no contradiction between maintaining (1) that all reality is in principle intelligibile by its own nature, and (2) that our minds are always less than omniscient and therefore in need of more questioning. In fact, the presupposition of questioning is the hope for an intelligible answer.

Reply to Objection 2: The infinite God is perfectly intelligible to the infinite mind of God. God is not fully intelligible to man, but He is fully intelligible in Himself. (He is "pure light, and in Him is no darkness at all." John 1:5) Lack of intelligibility *to any given mind* is not the same as lack of intelligibility in itself.

Reply to Objection 3: (1) To say that some domains of reality are intelligible while others are not, we would have to know the whole of reality first. For we cannot divide a genus into two species without knowing the genus. But we can know a thing only if it is knowable (intelligible).

(2) If we do not accept the principle of universal intelligibility *from the beginning*, and if we suppose instead that there *may* be some real beings, or some parts of reality, or some domains of reality, that are unintelligible, there is no way of knowing, before we investigate, whether or not the particular domain of reality we are now investigating might be one of those parts that is unintelligible. This results in universal skepticism.

Reply to Objection 4: This is a sophism. Or, if not, it is simply false; for "unintelligibility" is an intelligible concept, though a purely negative one, like darkness or nonexistence.

Reply to Objection 5: (1) It is true that the Principle of Intelligibility, like the law of non-contradiction, cannot be demonstrated from any prior principle without begging the question. The fact that it cannot be proved does not mean that it is not true, or that it is not certain. It is in fact self-evident, and necessarily presupposed, like the law of non-contradiction, as the objection itself shows.

(2) The objection assumes that everything must be proved. This is a self-contradictory assumption, for it cannot be proved.

Question III:
Natural Theology

Article 1: Whether natural theology (or philosophical theology) is possible?

Objection 1: It seems that it is not, for "theology" means "the science of God," and there can be no science of God, because science depends on reason, and reason depends on logic, and logic depends on definitions, and definitions depend on things having limits to define. But God, being infinite, has no limits, therefore no definition; therefore there is no logic, or reason, or science of God.

Objection 2: A given science must have a single real object. For instance, the object of physics is matter: not matter in dreams or matter in alternative possible universes that are merely theoretical, but the matter everyone recognizes as existent. But there is a different God for each different philosopher, each different religion, each different culture, and each different era. Therefore there is no single science of God.

Objection 3: God is the object of faith. But faith, even if it is true and does not contradict reason, is not a matter of reason, as science is. If faith does not go beyond reason, it is not faith. But if it does go beyond reason, it is not the object of science.

Objection 4: God is the object of "religion," which means a "binding relationship" which is personal. But the personal is not the object of science.

Objection 5: Human reason is too weak to be able to prove the existence and nature of God. And what is not proved, is not known with certainty, unless it is a self-evident first principle like the law of non-contradiction, which the existence of God is not. Therefore the existence and nature of God are not known with certainty. But science (whether physical, mathematical, or philosophical) seeks certainty, or at least measurable probability—which is also impossible regarding God. Therefore there is no science of God, or philosophical theology.

On the contrary, some of the most scientific philosophers of all time, such as Aquinas, Descartes, Spinoza, Hegel, and Shankara, have written elaborate rational defenses and explorations of the existence and attributes of God. Natural theology *exists.*

I answer that if God were altogether unknowable by natural human reason, we could not by nature desire, will, love, or seek Him, for we cannot desire what we do not know. But men do seek Him, even some men without faith, such as agnostics. Therefore He is not altogether unknowable by natural reason. And insofar as anything is knowable by reason, it can be the object of a rational science, whether physical, mathematical, or philosophical.

Reply to Objection 1: God can be defined negatively, as the non-finite being, the non-temporal being, the non-caused being, the non-potential being, etc. This clearly distinguishes God from all other beings.

Reply to Objection 2: What-*is* does not depend on what-is-"*for*"-you, i.e. on what you think—unless you are God the Creator and Designer of all reality except Yourself.

To say "there is a different God for each different philosopher, religion, etc." is simply a confused way of asserting atheism: that there is no real God. If this were true, of course there could be no science of God, or theology, since "God" is merely a dream or a myth, dependent on different minds. But this is precisely one of the questions of theology: is there one real God? Can God's existence be proved?

And the true answer to that question is not relative to different minds. As there is only one true answer to an equation in mathematics, even though there are many wrong answers "for" those who err in math, and as there is only one real universe, though there are many erroneous views of it "for" those who err in physics, so there is only one true God, though there are many false opinions about God "for" those who err in theology. And it is the task of theological science, as of mathematical and physical science, to use reason to discover the truth and refute errors insofar as human reason can do this.

Reply to Objection 3: The same God can be the object of reason or the object of faith, just as the same truth of physics or mathematics can be believed on the authority of another mind, or understood by one's own reason.

Insofar as faith goes beyond reason, it is not scientifically demonstrable (e.g. the Trinity). However, even then reason can (1) refute objections, and (2) provide analogies, clues, probabilities, or arguments from "fittingness," as Aquinas does. And insofar as reason *can* understand, discover, and prove (these are the three "acts of the mind") some truths about God (e.g. His existence, unity, intelligence, and eternity), it can generate the science of theology.

Reply to Objection 4: The same distinction answers both Objection 3 and Objection 4. The personal cannot be exhausted by science, but it can be partly understood, discovered, and proved by science. Thus psychology can be a science, though not the kind of pure and perfect science that mathematics is, or even the kind of exact, quantifiable science that physics is.

Reply to Objection 5: This statement about the weakness of human reason is an assumed dogma, not a demonstrated conclusion. We cannot tell whether or not our reason can perform a task *before* we try. The claims of philosophers like Aquinas to have done philosophical theology must be faced and evaluated *a posteriori*, not ignored or rejected *a priori* without examining the data (like the *Summa Theologiae*).

Article 2: Whether there is one primary meaning to the word 'God'?

Objection 1: It seems that there is not, for different religions differ about essential things like how many gods there are, whether God is one Person, three Persons, or no person, whether God has a will, whether God is the source of both good and evil or only good, and whether God is the creator of the universe.

Objection 2: The meaning of the word 'God,' insofar as it can be determined by philosophical reasoning, emerges from each argument for the existence of God: e.g. "first, uncaused cause of all caused causes," "necessary being on which all contingent beings depend," "most perfect being which gives place and rank to all imperfect beings," or "intelligent cause of design or intelligibility in nature," as in Aquinas. And since there are many arguments for God's existence and not just one, there are many meanings to the word 'God.'

Objection 3: There is no lowest common denominator among all the religions' different conceptions of God that can be used without prejudicial preference for some and against others.

On the contrary, believers in all religions agree with each other about *something* against the atheists; and that "something," however difficult to define, makes a great difference.

I answer that we can arrive at a minimal definition of "God" or "the religious object" that applies to nearly all religions, except for polytheism, which is not a "live option" today among the educated. For even if Anselm's "ontological argument" is fallacious, his definition of God as "that than which nothing greater can be conceived" would be agreed to by Christians, Jews, Muslims, Hindus, and even Buddhists and Taoists.   And from this definition of God, many attributes of God can be deduced, since it is more perfect to be actual, eternal, spiritual, omnipotent, intelligent, omniscient, wise, free, good, just, and benevolent than to be potential, temporal, material, weak, unintelligent, ignorant, foolish, unfree, evil, unjust, or malevolent.

Reply to Objection 1: These are differences *within* an already-agreed consensus, which is universal or nearly universal among all religions, that something exists that transcends the universe and humanity.

Reply to Objection 2: Different arguments for a conclusion do not entail different conclusions. These different arguments do not prove different Gods but different attributes of God. Even different definitions of God do not mean different Gods. If two definitions contradict each other, at least one is false; but both are attempts to define the same object.

Reply to Objection 3: (1) The lowest common denominator is religion itself. Even if the different religions cannot agree on a definition of the object of religion, the fact that we can speak meaningfully of different "religions" means that we have a working concept of the essential meaning of this term.

(2) They *do* agree on a "common denominator." For all religions teach that there is a single Ultimate Reality which transcends matter, time, space, finitude, and ordinary positive definition.

Article 3: Whether God's existence can be proved from the concept of God (Anselm's "ontological argument")?

Objection 1: It seems that it can, for the concept of God is natural to man and is universally understood. No other concept that is natural to man and is universally (or almost universally) understood fails to correspond to a reality.

Objection 2: Also, all men have an innate *desire* for God, or for union with God, at least implicitly, for they are never completely satisfied with anything else. But one cannot desire something that is unknown. Therefore all men innately know God, at least implicitly.

Objection 3: Anselm's argument proves that the existence of God is self-evident simply by analyzing the concept of God. It could be summarized most briefly as follows. Any proposition whose denial is self-contradictory is self-evidently true. But "God does not exist" is self-contradictory, therefore "God exists" is self-evidently true.

Proof of the minor premise: "God does not exist" is self-contradictory because "God" means "that than which nothing greater can be conceived," or "the being which possesses all conceivable perfections";

and objective, independent existence is a conceivable perfection. A God who exists independently of the human mind is more perfect than a God who exists only in the mind. So "God does not exist" means "The being which possesses *all* conceivable perfections does *not* possess *this* conceivable perfection: objective existence independent of the human mind." Since this is self-contradictory, its contradiction ("God exists") is self-evident.

On the contrary, the authority of common sense militates against Anselm's argument, for every time it is first explained, to any person but a philosopher, that person is suspicious and not convinced, even if he admires its cleverness and cannot refute it. (I can attest to this fact after presenting the argument to about 15,000 college students for almost fifty years.)

I answer that God's existence can be proved only by showing that something exists which could not possibly exist unless God existed as its only possible explanation and cause. But the "ontological argument" does not argue from the existence of anything except the concept of God in the mind, and it does not prove that the concept of God could not exist in the mind unless God existed in reality as its only possible cause. *That* line of thought (an argument of Descartes), like the argument from desire, is more impressive to most people, but it too is only a probable argument, for other causes have reasonably been brought forth by atheists to account for the presence of the idea of God in man's mind, such as the mind's extrapolation from a range of visible finite goods to an invisible infinite good, or wishful thinking.

Reply to Objection 1: The objection's argument has a weak, merely inductive and therefore merely probable step, which is the step 2 in the following progression.

Step 1 is data: All other natural and universal concepts correspond to realities.

Step 2 is an inductive argument from this data to the conclusion that therefore *all* natural and universal concepts correspond to reality.

Step 3 takes this conclusion as a major premise, adds the minor premise that "the concept of God is natural and universal," and draws the conclusion that "the concept of God corresponds to reality."

But inductive arguments like Step 2 do not yield certainty, only probability. The argument is very probable indeed, but not logically certain.

Reply to Objection 2: This argument is impressive and moving, but not certain, for:

(1) Not all men desire God, for to desire God is to hope that God exists, and not all men have that hope. All who desire God, will attain Him ("all who seek, find" – Matthew 7:8), and not all will attain Him (Matthew 7:21), therefore not all desire Him. The fact that men are not completely satisfied with anything else does not prove that they desire *God*, for one who despairs neither desires God nor is completely satisfied with anything else.

(2) The fact that men innately know the meaning of "God" does not mean that they innately know that God is real. Everyone knows that "God" does not mean a worm, or a paper clip; but not everyone knows that God is real, for there are atheists.

(3) Implicit unconscious knowledge of God is not the same as explicit rational knowledge of Him.

Reply to Objection 3: Anselm's argument commits the fallacy of equivocation. For it begins with the *concept* "God" and concludes with the proposition "God exists." The *concept* "God," like all concepts, is rightly put in quotation marks when made the subject of a proposition, while a reality is not. Thus "God" is used equivocally. The quotation marks are silently dropped in the conclusion. The proper conclusion should be: "Therefore the *concept* 'God' includes or contains the *concept* 'real, objective, independent existence.'"

Article 4: Whether God's existence can be proved from the cosmos?

Objection 1: It seems that it cannot, for the cosmos is finite and God infinite (since God is that than which nothing greater can be conceived, and the infinite is greater than the finite), and there is no proportion between the finite and the infinite. But no argument can validly move between two terms that have no proportion to each other. We have no positive concept of infinity; it is a purely negative term.

Objection 2: Not only are the ontological terms "infinite God" and "finite cosmos" disproportionate, but the very categories we use for things within the cosmos, such as "causality," may not apply beyond the cosmos to the infinite God, and so cannot serve as a mental bridge to bring our minds from the cosmos to God. Thus there is equivocation when we speak of God as "causing" the cosmos, using the same word we use for a bird "causing" an egg.

Objection 3: Either God did or did not create the cosmos. If God did not create the cosmos, His existence cannot be proved from the cosmos by way of causality since God would then not be the cause of the cosmos. But if God did create the cosmos, He must have done it by free choice rather than by necessity, for nothing finite can necessitate the infinite. But since God's free choices might have been different, there is no logical demonstration of them, for demonstration is only of the necessary and predictable, not of the free and unpredictable.

On the contrary, from observed facts in the cosmos such as (1) motion (change), (2) the causal dependence of one being on another for existence, (3) the existential contingency of finite beings, (4) degrees of perfection, and (5) order toward an end, Aquinas and others have validly proved at least a "thin slice of God," i.e. a being with divine (or at least, in the case of argument #5, superhuman) attributes such as (1) un-caused cause of change, (2) un-caused cause of existence, (3) necessary (non-contingent) and thus eternal being, (4) most perfect being, and (5) cosmic intelligence. If these proofs are invalid, the onus is on the critic to show how they contain ambiguous terms, false premises, or logical fallacies.

I answer that the literature on the subject of the cosmological proofs is immense, and not summarizable in one paragraph. The fact that Aquinas's "five ways" version of them, in the *Summa* (I, 2, 3), has remained the most well known and most popular for 750 years, among both philosophers and ordinary people, strongly indicates that that is the best summary of them.

And there is a sixth way available today due to modern scientific cosmology. It could be called "the Emo argument," and runs as follows:

(1) "The universe" (i.e. the physical universe) means the sum total of all matter, physical energy (prescinding from spiritual energy), space, and physical time (*chronos*, prescinding from spiritual time or *kairos*).

(2) The universe, it is now universally admitted, had a beginning about 14 billion years ago, in an event called the "Big Bang."

(3) Either this event was uncaused or it was caused.

(4) If it was uncaused, then the existence of the universe violates a fundamental principle of logic, science, philosophy, and common sense, namely, the principle of causality: that events have causes; that whatever happens has a reason for it happening; that the Pop! Theory is false (the theory that things can simply pop into existence for no reason at all).

(5) And in that case (if the Pop! Theory were true), it would be possible for anything to simply come into existence for no cause or reason at all, like a large blue rabbit with the name "Emo" tattooed on its tail (without a tattooer). For what is possible for all matter (the universe) is possible for some matter (Emo).

(6) This (Emo) is absurd.

(7) Therefore this event (the "Big Bang") must have been caused.

(8) It was not caused by matter, for all matter came into existence as its effect. (Remember our definition in step (1).)

(9) Therefore it was caused by something immaterial.

(10) But what is immaterial is spiritual.

(11) Therefore the "Big Bang" was caused by something spiritual that had the power to cause the entire universe to exist.

(12) And this is what we all call God. Nothing else fits that description.

This is only a "thin slice" of God, of course, not the "thick," fuller description of God in the Bible or any other specific scriptures. But it is enough to refute atheism.

Reply to Objection 1: Arguments may validly move between any two terms that are definable and clearly distinguishable. Although it is true that "infinite" is only a negative term to us, since we have no positive concept of infinity, nevertheless it is, like God Himself, negatively definable and clearly distinguishable from the finite.

Reply to Objection 2: Physical terms like "matter" and "time," and the kinds of causality that involve these things, do not, indeed, apply beyond the physical cosmos. But metaphysical terms like "being" and "cause of being" are absolutely universal and not limited to or dependent on the physical nature of this or any other cosmos; they apply to all being *qua* being. (See the previous articles on the legitimacy of metaphysics.) Their application to infinite being is, indeed, only analogically, not univocally, related to their application to finite being; but analogy is not equivocation.

Reply to Objection 3: When a human artist freely chooses to make a work of art, we may validly infer some things about the artist from the art. The same is true, by analogy, of the greatest of all works of art, the cosmos. We cannot, indeed, predict what will emerge from free choices, either human or divine; but we can validly infer some things about the cause from our experience of the effect, since everything in the effect is dependent on and explained by the cause, and since there is at least an analogical resemblance between effect and cause. For instance, marks of intelligence, such as order, are not adequately explained or caused merely by anything that lacks intelligence, nor is spirit adequately explained or caused by mere matter (though its activity may be *conditioned* thereby).

Article 5: Whether God's existence can be proved from human experience?

Objection 1: It seems that it cannot, for the same reasons it cannot be proved from anything else in the cosmos, as explained in the Objections in Article 4 above. For human experience is one of the events in the universe.

Objection 2: All human experience, including any experience of God that we may have, is fallible and subject to error and illusion. Thus it affords weak and uncertain premises for logical argument.

Objection 3: Human experiences can always be explained in a variety of ways. Thus at best they can point to the possibility, or even perhaps the probability, of God as their explanation, but they can never definitively rule out alternative explanations.

On the contrary, human experience, as data in the cosmos, has the same general relationship to God (as its ultimate cause) as other data in the cosmos. But from other data in the cosmos we can validly prove the existence of God, as we have seen in the previous Article. Therefore we can do the same from human experience.

I answer that human experience affords an even richer data base than any other cosmological arguments, for it includes facts like conscience, desire, and intelligence, which are lacking in the rest of the cosmos, and which afford the premises for proofs that are both more interesting, and more convincing, and more revelatory in their conclusions, i.e. which afford a "thicker slice of God," than other cosmological proofs.

(1) For instance, the **argument from conscience** argues from (a) the experience of absolute moral duty or obligation to (b) the reality of an absolute moral law, or "categorical imperative" known by moral or practical reason, and thus to (c) the reality of an absolute lawgiver as the only adequate cause of this absolute law. An imperative is not merely an ideal but a command. And a command comes from a commander, a will.

Cardinal Newman's version of this argument bypasses the intermediate step of establishing an objective and universal "natural moral law" (as, e.g., in C.S. Lewis's *Mere Christianity*, Book I) and argues directly from conscience—and from the fact that no one, not even the moral skeptic, believes it is ever right to deliberately disobey your own conscience—to God as the only possible ground for this absolute authority of conscience. For if conscience is only the contingent product of fallible causes such as society, parents, or natural selection, why should we bow to it as if it were a prophet of God? If we invented conscience, we can un-invent it. Thus Dostoevsky's

Nietzschean *Übermenschen* Raskalnikov in *Crime and Punishment* and Ivan Karamazov in *The Brothers Karamazov* reason logically. But they are refuted, and undone, by their own human nature and conscience. These two novels are, for many agnostics, the most powerful arguments for God.

(2) The **argument from desire** argues from the two premises of (a) the presence of our desire for total perfection, goodness, beauty, happiness, and/or joy (or from our dissatisfaction with the merely imperfect goods, beauties, happinesses, and joys that we experience), and (b) the principle that all natural, innate, and universal desires (though not artificial, conditioned and local desires like a world championship for the Cubs) correspond to real objects, to (c) the conclusion that nothing less than God could be the adequate reality corresponding to this desire.

To see the truth of premise (b), consider that all real hungers entail real foods. Desires, like ideas, are intentional; they point to something, like signs. The objects of ideas can be mere potential beings, or mere essences, like unicorns, but the objects of desires are real goods. (See *ST* I, 82, 3.)

(3) The **argument from intelligence** assumes the principle of causality (that an effect cannot exceed its cause, or the sum total of its causes) and argues that nothing *less* than human intelligence can be the adequate cause of the coming-to-be of human intelligence in the universe (though unintelligent physical forces such as evolution by random natural selection could have been used, as means, by such an intelligent cause). Nothing but a mind can program a computer with sufficient intelligence and reliability to justify our trust in it, and the human brain is (among other things) a computer that is programmed in such a way as to justify our trust in it. For if it were not, and if we therefore could not trust our own brains as the physical instruments used by our minds, then we would be back in a self-contradictory skepticism, and could not trust our minds when they tell us anything, including information about themselves or our brains or about reasons for skepticism. Therefore there must exist a superhuman mind with sufficient power and reliability to justify our trust in our own minds. And the only candidate that fits that description is God.

Reply to Objection 1: In addition to the answers to the objections above in Article 4, it may be added that human experience is not like anything else in the cosmos in that it is spiritual, personal, intelligent, free, and can have God as its object; and this is evidence, at least—a clue if not proof—of the existence of something beyond the cosmos.

Reply to Objection 2: Other human experiences afford valid premises for logical argument, in physics and in metaphysics. The objection's premise is thus either false, or leads to a total skepticism of all arguments from human experience. The Article on skepticism in the Question on Epistemology (VI, 1) will prove that this is self-contradictory.

Reply to Objection 3: This is an *a priori* assumption, which is refuted by the actual arguments in the body of the Article, each of which claims to do exactly the thing that this assumption claims is impossible: demonstrate that nothing less than God can possibly account for some human experiences.

Article 6: Whether God's existence as man's ultimate end can be proved?

Objection 1: It seems that it cannot, for not everyone seeks God as his ultimate end. For some seek God not at all, and others as only one among many goods, or as a means to another end such as personal satisfaction, or freedom from suffering in this world or the next.

Objection 2: If, as the three Abrahamic religions teach, God respects our free will so that "all those who seek, find," but *only* those who seek, find, then some do *not* find or attain God, and for them God is not their end. Therefore God is not all men's ultimate end.

Objection 3: With regard to events we do not plan, though their beginnings can be known from the beginning, their ends can be known only at the end. If our lives are planned by God, and we are not yet at the end of our lives, we cannot know yet with certainty whether God awaits us as our ultimate end.

Indeed, as scripture says, we hope for that which we do not see (*Romans* 8:24) as a matter of faith, not proof; for if it were a matter of proof, faith and hope would be unnecessary.

Objection 4: Man is not by nature capable of union with a supernatural being. So if this end is possible at all for man, it can be only by God's free choice to perform a miracle of grace. But God's free choices, miracles, and grace are not predictable or demonstrable.

On the contrary, the Argument from Desire above (Article 5) has already proved that nothing less than God can be man's ultimate, adequate end (happiness, joy, fulfillment).

I answer that the same causal proof by which we reason to God as the first efficient cause of what we now experience, both without (cosmologically) and within (experientially), can be used to reason to God as the last final cause or ultimate end. For nothing less than God can suffice as the ultimate cause in any order of causality. If God is not our ultimate end, then our conscious and unconscious teleology, our striving endlessly for good and our restless heart's dissatisfaction with all the finite goods that we do attain, would be inexplicable and meaningless. But this aspiration is the greatest thing in our nature, the highest natural sign of our supernatural destiny. Therefore if God does not exist as our final end, the greatest thing in our nature is meaningless.

If we weigh the idea of God, in the scales of the mind, against *all* other ideas and ideals that have ever appeared in all the minds of all the men who have ever lived, this single idea infinitely outweighs all others. For it is the idea of "that than which nothing greater can be conceived," the idea of an *infinitely perfect being.* What a dirty trick it would be if all the other ideals we could aspire to were real and attainable and this one alone, the greatest of all, were not. That would be like a long courtship without a marriage, or a perfect sequence of appetizers without a main course. It would indicate not randomness but the existence of a God behind this carefully designed trick, but his name would be Satan.

Reply to Objection 1: True, not all seek God (consciously, at least). But the real existence of God as our ultimate end does not depend on our seeking Him, just as the real existence of God as our first efficient cause does not depend on our knowing Him.

Reply to Objection 2: Those who do not attain God have failed to attain the Being that *is* in fact their end; thus they have failed to attain their own end. That is precisely why they are not happy. God is the ultimate "end" of all men in the sense of their *telos* or good, but not necessarily the ultimate "end" of all men in the sense of their *finis*, their "finish" or attainment.

Reply to Objection 3: Just as beginnings can sometimes be inferred from ends (e.g. the existence of parents from the existence of children, or artists from art), ends can sometimes be inferred from beginnings (e.g. the reality of children from parents' desire to have them, or from the biology of their reproductive systems; or the real possibility of art from artistic impulses). As the Greek myth teaches, human intelligence has both Epimethean (backward-looking) and Promethean (forward-looking) capacities.

That God is the object of Promethean hope does not necessarily entail the conclusion that He cannot also be the object of Epimethean reason and proof. (See above, Question 3, Article 1, Objection 3 and reply.)

Reply to Objection 4: Our success in attaining God as our supernatural end cannot be known with certainty, for this does, indeed, depend on a free gift of grace. But *our desire and need for it* can be known with certainty, for this depends only on observation of our present desires. And this is sufficient to prove the existence of God as our ultimate end. Thus from observing our hunger we cannot prove that we will not starve, but we can prove the existence of food.

Article 7: Whether God's relation to man ("religion") can be proved?

Objection 1: It seems that it can, for it has already been demonstrated that God's existence can be proved, and thus that God is known

75

by man. But knowing is a relationship. Therefore this relationship is provable.

Objection 2: If God had no relationship to man, then man would not desire God. But man does desire God, at least implicitly, as has been shown above. Therefore it can be proved that God has relationship to man.

Objection 3: The sense of common people, or common sense, should always be the primary sense in which terms are used. But common people's notion of God is the religious notion, the notion of the God who makes a difference to our lives and our experience. As William James says, if an idea's truth or falsity makes no difference to our experience, it is not in any meaningful sense of the word "true." (The point would have been more properly expressed if James had said that it is not, in any *true* sense of the word, *meaningful*.) Since God's existence can be proved, as shown above, and since this common religious notion of God is the only authentic and acceptable notion of God, it follows that the God who enters relationship to man can be proved.

On the contrary, Pascal says "the god of the philosophers is not the God of Abraham, Isaac, and Jacob." This does not mean there are two gods, or two contradictory definitions of God, but that the god of the philosophers is not known to be in a relationship with concrete men like Abraham, Isaac, and Jacob, only with the minds of philosophers.

I answer that true religion, i.e. a true relationship between God and man, is initiated by God, not by man. But God's choice to initiate this relationship by revealing Himself and His will for man is His free choice and not a natural necessity. Therefore it cannot be demonstrated by reason alone. As it comes from God's free and unpredictable choice to love us, it is offered to our free and unpredictable choice to love Him.

Reply to Objection 1: Mere knowing is not religion. To know a rock, or a crocodile, or a photon, is not to have a personal relationship with them. Only personal knowing (*kennen, connaitre*), not impersonal knowing (*wissen, savoir*), is a personal relationship. Such a relationship, unlike impersonal knowing, is always reciprocal. It depends on a free choice, and thus is not necessary or predictable or demonstrable.

Reply to Objection 2: As said above in the Reply to Objection 1, a personal relationship is always reciprocal. So if God did not meet man's desire toward Him by a desire or will toward man, there could be no personal relationship. But this will of God to meet man must be free and thus unpredictable and undemonstrable, as is argued in the *I answer that.*

Reply to Objection 3: The principle of accepting common-sense meanings as primary is correct. But the common religious notion of God, while richer and fuller than the philosophical one, is *not*, as the objection contends, "the only authentic and acceptable notion of God," even for common sense. For common sense believes that God must transcend common sense. Common sense also distinguishes matters of reason, such as impersonal rational proofs for the existence of God, from matters of religious faith, such as personal trust in God's love, which cannot be proved, but only believed.

Article 8: Whether the existence of evil disproves the existence of God?

Objection 1: It seems that it does, for, as Aquinas says, good and evil are contraries (opposites) and exclude each other. If good is infinite, evil has no ontological room to exist. If goodness were infinite, evil would be totally destroyed. But if God exists and is good, then good is infinite. So if God existed, evil would not exist. But evil does exist. Therefore God does not exist. (*ST* I, 2, 3, objection 1)

Objection 2: The three most non-negotiable attributes of God are infinite goodness (omnibenevolence, or totally good will), infinite power (omnipotence), and infinite wisdom (omniscience). Any being lacking in one or more of these attributes would not be God.

But if God is infinitely good, He wills only good. If He is infinitely powerful, He attains all that He wills. And if He is infinitely wise, He always infallibly knows what is best. So if He is all three, He would will, and know, and attain the abolition of evil. But this is not the case. Evil is not abolished. Evil exists. Therefore either God lacks goodness, or power, or wisdom, or existence itself.

Thus one of the following four propositions must be false:

(A) God is all-good.

(B) God is all-powerful.

(C) God is all-wise.

(D) Evil exists.

If A, B, and C are true, then D is false. There is no evil.

If A, B, and D are true, then C is false. There is no all-wise God.

If A, C, and D are true, then B is false. There is no all-powerful God.

If B, C, and D are true, then A is false. There is no all-good God.

All four of these conclusions, the only ones logically possible, contradict religious theism.

Objection 3: If God were totally good, He would will, and attain, our happiness. But we are not happy. Therefore He is not totally good.

On the contrary, the reality of God and the reality of evil are two of the most obvious truths of human life as taught throughout the Bible.

I answer that far from disproving the existence of God, evil is a powerful pointer to His existence, if not a proof of it. For our judgment that anything is evil, if it is a true judgment, presupposes that we know the standard by which a thing is to be judged as evil. That standard must be perfect goodness. For if it were imperfect goodness, mixed with evil, it would be a false standard for measuring things that are partly good and partly evil. The standard for measuring imperfect student exam scores is a perfect 100, whether any student attains that or not. But perfect goodness is found only in God. If there were no God, the standard of goodness would be either an objective reality that is imperfect or a wholly subjective ideal of perfection, existing only in our minds. In either case, it would not be a valid standard for objective judgment of good and evil. But the argument against God from evil assumes the objective reality of evil, for only an objective reality can prove or disprove another. So the argument against God from evil assumes the reality of God, and is thus self-contradictory.

Reply to Objection 1: As Aquinas answers, the existence of the infinitely good God and the existence of evil are compatible because of the existence of *time*. For an infinitely good God could allow evil to exist in order to bring out of it, in time, an even greater good than could have existed if evil had not been allowed to exist. Evil will, indeed, be totally destroyed, but in its proper time.

Evil is allowed to exist in order to preserve free will on the part of God's personal creatures. For it is more perfect, both for man and for the world, if man freely cooperates in the abolition of evil, than if he does not.

Also, the premise that evil *exists* is not, strictly speaking, true, for evil is not a substance, but existence is properly predicated only of substances. All that exists is good, because all that exists must be either (1) the Creator or (2) a creature, and (1) the Creator is infinitely good, and (2) all things created by Him are also good, since the nature of effects follows the nature of their causes.

Reply to Objection 2: God wills evil indirectly, in allowing it for the sake of preserving the good of the free will in man that caused it. God in His wisdom knows that part of goodness is the acceptance of the free will of other persons. And He also knows that part of power is the embracing of apparent weakness and defeat for the sake of that greater good, the free will of the other. Thus the four propositions, A, B, C, and D, are logically compatible.

Reply to Objection 3: True happiness (blessedness, beatitude) is not always identical with felt happiness (satisfaction of felt desires); for true happiness may require suffering, but satisfaction of desire is the opposite of suffering. God wills our truest and best happiness, according to His infallible wisdom, not according to our fallible wisdom and short-sighted desires. Since we are temporal, free, and fallen, we experience happiness gradually, through free choice, and through repentance, rather than instantly, timelessly, and with secure necessity, as God does.

Article 9: Whether human free will and divine predestination are logically contradictory?

Objection 1: It seems that they are, for (1) the absolutely first efficient cause of any event must be single, not double; thus (2) the first efficient cause of a human choice must be either God or man, not both. But (3) if this first cause is God, then man can only be an instrumental cause, a caused cause, as a character in a story is an instrument of the writer, but not a first cause. And (4) if this first cause is man's will, then God can be only the One who foresees and plans this, but does not carry it out as its first efficient cause. But (5) if it is God and not man who is the first efficient cause of a human choice, then there is divine predestination but no human free will. And (6) if it is man and not God who is the first efficient cause of a human choice, then there is human free will but no divine predestination, since predestination means not only that God knows, plans, and allows the event but is its first efficient cause. (7) Therefore the two ideas are logically contradictory.

Objection 2: The authority of common sense agrees with this conclusion, for all men wonder how these two things can both be true.

Objection 3: Scripture itself seems not only to affirm predestination (*Romans* 8: 29–30) but also to deny free will, when the Apostle declares that "it is not of him that willeth, nor of him that runneth, but of God that showeth mercy." (*Romans* 9: 16).

On the contrary, the authority of common sense tells us that these two things are both true. In fact all men know, at least unconsciously, that both predestination and free will are true. For every story ever told by man contains both predestination, on the part of the author, and free will, on the part of the characters. If there were no predestination on the part of the author, it would not be a story but the narration of an unpredictable series of random events. For "plotting" is one of the two most essential ingredients in any story. If there were no free will on the part of the characters (the other essential ingredient), it would not be a story but merely a narration of events that were caused deterministically by subhuman causes. This might make for good science or natural history but could never make good literature. Now if all men *know*, at least unconsciously, that both predestination (or destiny or fate) and free will are true, then they *are* both true, for only truth can be known, not falsity. It follows then they do not contradict each other, since only falsehood, and never truth, contradicts truth.

I answer that the reason predestination and free will do not contradict each other is that divine grace uses and perfects nature, and especially human nature, rather than diminishing, bypassing, destroying, perverting, or substituting for it. Thus divine predestination, which is to man a form of grace (divine gift), turns human nature, and the human free will which is an essential part of human nature, *on* rather than *off*. In using human free will, divine predestination makes it truly free, just as a good human author, in using one character to bring about the planned result in the life of a second character, does not change or remove either the personality or the free will of the first character but uses them. When a writer uses a pen as an instrumental cause, he does not change the character of the pen into something other than a pen; and when an architect uses an engineer as an instrumental cause of a building, he does not change the character of the engineer into something other than a human being with reason and free will. So there is no reason to think that God's predestining grace, when using human free will as the instrumental causes of His plan, changes the essential nature of man's will from free to unfree.

Reply to Objection 1: (1) The argument has a false hidden assumption: that in order for man's will to be free, it must be not only the real cause of his choices but the absolutely first, uncaused cause of them. This would require a man to be God.

(2) "God and not man" or "man and not God" are false alternatives, for God and man are not rivals in the same order, as two human characters may be rivals on earth, but are like a human author and

his story's character. Hamlet and Laertes are rivals, but not Hamlet and Shakespeare.

Reply to Objection 2: If common sense saw them as contradictory, it would not ask the question how they can be reconciled, for no one expects two contradictories to be reconciled—for instance, being alive and being dead. No one wonders how a man can be both alive and dead at the same time, for no one believes this is possible or actual. But we wonder how we can be both fated and free at the same time because we believe both are actual, and we wonder how it is logically possible.

Reply to Objection 3: (1) Scripture supplies data for faith (i.e. things to be believed) but does not claim to solve philosophical problems by reason. Thus it is not rightly used when it is quoted to solve *philosophical* problems.

(2) The passage in question is not addressing the question of whether or not man has free will, but the question of whether divine predestination is absolutely first and unconditioned. There are many other passages of scripture that do affirm the reality of free will, especially by affirming personal responsibility for choices, for we are not responsible for what we are not free to choose (e.g. our gender or eye color).

(3) The passage in question is taken out of context. Its first word, "it," refers not to the identity of the immediate cause of a man's choices, which is that man's free will, but to the absolutely first cause of all of human history, which is indeed God, not man. This is clear from what is said next: this "it" is "of God that showeth mercy." Human mercy is not referred to here, either to affirm it or to deny it, nor is human free will.

Article 10: Whether God changes (or is "in process")?

Objection 1: It seems that He does, for "God is love," and love is a change, either a passion or an action.

Objection 2: If God does not change, religion is impossible, for religion is a personal relationship between human and divine persons, and no human person can have a personal relationship with something that does not change, like an essence, or a truth, or a number, or even a being that changes very slowly, like a galaxy.

Objection 3: The Incarnation made possible a personal relationship to God that was not possible before. But to change is to add something that was not previously present. Thus if God by nature is eternal, and can change only when He incarnates Himself, it follows that the possibility of intimacy with God was not previously present, before the Incarnation. But in that case Judaism and Islam, which deny the Incarnation, are not religions—which is absurd.

Objection 4: The power to change is a power. If God has all power, He also has the power to change. If He does not have the power to change, He lacks a power and is not all-powerful.

Objection 5: Scripture constantly refers to God changing, e.g. "repenting" at the wickedness of man or "relenting" from His judgments when man repents.

Objection 6: The personal and the eternal are contradictories. This is why Vedanta Hinduism and Buddhism deny the personal character of ultimate reality: to preserve its eternity. Christianity, to affirm God's personality, must deny His changelessness.

On the contrary, God Himself reveals His eternity: "I am the Lord; I change not." (*Malachi* 3:6) It takes no remarkable leap of faith or reason to believe that God knows how to describe Himself truly.

I answer that all change either adds or subtracts something. If the thing added is a perfection, or if the thing lost is an imperfection, it is a change from worse to better; and if the thing added is an imperfection, or if the thing lost is a perfection, it is a change from better to worse. In each of these cases (and they are the only ones logically possible), the changing being is at one point less than perfect. And this cannot be said of God. Therefore by His essential nature God does not change.

Reply to Objection 1: God's love is not a passion, for it is the act of *agape* (the willing of good to the other), not the passion of *eros* (desire). As C.S. Lewis says in *The Problem of Pain*, God does not fall in love for the same reason the sea does not get wet.

God's love is an act. There are two kinds of act. (1) "First act," or actuality (as distinct from mere potentiality), does not necessarily imply change. (2) "Second act," or activity, follows and depends on first act, and implies change in its object, but not necessarily in its subject. An unchanging cause can produce changing effects, and this would also entail change in the relationship between them. An imperfect image of this is the (changing) relationship between the (relatively) unchanging sun and a man who moves into and out of the sunlight. Thus God's love to man implies change in man, whose being is temporal, and in man's relation to God, but not in God Himself, whose being is eternal.

Two other ways to this conclusion are (1) from the premise that God *is* love, which is perfect, essential, and complete, and there is no need for change in that which is perfect, essential, and complete; and (2) from the premise that God is infinite in all His perfections, and what is infinite does not increase.

Reply to Objection 2: This is the essential argument of "process theology." However, a relationship between the changing and the unchanging is possible, as we have seen in the Reply to Objection 1, and this will be a changing relationship, like the relationship between unchanging sun and the changing man, or like the relationship between the swinging ball of a pendulum and its fixed hinge. For the pendulum's arm, which relates these two terms, does move through an arc and change. This is also the (changing) relationship between unchanging moral principles and changing applications of them to changing situations.

Reply to Objection 3: There are two kinds of differences, essential and accidental. Christianity is not an *essentially* different kind of religion, *qua* religion, from Judaism and Islam; for what the Incarnation made possible for the first time was not personal intimacy as such, but a kind and a degree of intimacy that was not present before. For even before the Incarnation, in Old Testament Judaism, and among those who deny the Incarnation, like Muslims, especially the Sufis, we find the possibility of personal intimacy with a personal but eternal God.

It may be true that God's will to incarnate Himself is the only thing that in objective fact makes this intimacy possible; but this fact need not be explicitly known subjectively by the man who enters this intimacy. A parallel case: Christianity declares that it is Christ alone who makes salvation ontologically possible, but those who through no fault of their own seek God without consciously knowing Christ may still be saved by Christ.

Reply to Objection 4: The power to change is a positive power only in a being which lacks some perfection. But in an infinitely perfect being, the power to change would be the power to lose some perfection, which is not a positive power at all. The imprecision of our language deceives us here. The "power" to sin, or to err, or to die, are not really powers at all but weaknesses.

Reply to Objection 5: Scripture constantly uses figurative and anthropomorphic language when speaking of God, for language describing the invisible must be taken from the realm of the visible. Scripture uses anthropomorphic language because there is no higher analogy for God in our experience than man, who alone of all creatures bears the image of God, however imperfectly and temporally.

Reply to Objection 6: This is precisely the fundamental erroneous theological assumption of Vedanta Hinduism and Buddhism, which God corrected when He spoke His own personal yet eternal name to Moses in the burning bush: "I AM." Thus God is both Person ("I") and Being Itself. (See Norris Clarke, S.J., *Person and Being.*)

Question IV:
Cosmology

(Note: the ten preceding Articles were a tiny sample of a rich, complex, and ongoing field of philosophy: philosophical theology and its related and partly overlapping field, philosophy of religion. In contrast, many of the questions that ancient and medieval philosophers treated in cosmology have been resolved by modern science. This is why this following section is shorter than the preceding one. However, there are a number of important philosophical questions which remain in this field.)

Article 1: Whether the order in the cosmos is teleological?

Objection 1: It seems that it is not, for this philosophical assumption of teleology, or objectively real purpose- or end-directed action in nature, which characterized all premodern cosmologies except ancient Greek and Roman atomism and materialism, has been rejected by modern science; and this rejection was a precondition for scientific progress. Science flourished when it began to measure the visible instead of speculating about the invisible. ("Purposes" or "ends" are invisible.)

Objection 2: "Purpose" is a personal, subjective, psychological concept. Only minds have purposes. Thus the concept of purpose belongs in psychology, not cosmology.

Objection 3: Teleology inevitably involves theology, via the argument from "intelligent design" in nature to a cosmic Designer. Teleology in nature thus assumes a God behind nature; it sneaks God into science.

Objection 4: Ockham's Razor, or the principle of parsimony, dictates that entities are not to be multiplied beyond necessity; that simpler explanations are always to be preferred to more complex ones. But

everything in nature can be explained by efficient and material causes, without the addition of formal causes ("essences") or final causes
(ends).

On the contrary, both common sense and nearly all traditional, pre-
modern philosophers share a teleological world-view. It is a kind of
mental tyranny to forbid any use of these natural categories, and a
kind of intellectual murder to try to eliminate two of the four meanings of the question "why," i.e., two of the four causes.

I answer that if objective teleology is an illusion, then eyes are not
really "for" seeing, ears "for" hearing, legs "for" walking, or stom-
achs "for" digestion; and we should stop speaking of "the reproductive system," "the digestive system" and so forth. But this is absurd.

Teleology is not an ideology, a superstition, a fallacy, a faith, or a
projection, but a fact. We *observe* that every visible thing in nature
acts for an end (final causality) and according to its essence or distinctive nature (formal causality). Birds grow wings and fly; fish grow
fins and swim. Even chemicals act for ends: water freezes at 32° F. If
there were no end-directed, end-determined action, things would act
randomly. They do not. Therefore there is.

An efficient cause determines matter to be shaped into one form
or another, but a final cause answers a different question: why the
efficient cause produces this given effect rather than some other. We
cannot confuse the two questions, or reduce either one to the other:
(1) *What* caused this effect? and (2) *Why* did it produce this effect
rather than some other one? Efficient causality supplies the power,
but final causality focuses it.

Reply to Objection 1: Teleology has been rightly rejected as a
methodological principle in the natural sciences, for "order to an
end" or "purpose" is a concept that is not "scientific" in the strict,
modern sense, since it cannot be detected, verified, or falsified empirically or quantitatively, but only intuitively. But this does not entail
its unreality, or the need to reject it in philosophical cosmology,
unless we accept the highly questionable premise that whatever is not
"scientific" (i.e. subject to empirical detection or quantitative meas-
urement) is not real, and not a proper subject for philosophy. But

there are many other things which are not "scientific" but are nevertheless real. Three of these are (1) mind, thought, self-consciousness, subjectivity, personhood, or spirit; (2) moral values, good and evil; and (3) beauty.

Reply to Objection 2: The Objection begs the question. There are philosophical arguments that claim to demonstrate the existence of objective teleology in nature; these arguments are not refuted simply by stating, rather than proving, that purposes are not objective but only subjective.

Final causality is an *analogical* concept. Its clearest example is (1) human conscious and free choices; but analogous examples are (2) conscious but un-free animal instincts and (3) the unconscious and un-free natural tendencies of plants and minerals such as tropism and gravity.

Reply to Objection 3: (1) Design may *entail* God but it does not *assume* God.

(2) A concept ("purpose or design in nature") is not refuted merely by claiming that it entails another concept ("God") unless (a) the entailment is proved to be logically inevitable *and* (b) its conclusion is proved to be absurd. (In that case we have a *reductio ad absurdum* argument.) But neither of these two things has been shown at the beginning of the inquiry. Perhaps design does not entail a divine designer, or perhaps the concept of a divine designer is not absurd.

(3) There is no "sneaking" of God into science here, for teleology does not begin with God and it does not end with natural science. It begins with a *philosophical* reflection on our observation of how things in nature behave (they move in ordered ways to natural ends), and it ends with a *philosophical* conclusion about teleology. "Intelligent design" is not a scientific concept, for it is not empirical or quantifiable; nor is it a religious concept, for it does not depend on any personal God (i.e. any God-who-is-a-Person), any divine revelation, or any personal relationship with God. It is a philosophical (and commonsensical) concept.

Reply to Objection 4: (1) Ockham's Razor is a good methodological principle for modern science, but it is not a good ontological principle; for the real universe, as distinct from scientific explanations, is much fuller than it needs to be. There is no need for ostriches. Yet they exist.

(2) Even if there are no good scientific reasons for affirming the reality of formal and final causes, there are good philosophical and commonsensical reasons for doing so.

Article 2: Whether the cosmos exists for man?

Objection 1: It seems that it does not, for man is only an insignificantly tiny accidental latecomer into the cosmos. Anthropocentrism, like geocentrism, is an illusion of perspective that has been refuted by modern science. Astronomically speaking, man is insignificant.

Objection 2: The vast majority of all times, places, events, and entities in the cosmos are unknown and unused by man in any way. It is absurd to say that each atom in each galaxy for 14 billion years is "for" man, since man has no knowledge or care about them and they make no difference to him.

Objection 3: To say that the cosmos is "for" man presupposes a God who designs it thus; and this is an unwarranted intrusion of religion into cosmology.

On the contrary, The idea of man's centrality (in meaning, not in space) is confirmed by the authority of tradition in all cultures, by religion, and even by science (the "Anthropic Principle"), as well by common sense, according to which the physical universe appears like the setting for a play or a story, in which we are the characters and human life is the plot. What the point or theme of the story is, is one of the great questions of philosophy, and the question religion claims to answer.

I answer that as far as anyone knows, the universe has never produced or evolved any entity as perfect and complex as man, or any other entity which can understand laws that are true of the entire universe (and, in fact, even of all possible universes, such as the law of non-contradiction). One could say, with Alan Watts, that "the universe *humans* as a rosebush flowers." Furthermore, man alone, of all known entities in the universe, has a trans-spatial, trans-temporal, and trans-material destiny and immortality, as will be demonstrated in the section, on philosophical anthropology.

Reply to Objection 1: There are at least six fallacies or confusions in this short objection.

(1) Man is not insignificant simply because he is tiny—unless size is an index of importance, in which case elephants are more important than humans, fat humans more important than thin ones, and the planet Jupiter more important than the planet Earth.

(2) The objection also begs the question by *assuming* that man's appearance on earth is accidental.

(3) It is also fallacious to identify late-coming with insignificance. By that argument, horseshoe crabs are more significant than man.

(4) No *spatial* centrality is claimed for man or for planet Earth, only a centrality of purpose or significance. In fact, *no* place in the universe can be central, since space is relative, not absolute; so earth is as central as any other place.

(5) Anthropocentrism is not refuted by modern science. If anything, it is confirmed by the "Anthropic Principle," according to which the cosmos appears to be very finely calibrated to evolve man through very many, very tiny "windows" of opportunity.

(6) Astronomically speaking, man is not insignificant, for astronomically speaking, man is the astronomer.

Reply to Objection 2: (1) The very fact of the universe's vastness and independence of man gives man an opportunity for awe, wonder, and humility.

(2) Man does have knowledge of each atom, not individually but through general principles, both physical and metaphysical, that apply to every atom.

(3) Everything makes a difference to everything because it is a single universe. See, e.g., the famous Ray Bradbury story "A Sound of Thunder." Gravity, e.g., pervades all physical relationships in the cosmos, so that, in the words of Loren Eiseley, "one could not pluck a flower without troubling a star" ("the butterfly effect").

Reply to Objection 3: Like the Argument from Design, this idea may *entail* God (or it may not: that has not yet been demonstrated) but it need not *presuppose* God. And from the cosmological evidence available to unaided human reason alone, only "nature's God," not religion's God, can be inferred. (See Question 3, Article 7.)

Article 3: Whether the uniformity of nature is a necessary philosophical presupposition of all physical science?

Objection 1: It seems that it is not, for science cannot thus depend on philosophy. For the more certain cannot depend on the less certain.

Objection 2: Granted that this principle cannot be proved by science but must be presupposed, it does not follow that it must be proved by philosophy, for it need not be proved at all, since it is a merely procedural or practical presupposition for science, not a necessary theoretical one. Nothing is ever deduced from it in science.

On the contrary, P.F. Strawson says (in "The Justification of Induction," from *Introduction to Logical Theory*) that if we are to undertake science with any hope of success, we must believe that "the universe is such that induction will continue to be successful." But if nature is not uniform, the universe is not such. Therefore we must believe that it is. But we cannot prove this belief inductively, for that clearly begs the question. Therefore we must either not prove it at all, or prove it deductively by philosophy.

I answer that if nature were not uniform, i.e. if it were not indubitably certain that at least some of the same laws and principles were true in all places and times in the cosmos, then we could not know, or predict, or reliably assume, such things as gravity, the speed of light, the convertability of mass and energy, or the atomic table of chemical elements in other galaxies or in past millennia (at least since the first few seconds after the 'Big Bang'); and this would make sciences like astronomy and geology impossible. Therefore science must *assume* the uniformity of nature, since science cannot *doubt* this principle and cannot *prove* it by its own methods. Therefore if this assumption must be proved, it must be proved in other fields and by other methods, such as philosophy.

Reply to Objection 1: It has not been proved that science is more certain than philosophy. In fact, it is often the reverse, since philosophy investigates unchanging and necessary truths while science investigates the changing world, which is contingent.

Reply to Objection 2: (1) True, *the working scientist* need not prove all his presuppositions. But *the philosopher of science* should. The uniformity of nature is a principle that must be true for any science to "work." To leave such a principle entirely unproved would be to erect a great skyscraper on a foundation of clouds.

(2) True, nothing is *deduced from* it in science. But much is *reduced to* it. For only if it is true can science yield any certainty or any predictability. For if the fundamental laws of nature were to change at any time, all scientific demonstration would fail. That would be like waking up from one dream and entering another, which had fundamentally different laws.

Article 4: Whether science presupposes real causality?

Objection 1: It seems that it does not, for (1) science cannot depend on philosophy, but (2) the reality of causality can be proved only by philosophy, not by science.

Objection 2: As Hume demonstrated, causality itself is not a scientific notion because it is not empirically observable, since it is neither an entity nor an event but a relationship (he called it a transference of invisible power from cause to effect).

On the contrary, Hume says, "All reasonings concerning matter of fact seem to be founded on the relation of *Cause and Effect.* By means of that relation alone can we go beyond the evidence of our memory and senses." (*An Enquiry Concerning Human Understanding* IV, 1)

I answer that science uses the principle of causality in all its explanations, for it explains effects by their causes, eliminating inadequate explanations as inadequate causes. Also, it assumes that nothing just happens without a cause. If this were not so, anything might pop into existence at any time and place for no reason at all; and this "pop theory" would make all science, philosophy, and common-sense explanations invalid and dubitable, leading to total skepticism. Thus science must "borrow" the principle of causality from philosophy rather than proving it by its own methods. It is not the business of science to prove its own philosophical presuppositions.

Reply to Objection 1: The second premise is true but the first is false. It is simply an ideological or philosophical prejudice, and is assumed without proof. It is contrary to the scientific method to make unquestioned assumptions at the outset, without investigation, whether those assumptions are scientific assumptions or assumptions about the relation between science and philosophy.

Reply to Objection 2: Hume's argument assumes that science cannot use any notions which are not empirically observable. But this is not true, for science assumes the principles of logic and mathematics, which are not empirically observable.

Article 5: Whether there are four causes (formal, material, efficient, final)?

Objection 1: It seems that there are not, for this is an outdated philosophical theory of Aristotle and no longer assumed or used by most modern philosophers, much less scientists.

Objection 2: We no longer use the word "cause" to refer to the two internal elements or dimensions that Aristotle called "formal" and "material" causes.

Objection 3: Science no longer uses explanations by final causality.

Objection 4: Platonists would add a fifth causality, viz. exemplary causality. These are the Platonic Forms or Ideas.

On the contrary, Aristotle says: "It appears, therefore, from their failure to discover a fifth kind (of cause), that earlier thinkers confirm my account of the number and nature of the causes; and that all principles (causes, explanations) must be sought for along such lines." (*Metaphysics* A, vii)

I answer that the four "causes" is one of the most universally useful ideas in the history of thought. All explanations, in all fields, can be classified under these four kinds. For a cause is either intrinsic or extrinsic to its effect. (Let us call the effect X.) If it is intrinsic, it is either (a) *what* X is, i.e. its essential nature or essence (e.g. a house)—and this is the "formal cause"—or (b) what X is *made of or made from*: the raw material that was formed, shaped, or determined to be X rather than Y (e.g. wood)—and this is the "material cause." If it is extrinsic, it is either (c) the agent or origin that made or changed X (e.g. the carpenter)—and this is the "efficient cause"—or (d) the end or purpose of X, whether unconscious or conscious (e.g. to shelter a family)—and this is the "final cause." Thus for every X, there is (a) *that which,* (b) *that out of which,* (c) *that from which,* and (d) *that for which* X is.

Reply to Objection 1: This is what C.S. Lewis calls "chronological snobbery": trying to tell the truth with clocks and calendars instead of evidence and arguments.

Reply to Objection 2: (1) Changing the labels on a container does not change the contents contained. A cause by any other name still smells as sweet.

(2) We still use the word "because" for all four causes, even though we no longer use the word "cause" for the first two. E.g. we say that an enclosed plane figure is a triangle "because" it has three angles (formal causality), or that paper towels mop up liquid "because" of their capillary structure (material causality).

Reply to Objection 3: See Article 1.

Reply to Objection 4: Exemplary causality is a kind of formal causality, but with the form separated from the matter (as in Plato) rather than together with it in the substance (as in Aristotle). And if forms exist both in matter (e.g. humanity in human beings) and separated from matter (e.g. the Idea of Man in the Mind of God), the second may be called "exemplary" causality, but it is still the exemplary *form*, and thus included under formal causality. Thus both (a) Platonists, for whom forms exist separated from matter, and (b) Aristotelians, for whom forms exist in matter, and (c) theists like Augustine and Aquinas, for whom forms exist in both states, speak of formal causality here, not a fifth kind of causality.

Article 6: Whether the cosmos is infinite in space?

Objection 1: It seems that it is infinite in space, for there is no wall at the edge of space. If an object travels through space indefinitely, it will never reach an end. If there were a "wall at the edge of space," that wall would be in space, with space on both sides of the wall, and thus it would not be the edge of space.

Objection 2: It is infinite in space because space keeps expanding, with no limit. What has no limit is infinite. Therefore space is infinite.

Objection 3: It is infinite in space because it could be limited only by a body. But that body, in turn, must be in space; and that space, in turn, must be infinite because it could be limited only by another body, et cetera.

On the contrary, God alone is infinite, and the universe is not God, therefore the universe is not infinite. And space is not more than the universe, since the universe is the sum of all space and matter. Therefore space is not infinite.

I answer that the universe as such is finite, and therefore every aspect of it is finite. Space is an aspect of the universe, therefore space is finite actually, though it, like time and number, is potentially infinite. This does not mean it has a positive power to be or become at any time actually infinite, but merely that its potentiality for expansion is not limited by anything actual like a "wall at the end of the universe."

Every body has a surface boundary, which makes it finite spatially. But the universe is the sum total of all bodies. Therefore the universe is finite spatially.

Reply to Objection 1: Space is finite, because space is relative to matter, and the amount of matter in the cosmos is finite. (It follows that the amount of energy is also finite, since energy and matter are convertible.) The reason there is no "wall at the edge of space" is that space has no edge, being curved by matter, as Einstein showed, rather than uniform and absolute, as Newton thought.

Reply to Objection 2: There is no absolute Newtonian space into which the universe expands. Space (and its expansion) is *potentially* infinite, like the series of positive integers, since no limit is set on its expansion, but it is never actually infinite.

Reply to Objection 3: Space is not limited by bodies, nor bodies by space, as if space were itself another body. Rather, space is one aspect or dimension of bodies, and is relative to and measured by bodies rather than bodies being relative to and measured by it, since there is no absolute Newtonian space.

Article 7: Whether time is infinite?

Objection 1: It seems that it is, for the contrary notion, that time is finite, is internally self-contradictory. For to say that time is finite is to say that time had a beginning. But every beginning is a beginning *in* time, therefore it cannot at the same time be a beginning *of* time. It must be a beginning in time because a "beginning" means the coming to be of an event which is preceded by some time in which the event does not yet exist.

Objection 2: Just as there is no "wall at the end of space," for that would entail a space outside of space (on the other side of the wall), so there is no time at the end of time. Therefore time is infinite.

Objection 3: The reason people think time is finite is that it had an absolute beginning, some 14 billion years ago, in the "Big Bang," and they think that whatever has a beginning has an end, as Buddha taught ("Whatever is an arising thing, that is also a ceasing thing."). But this Buddhist premise is not true, for angels and human souls (and resurrection bodies too) have a beginning but no end.

Objection 4: If time had an end, that end would be at a certain point in time. It could not be both an end *in* time and an end *of* time.

On the contrary, we know by faith that there will be an "end of the world (*aeon,* era)" when God will end the history of the universe, and thus end time itself (i.e. *kronos,* the time that is dependent on the universe's matter, as distinct from *kairos,* the time of spirits and their thinkings and purposings).

I answer that like space, time is potentially infinite in that it could continue forever in the future, from its absolute beginning (in the "Big Bang"), as space could expand forever from its point of maximum smallness (the 'Bang'). But it is improper to speak of *time's* past or future, for time is not a *thing* that continues or moves, but the measure of the continuing or moving of things.

Nevertheless there is a difference: nothing prevents space from expanding infinitely, but the Second Law of Thermodynamics ("entropy") prevents time from continuing forever. For entropy eventually would produce homeostasis, when all energy in the universe is homogeneously distributed, and in that case there would be no more change. Since time (i.e. material time, *kronos*) is the measure of material change and thus relative to it, time would then also cease when change ceased, if God did not intervene before that time to end the universe and its time—which event could not, of course, be predicted by human reason, any more than His creation of the universe could.

Reply to Objection 1: The objection misconceives of the beginning of time as an event. The beginning of every *event* is preceded by some time in which that event is not, but the beginning of time is not the beginning of an event. What is internally self-contradictory is not the notion that time is finite but the notion that the beginning of time was preceded by some time.

Reply to Objection 2: (1) The two cases are not alike. It is not necessary to posit a time after time in order to conceive time having an end, just as it is not necessary to posit a time before time in order to conceive time having a beginning.

(2) The two cases are alike in this, that the lack of a "time wall" does not show that time is actually infinite, any more than the lack of a "space wall" showed that space was actually infinite.

Reply to Objection 3: It is true that Buddha's principle is false. But this proves nothing, for the falsity of the premise of an argument for a certain conclusion does not *dis*prove that conclusion.

Reply to Objection 4: Just as there is an absolute beginning *of* all time which is not *in* time (i.e. not surrounded by both *a prior* and *a posterior* time), so there can be an absolute end of all time. As the beginning term of the continuum of time has an "after" but no "before," so the end term of the continuum of time can have a "before" but no "after."

Article 8: Whether time travel is possible?

Objection 1: It seems that it is not, for if it were, then I could travel back in time and murder my own grandfather. But that is logically impossible, for if I murdered my own grandfather when he was a child, he would not be able to cause my father's, and thus my, existence, and thus I would not exist. But what does not exist cannot commit murder because what does not exist cannot act or change anything. Therefore time travel involves a logical self-contradiction. And what is logically self-contradictory is physically impossible.

A. 8: Whether time travel is possible?

Objection 2: Time travel has appeared very frequently in science fiction, but never in science, either in fact or even in accepted theory. No one has ever demonstrated its actuality or even its possibility.

On the contrary, Aquinas says the resurrected body will have the power of "levity," i.e. of moving to any place desired simply by an act of will, which power is presently possessed by angels. Its presence in human beings is also confirmed by literally millions of people who have had out-of-body experiences. It is at least reasonable and probable that this will be true not only of body and space but of time also: that at or after death time will become malleable to the enlightened and perfected soul.

I answer that time travel, of the mental rather than physical variety, is not only possible but actual. For we all experience a mild form of time travel (a) in memory, (b) in anticipation, and (c) in telling or hearing stories about other times. In all of these, our consciousness enters into other times, and occasionally does so with extreme vividness, such as at the moment of death when, according to widespread testimony, one's entire past life often appears in perfect order and detail before one's consciousness as vividly as it appeared in life; or in prophecy, though this seems to lack vividness and clarity; or in unusual literary "out-of-body experiences" in which one who reads a story or sees a play or a movie enters into the time and place of a story with such vividness that the world and the story *in* the book, play, or movie appears more real than the world *outside* it. There have been many well-documented cases of people (usually "primitives") entering other times and places with their consciousness, e.g. "dream time" or "the dreaming" among the Australian aborigines.

All of this is, of course, highly speculative and uncertain. The point of this Article is only to open minds, imaginations, and possibilities, especially for God's future actions in man.

Reply to Objection 1: This argument refutes not time travel as such, but time travel (a) in this life (b) into the past (c) so as to produce physical changes. It leaves open the possibilities of (a) time travel after death, (b) time travel into the future, and (c) time travel in which only mental awareness does the "traveling," and not any physical powers.

Reply to Objection 2: (1) What is said here is true of many of the technological advances in the history of science.

(2) Science fiction often predates science fact.

(3) The fact that a thing is not yet actual is no proof that it is not possible.

(4) There are actually some (highly speculative) theories in physics in which time travel is a theoretical possibility.

Article 9: Whether matter is only a projection of mind?

Objection 1: It seems that it is, since all matter manifests order and intelligence, and these cannot exist except in a mind.

Objection 2: When we imagine or dream, our minds conjure up material things that may not exist outside our minds. Thus it is possible that all matter is the product of the divine imagining or dreaming.

Objection 3: Since it is logically possible, and not self-contradictory, that matter exists only in mind, and since what does not involve a contradiction is not logically provable, it is not logically provable that matter exists outside of mind. Thus it is merely an article of faith that the matter that exists in our consciousness, or our experience, also exists outside it.

Objection 4: As Bishop Berkeley argued, "Is it not a great contradiction to *think* that a thing exists when we do *not think* it?" It is impossible to point to any matter existing independent of mind because the act of pointing is an act of mind.

On the contrary, both divine revelation (of God's creation of the universe), and common sense, and the nearly universal human consensus and tradition believe in the reality of matter independent of our minds.

I answer that the universal experience of the difference between physical *discovery* and mental *creation* (e.g. between not being able to actually unlock a door and imagining it open) shows the difference between the matter that is merely a mental projection and exists only in the mind or the imagination, and the matter that is objectively real. If matter were merely mental projection, it could be changed merely by thinking, and no one would ever have to endure pain or death.

If it is replied that matter is merely mental projection to God though not to us, since what is subjective to God can appear objective to us, then the main point at issue is admitted, for matter is then objective to us.

But if God chose to dream, rather than to create, the universe, He would be a deceiver because He dreamed (or created) us with a natural tendency to *believe* that the universe is independently real and not merely a dream. This is shown by the fact that the doctrine of God's creation of the universe, as in Judaism, Christianity, and Islam, even though it is an article of faith, strikes common sense as obvious, while the doctrine of God's dreaming of the universe, as in Hinduism, is presented as a mystical secret known to be true only by an altered state of "enlightened" consciousness.

Reply to Objection 1: Although intelligence can exist only in minds, order can exist both in mind and in matter. Matter *contains* order and *manifests* intelligence but does not *contain* intelligence.

Reply to Objection 2: What is possible is not necessarily actual. God could have willed to merely imagine a universe that existed only in His own mind, *or* He could have willed to create a universe that existed outside His mind. He has both the power and the freedom to choose either option. He chose the second (or rather *chooses* it, for creation is not an event *in* time).

Reply to Objection 3: Demonstration is *not* limited to what can be reduced to logical contradictions. This was one of Hume's mistakes, and led to his skepticism. If that were true, then only tautologies could be demonstrated. Between such tautological demonstrations, on the one hand, and unprovable faith on the other hand, lies most of philosophy and its demonstrations—for example Plato's long demonstration in the *Republic* that justice is more profitable than injustice. His demonstrations in Book I were merely formal and tautological, and that is why they were not fully persuasive, as Socrates admitted at the end of this Book. They were merely negative and demonstrated only that Thrasymachus's definition was self-contradictory. But the demonstrations in Books 2–9 were positive and persuasive because they involved understanding (the "first act of the mind") as well as formal logical consistency (the product of the "third act of the mind").

Reply to Objection 4: We can find the fallacy of amphibology, or grammatical equivocation, in Berkeley's argument. The adverbial phrase introduced by "when" can modify either "think" or "exists." It is indeed a contradiction for us to think when we do not think, but it is not a contradiction for a thing to *exist* when we do not think it, or for us to think *that*.

Article 10: Whether mind is only a projection of matter?

Objection 1: It seems that it is, for every mental activity, including philosophical reasoning, mathematical calculation, religious faith, creative imagination, sense perception, and all emotions, can be adequately explained in terms of the physics and chemistry of the brain and nervous system, by cybernetic science. There is no thought or sensation, X or Y, that cannot be explained as the product of physical-chemical acts X^1 or Y^1 in the brain. By Ockham's Razor, or the principle of parsimony, then, there is no need to posit anything beyond material causes.

Objection 2: Science has proved that material biological forces, through evolution by natural selection, are in fact the causes that produced human brains. And brains produce thought, since a blow to the brain takes away thought. Therefore material forces are the causes of mental acts.

Objection 3: No one can think without a brain. Yet brains can exist without thinking. Therefore brains are the cause and thinking the effect.

On the contrary, the authority of immediate experience speaks against this reduction of mind to matter. For all persons are immediately aware of their thinking whenever they think, since ordinary thinking is simultaneously self-reflective or self-aware. This is data as immediate and indubitable as empirical data, and distinct from empirical data, since it does not depend on sensation and can be purely abstract (e.g. "I think, therefore I am").

I answer that materialism (the reduction of all real things, including mind, to matter) is immediately self-contradictory, for it is an "ism," a theory, a *thought*. It can be held only by turning away from the above data (in the *On the contrary*) by an act of will or inattention.

The categories that apply to matter, such as color, size, mass, and shape cannot be made to apply to thoughts. (Are logically sound thoughts green? Are abstract thoughts rounder than concrete thoughts?) And the categories that apply to thoughts, such as true and false, cannot be made to apply to matter. (Are positive ions "true" and negative ions "false"?) Therefore neither can be reduced to the other.

To claim that there are no minds, only material brains, which are like computers, is like claiming that there is no person behind a computer who designed or programmed it. No one would trust such a computer. So why does a materialist trust his brain?

Reply to Objection 1: (1) The same principle of parsimony could equally lead to the "mentalist" conclusion that there is no need to posit anything beyond *mental* causes, since no one can point to a physical cause except by an act of thinking, which is a mental cause.

(2) The facts are most adequately explained by the hypothesis of a psychosomatic unity of form and matter between mind and body, similar to the unity between the meaning and the words of a speech. This would account for the fact that it is impossible to produce any event in either realm absent a corresponding event in the other; for the only way to change the meaning of a speech is to change the words, and vice versa: every change of meaning is a

change of words and every change of words is a change of meaning.

(3) To produce an "explanation" of X in terms of X¹, and Y in terms of Y¹, is not yet to have proved that X¹ and Y¹ efficiently *cause* X and Y. If they occur simultaneously, it may be that X¹ and Y¹ are *caused by* X and Y. Or it may be that both are caused by a third thing.

Reply to Objection 2: (1) Evolution is not empirical data, it is a *theory.*

(2) Even if science proves that evolution by natural selection was the material cause of human brains, that does not prove that this material cause was the *sole* cause. If it is proved that a certain pen wrote a certain letter, that does not prove that a man with a mind did not hold the pen.

(3) And even if evolution is the *sole* cause of *brains*, that does not prove that it is the sole cause of *thought* unless it is also proved that brains are the sole cause of thought.

(4) That fact that a blow to the brain takes away thought does not prove that the brain is the sole cause of thought, any more than the fact that demolishing a microphone makes the speaker's voice inaudible proves that the microphone was the sole cause, or even the cause at all, of the voice.

Reply to Objection 3: (1) If no one can think without a brain, this could be either because (a) the brain is the *cause* of thought, or because (b) the brain is the *instrument* of thought, or because (c) the brain is one of the necessary *conditions* for thought. A necessary condition is not the same as a sufficient condition.

(2) It is not true that no one can think without a brain. There are many examples of correct thinking (e.g. accurate reports of words spoken by others or of the location of lost objects) by patients whose brains were not acting at all because they were "brain dead" and having out-of-body experiences. (See the research done at the University of Connecticut on this.)

Question V:
Philosophical Anthropology

Article 1: Whether all human beings are persons?

Objection 1: It seems that they are not, for all persons have rights, but the unborn products of human conception do not have rights, not even the first of rights, the right to life, therefore they are not persons.

Objection 2: "Person" is a legal term, and thus it is as socially relative as the law is.

Objection 3: There are no other "persons" besides human persons. But there are other humans (those without legal rights) besides persons (those with legal rights).

On the contrary, a person by nature is a rational, self-conscious being. The verbal indicator of personhood is the word "I." And all human beings by nature are capable of rationality and self-consciousness, even if that capacity is presently undeveloped or blocked, as, for example, in the unborn, the severely retarded, those in deep sleep, and fans of the New York Yankees. Therefore all human beings are persons.

I answer that obviously all human beings have essential human nature. If not, we could not call them human beings. Now there are only two possibilities: either (1) *all* human beings are persons, with the natural rights of persons (i.e. the rights following from their essential nature), or (2) only *some* are persons. All the tyrants, murderers, terrorists, sociopaths, rapists, robbers, slavers, and oppressors in history have embraced the second philosophy; because in order to *treat* someone as subhuman, we must *think* of them as such. On the other hand, all the defenders of human equality, human liberty, and human rights in history have embraced the first philosophy. The competition between these two philosophies has been the main theme of human history. "By their fruits you shall know them." No further argument should be necessary.

Reply to Objection 1: If we speak of *natural* rights here, the argument from human legislation proves nothing, for human legislation is not the author of human nature, on which natural rights depend. If, on the other hand, we do not speak of natural rights here but only of legal rights given or refused to some humans by other humans—humans who may be either wise or foolish, good or evil—then again the argument proves nothing. For the Nazis, for example, denied legal rights to the Jews, but that said nothing about who the Jews really were, only about who the Nazis really were: those whose will was for the Jews not to be. Similarly, *Roe v. Wade* and *Dred Scott*, in declaring that two classes of human beings (the unborn and Blacks) were not *legal* persons, said nothing about the *nature* of the unborn or Blacks, only about the will of the legislators against them.

Reply to Objection 2: "Person" is not *merely* a legal term. Many and even most "legal terms" have a prior, pre-legal meaning.

Reply to Objection 3: The Divine Person or Persons, angels, and possible rational extraterrestrials are examples of other persons besides human persons. "Person" is a broader term than "human" because there are nonhuman persons; but "human" is not a broader term than "person" because all humans are persons, with the rights of persons that follow from their nature as persons. One must first depersonalize some sub-class of humans (slaves, Blacks, Jews, the unborn) by an act of will before one can declare them non-persons by the mind. One does not *discover* or *receive* this by the mind, as *data*; one *decrees* or constructs or creates it by the will.

Article 2: Whether all persons are intrinsically valuable?

Objection 1: It seems that they are not, for *human* persons are part of the universe, and in the universe everything is relative to everything else. Therefore the value of any part of the universe, however great, is a value that is not intrinsic, or absolute, but relative to other entities in the universe.

Objection 2: Only God is intrinsically and absolutely valuable, for God is the only absolute. All creatures, as is evident by that very term, are relative to their creator and receive their meaning and value, as they receive their existence, from the fact that God created them and values them. Thus since their value is relative to God, it is relative and extrinsic, not absolute and intrinsic.

Objection 3: Christ said "No one is good but God alone." (*Mark* 10:18) If he meant by "good" "intrinsically good," the point is granted. But if he meant "good" simply, the point is also granted, for if no one but God is good at all, then *a fortiori* no one but God can be good intrinsically.

On the contrary, the single most widely accepted principle of morality today is Kant's "categorical imperative," one formulation of which is to treat all persons with *respect* rather than *use*, i.e. as *ends* rather than *means*, and this means they are to be treated as having intrinsic rather than instrumental value. This imperative or rule of practice could not be morally valid if it were not *true*. Kant himself, though skeptical of objective ("transcendent") metaphysics and anthropology, explicitly grounded this imperative in the fact that all persons *are* ends rather than means.

I answer that the intrinsic value of every person can be demonstrated in six steps: (1) In nearly all wisdom traditions (e.g. Christianity, Buddhism, and "Enlightenment" humanism), the two supreme values are wisdom and love, truth and good will, honesty and compassion, *prajna* and *karuna*. These are also the two values which all who have had near-death experiences (apparent foretastes of the next life) come back with and devote their lives to, though they seldom saw this wisdom clearly before their experience.

(2) These two values are one. For the supreme wisdom *is* to live a life of love, which is the supreme value. Love and wisdom, heart and mind, goodness and truth, cannot contradict each other, unless the human self is so badly twisted that its two greatest values contradict each other.

(3) Now the eye of love always perceives the beloved as intrinsically valuable.

(4) Therefore if this love (*agape*, not *eros*) is wisdom and truth, all persons loved *are* intrinsically valuable.

(5) But this love (*agape*) is universal, not particular, as *eros* is. *All persons are to be loved with charity.*

(6) Therefore all persons are intrinsically valuable.

Reply to Objection 1: Persons, though parts of the universe, are not *merely* parts of the universe. This is proved by the fact that they can know some truths about the entire universe and even judge the universe. This cannot be done except by abstracting themselves from it and making it their object. But the subject of knowing and judging cannot be merely a part of the object known or judged, as light cannot be itself one of the objects lit up. Therefore persons are not merely parts of the universe. The premise is false.

Reply to Objection 2: This is true for all *things*, but *persons* are not merely things, i.e. objects, but are subjects. Theologically put, they are created in God's image ("I-hood": cf. *Exodus*. 3:14). In the words of John Paul II, quoting Vatican II, "man is the only creature God created for its own sake" (as end, not means).

Reply to Objection 3: Christ was testing his interlocutor here. He meant neither intrinsic nor non-intrinsic *ontological* goodness, but *moral* goodness, i.e. moral perfection, which indeed resides in God alone. The authority Christ always appealed to, Jewish scripture, tells us that God himself declared all that he had created to be (ontologically) "good" and mankind "very good" (Genesis 1). According to Christian doctrine, even when mankind lost moral goodness, its ontological goodness was so great that God made the supreme sacrifice of Himself to redeem it. We are not junk.

Article 3: Whether man is essentially distinct from animals?

Objection 1: It seems that he is not, for animals are more like humans than the traditional view allows. Every human attribute and activity also can be found to a lesser degree among the animals, so that the difference seems to be one of degree rather than kind. Every biological characteristic in man is also found in some animals, and vice versa. And with regard to the supposedly nonbiological, or spiritual, attributes, such as language, creativity, or intelligence, there is a greater gap between lower animals such as worms or amebas and higher animals such as porpoises and chimpanzees, than between these higher animals and man, as is evident by observation.

Objection 2: Not only are animals more like man than the traditional view allows, but man is also more like animals than the traditional view allows. Science keeps discovering biological, genetic, and cybernetic bases for all features previously thought to be spiritual and distinctively human, such as religion, morality, and mathematical ability. Therefore man is only the most intelligent among the animals.

On the contrary, no society in history has ever treated humans in the same way as it has treated animals, or treated animals in the same way as it has treated humans.

I answer that we find at least ten differences in kind between animals and humans. (1) Animals have absolutely no signs of religion, of an awareness of God or immortality. (2) They are conscious of the world of objects but not of themselves as personal subjects. Their consciousness is not self-reflexive. And therefore (3) though they can be trained to *behave* in ways that humans find acceptable, they have no moral *conscience* (they have social *shame* but not individual *guilt*). (4) Their creativity is routine and circumscribed by their instincts: e.g. a given species of bird will always build its nest in exactly the same way. (5) Their languages are not articulate, not invented, and do not change or progress through time. (6) Their thought is concrete, not abstract. They have precepts but not concepts. (7) They have immediate intuition but not demonstrative reasoning. (8) They do not produce technological inventions, because (9) they do not formulate scientific theories. (10) They have no sense of artistic beauty, or beauty for its own sake.

And even among the biological and nonspiritual attributes such as sex, death, and food, we find that humans imbue these biological activities with spiritual meanings that are incomprehensible to animals. For instance, romance, funerals, and ceremonial feasts transform sex, death, and food into spiritually significant mysteries.

Reply to Objection 1: The biological differences are indeed only differences in degree, or in biological species rather than essential genus. But there is a difference in essence, or in kind rather than in degree, between humans and animals with regard to every attribute that is spiritual rather than merely biological, as is shown in the body of the Article.

Reply to Objection 2: This biologism or materialism has already been answered in Question 2, Article 9, and Question 4, Article 10. See also Mortimer Adler, *The Difference in Man and the Difference It Makes.*

Article 4: Whether gender is more than something social plus something biological?*

Objection 1: It seems that it is not. For man may be considered under three dimensions: (1) externally, in his relationships with others (and this is the social dimension); (2) internally in his body (and this is the biological dimension); and (3) internally in his soul (and this is the spiritual dimension). (1) Social gender roles and identities are for the most part constructed by society and relative to different societies, as can be shown by anthropological data. This accounts for the relative and changing face of gender. (2) Biological gender identity, on the other hand, is given at birth and is not wholly relative to society, culture, time, or place; and this accounts for the absolute and unchanging face of gender. (3) So there is no need for the spiritual dimension to account for either relative or absolute gender identity. The other two dimensions are sufficient.

Objection 2: Speaking of male and female souls is a category confusion. Maleness and femaleness are biological categories. Souls are free from gender as they are free from matter.

Objection 3: Speaking of masculine and feminine souls invites sexual stereotyping: "the feminine mind" and "the masculine mind."

* See also Sample Q.7, p. 237.

A. 4: Whether gender is more than social and biological?

Objection 4: In most languages, the word for "soul" is feminine only. If souls were in fact masculine (in men) and feminine (in women), there would be two words, or two grammatical genders for the word.

On the contrary, almost every language in the world except English has masculine and feminine nouns, which indicates a belief that all things (which are designated by nouns) have gender in some analogical way. Therefore souls also have gender.

I answer that the innate gender identity of souls can be demonstrated from the two premises of (1) the universally admitted innate gender identity of the body and (2) the psychosomatic unity, according to which soul and body are not two independent substances but two dimensions of one substance, the form and the matter, like the words and the meaning of a book. The fact that both premises are almost universally admitted, yet the conclusion is not, attests to the lack of logic in media-influenced fashionable thinking.

Reply to Objection 1: We cannot determine whether or not gender exists *in souls* simply by noting that, of the *other* two human dimensions, one is relative and one absolute. We are not the inventors of humanity and cannot apportion *a priori* the proper place of gender. We must find this from the data.

Reply to Objection 2: (1) We speak of masculine and feminine souls, not male and female souls. The existence of these two different sets of words, one personal and the other biological, indicates the existence of sex or gender in the psyche as well as in the soma.
(2) Because of the psychosomatic unity, this is not a category confusion, any more than it is a category confusion to speak of "seeing" with the mind as well as the eye, or having an emotional "heart" as well as a biological one. A meaningful *analogy* is not a confusion but an insight.

Reply to Objection 3: (1) There *is* such a thing as an innately different feminine mind and masculine mind, as is evident from abundant psychological research.
(2) The fact that a difference is innate does not necessarily make

it absolute. There are innate but relative tendencies, or typical patterns, in men and women, psychologically as well as biologically (e.g. the range of voices among sopranos, contraltos, altos, tenors, baritones, and basses). Men and women are not two different *species*, either in soul or in body.

(3) A stereotype is created by social prejudices, which can be traced to a certain time and place, while the difference between masculine and feminine is created by nature and exists in all times and places. It is an archetype rather than a stereotype. Insofar as such stereotypes do exist, they do not disprove the archetypes of which they are perversions. *Abusus non tollit usum.*

Reply to Objection 4: (1) The word for "soul" is feminine because it is taken metaphysically, in relation to God. To God all souls are feminine; that is why God has always been spoken of as "he" by Jewish, Christian, and Muslim theists.

(2) Bodies are innately gendered, yet there are not two words for bodies, one for men's bodies and another for women's. The same can be true for souls.

Article 5: Whether there is free will in man?

Objection 1: It seems that there is not, for nothing can happen without a cause; but a cause determines its effect; therefore all that happens is determined by its causes. But free will would be the opposite, the contradiction, the alternative, or the exception to this universal determinism. Therefore, since determinism is true, free will cannot exist. Nothing in nature can be uncaused, unless we embrace the utterly irrational "Pop! Theory."

Objection 2: What is not cause of itself is not free. And man is not cause of himself, for only God is that.

Objection 3: Science has discovered causes for all the actions and choices thought to proceed from free will, whether these be biological, emotional, environmental, or motivational factors. It is impossible to point to a single act of free will that science cannot explain by pointing out its determining causes.

Objection 4: We experience our own lack of free will, as when St. Paul says "The good which I will, I do not, but the evil which I will not, I do." (Romans 7:19).

Objection 5: Divine sovereignty contradicts human free will. For divine sovereignty means that God is the first cause of everything in the universe, including man's choices and actions, in which case man can at best be only an instrumental cause, as a pen is an instrumental cause of a book; while free will means that a man is the first cause of his own choices and actions, as an author is the first cause of his book.

Objection 6: In the presence of two known goods, the will is necessarily attracted more to the greater one; and in the presence of known good and known evil, the will is necessarily attracted to the good and repelled by the evil. Thus, as Plato argues, all choice of evil is due to ignorance, for evil could not be chosen unless it appeared good, i.e. desirable. It is not under the competence of the will, however, but of the intellect to discriminate between real and apparent goods; thus the cause of evil choices is not a free will but an ignorant reason.

Objection 7: (a) If our reason is *not* operating, we cannot be rightly praised or blamed and we cannot make a free choice. Thus ignorance is a moral excuse. (b) But if reason *is* operating, it is operating by necessity, for reason perceives necessary connections between terms in making propositions, and between propositions in making arguments. The will has no freedom to contradict reason. When we understand that "2+2=4," or that "good is to be done and evil avoided," we have no free will to doubt it. Thus reason makes will unfree. So in either case, whether our reason is operating or not, there is no free will.

On the contrary, William James argues for free will from the premise of the *un*certainty of all arguments for and against it, for this uncertainty leaves one free to choose to believe or not to believe. (See "The Dilemma of Determinism.")

I answer that (1) If free will does not exist, all moral language becomes meaningless. For it is meaningless to praise, blame, reward, punish, counsel, command, forbid, or exhort an unfree agent such as a machine or a "dumb animal." When the Coke machine fails to deliver a Coke, we do not accuse it of sin and tell it to go to confession; we kick it.

(2) And since rewarding and punishing are the acts of justice, if free will does not exist, justice itself becomes meaningless. But without justice all higher moral values such as mercy and forgiveness and even love are meaningless. And without love, human life itself is meaningless. Therefore if there is no free will, human life is meaningless.

Reply to Objection 1: Free choices are not uncaused but self-caused, not undetermined but self-determined. The universal causality and free will are compatible.

Reply to Objection 2: Man is indeed the cause of himself (i.e. his own choices), but not the absolutely *first*, uncaused cause. Only God is *that*. And even God is not *self*-caused (*causa sui*) as Spinoza says He is, but *un*-caused. For nothing can be simply the efficient cause of its own existence, since nothing can be prior or posterior to itself.

Reply to Objection 3: (1) This is a claim not about what science has in fact already done but about what it will be able to do if challenged. Thus it is an act of faith or hope in the future, and this is not part of the scientific method.

(2) The "causes" of free choices that science has discovered are all conditioning causes, not determining causes. Our choices are indeed conditioned by many factors, but not necessitated by them, for we are not merely *patients* but *agents* and thus responsible for our actions. These factors are *influences*, whether from without (the environment), from the body (heredity), or from the soul (motivations), which make up only some of the multifarious factors in a human choice, and they are influences which can and often are resisted. If any such influence simply *cannot* be resisted (e.g. in delirium or serious chemical addiction), the choices which such influence necessitates are by definition unfree. They are then the internal equivalent of another, stronger man holding and controlling the hand of the agent.

Reply to Objection 4: The very fact that St. Paul complains about this shows that it is a pathological and particular situation, not a natural and universal one. Often, but not always, our will is moved more by our passions than by our reason and conscience. Yet even then it is free, for we rightly feel guilty for yielding to temptations; but if the effect were necessitated, there would be no reason for guilt.

Reply to Objection 5: Just as light, because it transcends all colors rather than being a rival color, brings out and perfects all colors, so divine grace, since it transcends nature rather than rivaling it, perfects nature rather than setting it aside. Thus when God moves unfree things He moves them unfreely, according to their nature; and when He moves man's will He moves it freely, for that is its nature. He turns man's free will on, not off. Just as God's presence in a dog makes a dog more doggy, not less, it makes man more human, not less; and free will is an essential part of what it means to be human. As Augustine says, God is the "Interior Master," not an external rival or tyrant.

Reply to Objection 6: We all know by experience that Plato's teaching is not true, for we all experience occasions of choosing evil even when we clearly know it is evil. The reason is that the free will can choose to side with the passions and blind the reason, commanding it not to attend to the fact that an act is evil, but only to its desirable consequences.

Reply to Objection 7: Reason makes the will free, not unfree. For reason has the power to abstract from the particular concrete good and rise to an understanding of goodness in general (this is how it is able to formulate universal principles), thus leaving the will free to choose between alternative contingent particulars as different possible instances or incarnations of the necessary universal or means to the good end. The will cannot choose evil *qua* evil, or evil in general over good in general, any more than the mind can believe falsehood qua falsehood, or known falsehood over known truth. But just as the mind can believe particular errors, the will can choose particular evils.

Article 6: Whether the will is higher than the intellect?

Objection 1: It seems that it is, for loving is higher and more valuable than knowing, but loving is an act of the will, while knowing is an act of the intellect.

Objection 2: The will is the king and captain of the whole soul, commanding the intellect to think or not to think. Thus the act of the will is the cause and the act of the mind is the effect. No effect can be greater than its cause, and therefore the act of the intellect cannot be greater than the act of the will.

Objection 3: If, as has been proved, there is free will, then the will must be the first cause (prescinding from divine causality), else it is not free. Thus it is the will that is primary.

On the contrary, Voluntarism, the prioritizing of the will over the intellect, leads to theological and moral absurdities, as shown in Plato's *Euthyphro*. See also Pope Benedict XVI's Regensburg Address and Robert Reilly's *The Closing of the Muslim Mind*.) It is no accident that the title of the most influential Nazi propaganda film is *The Triumph of the Will*. It is the formula for timocracy, tyranny, and terrorism.

I answer that since both intellect and will are aspects of the divine image, and since both truth and goodness, their respective objects, are absolute values and divine attributes, neither one is simply and absolutely higher than the other. No one can ever have too much of either truth or goodness, and no one should ever compromise or act contrary to either truth or goodness. Asking which is higher is putting them into competition, and that is analogous to, and as mistaken as, doing the same to the Persons of the Trinity.

Reply to Objection 1: Loving persons, divine and human, is higher and better than knowing them, but knowing things and principles is better than loving them. For love draws and conforms the lover to the beloved, while knowledge subjects the thing known to the exigencies of the knower. For a thing is known according to the powers of the knower; thus to know God is to know him according to the limitations of the human mind. But to love Him is to be drawn to Him and to become more like Him. So to know ice cream is to raise it up to the level of a spiritual concept, while to love it is to become more like it by filling one's mind and desires with it.

Reply to Objection 2: It is true that the will can rule and command the intellect, but it is also true that the intellect rules the will, for the will cannot will anything—any X rather than non-X—until the intellect presents the nature of X and non-X to the will. The will is the efficient cause of the intellect's act, but the intellect is the formal cause (the specification) of the will's act.

Reply to Objection 3: (1) Primacy in time or causality is not the same as primacy in value.

(2) The mutual causality (formal and efficient) between intellect and will which is described in the previous Reply is simultaneous. Neither causality comes before and without the other.

(3) However, we *can* contemplate a thing with our intellect without desiring it with our will, though this requires a previous act of the will-to-contemplation, unless the object of the intellect appears involuntarily to the mind as a sight does to the eye.

Article 7: Whether soul and body are distinct substances?

Objection 1: It seems that they are, for, as Descartes shows, they are two clear and distinct ideas. A (human, rational) soul can think (and choose) and is not extended in space, while a body cannot think or choose and is extended in space. Two clear and distinct ideas indicate two distinct substances. Therefore soul and body are two distinct substances.

Objection 2: Since the soul is immortal and the body is mortal, and since no single substance can possess opposite attributes at the same time, therefore soul and body are not a single substance but two substances.

Objection 3: If the soul were not a distinct substance from the body, it could not be immortal. But it is immortal. Therefore it is a distinct substance from the body.

Objection 4: If the soul is not a substance, it is either the form of the (mortal) body or an accident of the (mortal) body or an effect (an epiphenomenon) of the (mortal) body. But in all three cases it would be mortal. It is not mortal, therefore it is a substance.

On the contrary, every good psychologist, common sense, and daily experience all recognize the psychosomatic unity. But the theory of two substances contradicts the psychosomatic unity.

I answer that if soul and body were two substances (if the soul were "the ghost in the machine"), then the experienced causal interaction between them could not be explained. For a ghost cannot manipulate the levers of a machine, having no fingers; and the atoms of a machine or any other physical thing cannot cause pain in a ghost, who has no pain nerves. The only hypothesis that explains all the experienced data is some kind of hylomorphism. The body is the matter (hylè) and the soul is the form (morphè) of the one substance, the person.

Reply to Objection 1: Two clear and distinct ideas do not always indicate two distinct substances. For instance, the notes of a piece of music and the beauty of the music, or the arguments in this book and the syllables in this book, or the life of a tree and the molecules of the tree, are examples of two clear and distinct ideas but not two different substances.

Reply to Objection 2: The matter and the form of one substance can possess opposite attributes at the same time, such as the three examples in the Reply to Objection 1.

Reply to Objection 3: The soul is both a substance (and thus can be immortal) and the form of the mortal body. It is the body that is not a distinct substance, but only the matter for the soul.

Reply to Objection 4: The soul can be both a spiritual substance (and thus capable of immortality) and at the same time function as the form of the body, the life of the living body. We do not have two or three souls, but one. It is the same single form (soul) in us that (a) gives biological life to the mortal body, (b) performs the actions of sensation and animal appetites and instincts in the mortal body-soul compound, and (c) is capable of reason and free will through its immaterial, spiritual nature. Although the human soul is such an unusual case that it is unique, there is no inherent logical contradiction or metaphysical impossibility here.

Article 8: Whether the soul is immortal?

Objection 1: It seems that it is not, for souls, like bodies, have a beginning, and the law of nature is that whatever has a beginning has an end, as Buddha says in his "diamond sutra."

Objection 2: There is empirical evidence that nothing in us survives death. For we observe that (1) without a brain there is no self-consciousness and that (2) at death the brain decays, like the rest of the body. Therefore after death there is no self-consciousness.

Objection 3: We use empirical data as criteria to identify and distinguish each other. But souls without bodies have no senses and thus no empirical data or criteria. Therefore they cannot be distinguished and identified after death.

Objection 4: If the soul's immortality is proved, the premises must be taken either (a) from what is above the soul or (b) from what is below the soul, or (c) from the soul itself. (a) They cannot be taken from what is above the soul because this is God, and we cannot predict what depends on God's will: He could create mortal souls or immortal souls. (b) They cannot be taken from what is below the soul because no data concerning bodies can prove any conclusion about spirit. (c) And they cannot be taken from the soul itself because we have no access to the soul itself except through bodies, since all knowledge depends on sense perception; and as we have seen, data about bodies do not entail conclusions about spirit.

On the contrary, if there is no life after death, nearly all humans who have ever lived, including the wisest, holiest, and best of us, have lived by a false and illusory hope.

All the religions of the world and the vast majority of all human beings in all cultures throughout history have believed in life after death. Most of the unbelievers are found in only one time (modernity) and one place (Europe and North America).

I answer that the existence of life after death through the immortality of the soul can be proved in many ways. If only *one* of these arguments is valid, immortality is proven.

(1) Plato argues in the *Republic* that we observe many lethal bodily diseases that can kill bodies but no spiritual diseases that can kill souls. For the two main diseases of souls are ignorance (or folly, the opposite of wisdom) and vice (or immorality), and neither of these is capable of killing souls, only wounding them.

(2) Plato argues in the *Phaedo* that souls give life to bodies, and what gives a power by nature has that power by nature. But what has that power by nature (i.e. by essence, by its Form) cannot lose it. Therefore souls cannot lose life.

(3) (a) The only two ways in which a thing can die are decomposition into parts or annihilation. (b) But souls cannot be decomposed because they were not composed. Souls, unlike bodies, are simple, not compound. You can't cut souls into pieces. Therefore, not being composed, they cannot be decomposed. (c) And nothing is simply annihilated as a whole. (d) Therefore souls cannot die.

(4) Kant argues that if there is no life after death, justice is not done, for it is not perfectly done in this life. And the demand for justice is absolute, not conditional.

(5) The soul can know its body as an object. The body cannot do this. This power to objectify the body cannot be a bodily power. For

to know X, I must be more than X, since the knowledge of a thing as an object is not one of that thing's parts. Therefore the soul has a power that is not a bodily power. Thus the soul is more than the body. And what is more than the body need not be subject to the body's mortality.

(6) The soul can also perform two immaterial operations: abstract conceiving, judging, and reasoning, as distinct from sensing; and free choice, as distinct from animal instinct or desire. These are not operations of the body for the body supplies only the biological instruments (brain and nervous system) for them. What can perform an immaterial act is immaterial, and what is immaterial is not subject to physical death.

(7) If we love another person with the love of charity rather than cupidity (*agape* rather than *eros*), we perceive the intrinsic value and indispensability of that person. (See Question 5, Article 2.) It is morally intolerable that that which is in fact indispensable be dispensed with. If reality does that to persons, it offers us no ground for morality, which commands us *not* to do that to persons (Kant's "categorical imperative"). But if morality is not grounded in reality, it loses its authority and force, being grounded only in our own will, like the rules of a game. Therefore either persons are immortal and not dispensed with at death, or the morality of respect for persons loses its ground and authority and force. (See Gabriel Marcel for a version of this "Personalist" argument.)

Reply to Objection 1: The human soul is the exception to this law of nature, for it comes not from nature, by evolution, but from God, by creation.

Reply to Objection 2: The first of these "observations" is not an empirical fact but a philosophical assumption, for self-consciousness is not empirical. It is true that while united to the body the soul's activity is dependent on the brain, but this fact does not necessarily entail the conclusion that the soul cannot also act on its own, even as a man whom we see being carried by a horse may also be capable of walking by himself. In fact there is data to show that this is so, based on scientific studies of out-of-body experiences and near-death experiences.

Reply to Objection 3: Even while joined to the body, each individual soul uses also nonempirical criteria for identifying itself, and, by analogy, other souls. We speak of others' personalities, not just of others' bodies. "Personality," though communicated empirically, is not itself an empirical concept. (It has no size, shape, or color.) Even though the nonempirical aspects of personality are mixed with and dependent on the empirical aspects in this life, since the soul is the form of the body, yet we all recognize that these nonempirical aspects of a person exist, and this makes it metaphysically *possible* for them to exist separated from the empirical aspects of personality, *if* it is metaphysically possible for the soul to exist apart from the body, which is demonstrated in the "*I answer that.*" For a thing's existence is not dependent on its mode of communication, which is its property or accident. In short, even if the premise were true that in this life all ways of identifying souls depend on empirical data, that does not entail the conclusion that in the next life there can be no other ways of identifying souls.

But even in this life it is not true that all ways of identifying souls depend on empirical data. Mental telepathy shows that it is sometimes possible to identify souls nonempirically.

Reply to Objection 4: (a) Reason can know some truths about God, from which we may be able to deduce conclusions about the souls He creates. For God's will is not arbitrary. For instance, if God is trustable, He would not create us with innate longings which cannot be fulfilled; but we have an innate longing for immortality.

(b) Since souls, bodies, and nature form a single universe designed by a single mind, there may well be clues and analogies in the lower world that strongly point to truths in the higher world, even if they do not logically demonstrate them. For instance, if even matter is immortal (since nothing in nature can either create matter/energy or destroy it), it seems even more likely that spirit is immortal.

(c) And because of the soul's substantial unity with the body, data about bodies are as relevant to conclusions about souls as data about words are relevant to conclusions about thought. All of the arguments in the "*I answer that*" are taken from this source, the nature of the soul itself.

Article 9: Whether artificial immortality is desirable?

Objection 1: It seems that it is, for artificial immortality is immortality, and immortality is intrinsically desirable. The desirability of a thing in itself cannot depend on how that thing is acquired. For instance, even if a jewel is acquired by theft and murder, if it is worth a certain sum before it is acquired, its worth remains the same afterwards.

Objection 2: Since divine grace perfects human nature, it is not contrary to the divine order that man technologically create his own immortality.

Objection 3: Artificial immortality would produce great happiness, since it would fulfill a universal, natural desire and overcome a universal, natural fear (death).

Objection 4: "Man's conquest of nature" is one of man's natural tasks, and its history has been the history of continual progress. Death is the one aspect of nature that man has not yet conquered. It is nature's trump card. So the conquest of death would be the consummation of the conquest of nature.

On the contrary, many wise old myths like "Tithonius the Greek," "the Wandering Jew," and "the Flying Dutchman," as well as wise modern science fiction stories like Arthur C. Clarke's *Childhood's End*, Natalie Babbitt's *Tuck Everlasting*, and Robert Heinlein's *Time Enough for Love*, all teach the need for death, and the curse that deathlessness in this world would be.

I answer that if (a) our individual progress through the different stages of life is part of God's and nature's purpose for our eventual perfection and happiness, then (b) arresting that progress at any point would be detrimental to us, like staying in kindergarten forever. But it is at least very likely, by argumentation from analogy, from religious faith, from universal human experience, from the wisdom of human authority, from intuition and instinct, and from philosophical reasoning, that this antecedent, or premise (a), is true. Therefore it is at least very likely that its consequent, or conclusion (b), is also true—i.e., that artificially arresting our natural progress would be detrimental. But preventing natural death by artificial immortality would be arresting that progress. For the experience of death is an essential part of human progress in wisdom and experience. Therefore it would be detrimental.

This is true if and only if we live through the experience of death, of course, for we cannot learn any wisdom if we do not exist any more. The implicit assumption of this argument, therefore, is the existence of natural immortality, which has been demonstrated in the previous Article; and the implicit assumption of those who favor artificial immortality is the denial of natural immortality. If we are already immortal, we need not make ourselves immortal.

Reply to Objection 1: (1) Sometimes, the mode of acquiring a thing changes the nature of the thing itself. For instance, pregnancy by rape is essentially different from pregnancy by loving consent; and political power acquired by murder, deceit, and terror is an essentially different kind of power than that obtained by justice and consent, and can be maintained only by the same forces with which it was acquired. Thus natural immortality (immortality from the intrinsic nature of the soul) is never threatened with death, for nothing can lose its essential nature; while an immortality that was obtained through technological means could also be undone by technological means.

(2) The end result of artificial immortality, like its beginning, would be essentially different from that of natural immortality. For it would ensure an immortal life in this fallen body and in this fallen world rather than in a new, unfallen body and a new, unfallen world recreated by God. Since natural immortality and the promise of an unfallen body and an unfallen world has already been given to us, it is infinitely foolish to exchange this for what is not only lesser but also inherently corrupted and corrupting, a downward spiritual

gravity uncorrected by grace. As C.S. Lewis has said in *Mere Christianity*, "We are like eggs at present. And you can't just go on being a good egg forever. You must hatch or go bad." To discover what artificial immortality would produce, leave a dozen eggs out on your kitchen table for a year.

Reply to Objection 2: It is contrary to the divine order, and to the divine respect for nature, that the essential nature of a thing be changed.

Reply to Objection 3: Our foolish and fallen desires and fears are no infallible index of wisdom. We also desire great worldly power and wealth, but both corrupt us.

Reply to Objection 4: (1) There are progressions whose last term undercuts all previous progress, as C.S. Lewis shows at the end of *The Abolition of Man*.

(2) Man's task is not to conquer nature, as if she were an enemy, but to care for it and perfect it. Man's nature is to die; so bypassing death would not be caring for or perfecting human nature.

(3) Conquering nature does not include conquering our own nature, for that would be conquering the conqueror, thus *being* conquered.

Article 10: Whether there is reincarnation?

Objection 1: It seems that there is, for there are many cases of people who remember past lives, and some of these are empirically verifiable, e.g. by correctly revealing the location of items hidden by ancestors, or other long-lost historical information revealed during hypnotic "past life regressions."

Objection 2: Few if any of us are "finished," i.e. perfected, at death. Physical death by itself is not sufficient to cause the change from sinner to saint, from the intellectually and morally imperfect state we are in when we leave the body to the wisdom and virtue of Heavenly perfection—unless one radically underestimates either our present follies and vices, or our Heavenly perfection, and the greatness of the gap between them. Since we need reincarnation to be complete, nature and God would supply it.

Objection 3: Reincarnation is believed (1) by many ancient religions, (2) by two of the higher religions, Hinduism and Buddhism, and (3) by many independent thinkers in the West even contrary to their own Western secular or Biblical traditions. All this shows at least that the idea is natural to man.

On the contrary, "it is given unto man *once* to die and after this the judgment." (*Hebrews 9:27*)

I answer that the idea of reincarnation contradicts (1) the official teachings, scriptures, and historical tradition of all three theistic religions (Judaism, Christianity, and Islam); (2) the unique dignity of the unique individual, since according to reincarnation "I" was once another individual; (3) the importance of this life, since reincarnation allows as many "re-tests" as we need, thereby draining away the drama of all tests, including moral tests; (4) the personality of the body, since according to reincarnation bodies are not aspects of one's personality but merely temporary locations, like motel rooms; (5) the psychosomatic unity, since according to reincarnation souls are indifferent to and compatible with many different bodies; and (6) the free will to choose damnation, since according to reincarnation everyone must eventually "make it" to Heaven, or full Enlightenment.

Reply to Objection 1: These cases could all be hoaxes; or, if not, they could be due to mental telepathy from ghosts (the souls of dead humans) or fallen and deceiving angels (evil spirits) pretending to be human souls.

Reply to Objection 2: The premise of our "unfinishedness" is profoundly true, but it does not prove that *reincarnation* is the way this is overcome. *Purgatory* overcomes it just as well, and is a more reasonable hypothesis (quite apart from religious authority), since nature never simply repeats stages of growth. Belief in reincarnation stems from the juxtaposition of (a) the insight into this true premise with (b) the failure to imagine a different kind of spiritual growth, outside this body and this world.

Reply to Objection 3: (1) These ancient religions are mistaken about many other things (e.g. polytheism and magic), so they are no reliable index of wisdom. (2) In Hinduism and Buddhism, reincarnation is closely tied to a theology of pantheism or monism and an anthropology of karmic fatalism. (3) What we today call "independent thinkers" used to be called "heretics." *Many* errors are "natural to man."

Question VI:
Epistemology

Article 1: Whether skepticism is refutable?

Objection 1: It seems that it is not, for the skeptic can simply subject any refutation of skepticism to more skeptical questioning.

Objection 2: Skepticism is refutable theoretically only by demonstrating some truth with certainty. But every valid proof or demonstration rests on premises. For an idea can either be believed without reason (premises), or with reason. If without reason, there is no proof that it is true, and no refutation of skepticism. If with reason, the skeptic can question the premise, as he questioned the conclusion; and this premise is subject to the same alternatives as before: either it is believed without reason or with reason, and if with reason, then the premises of *that* reasoning can be questioned, et cetera *ad infinitum.*

Objection 3: Skepticism can be justified for practical reasons. For skepticism always keeps an open mind, and this is the only pathway to progress. All errors consist in believing to be true that which in fact is not true; and only practical skepticism avoids that.

Objection 4: As the ancient Roman skeptics pointed out from experience, peace of mind can be attained by the suspension of all judgment that comes with skepticism.

Objection 5: As Socrates showed in practice, skepticism is always the appropriate attitude. For there is no idea which cannot and should not be doubted. To refuse to doubt is to have a closed, narrow, small, dogmatic mind.

Objection 6: There are moderate forms of skepticism, such as skepticism of certainty, but not of probable knowledge, or skepticism of absolutes, or of universals, or of objectivity.

On the contrary, no great thinker has ever been a simple and complete skeptic. To practice skepticism is to cease to speak, like Cratylus, who would only move his finger.

I answer that (1) The skeptic is not skeptical enough, for he is not really skeptical of his skepticism.

(2) The skeptic never lives his philosophy, for he makes judgments about matters of life and death, such as what is and is not the edge of a cliff, as if he had genuine knowledge. Thus to be a theoretical skeptic is to be a hypocrite, if a hypocrite is one who lives the opposite of what he says he believes.

Reply to Objection 1: This is not a logical argument but a child's willfulness. It is essentially the four-year-old asking "why?" to every answer his mother gives him, with no regard for the cognitive content of her answer, even if the answer is a valid refutation of skepticism.

Reply to Objection 2: As Aristotle showed, this "backwards doubt" terminates in two places: psychologically indubitable immediate sense experience and logically indubitable first principles such as "X is not non-X" in theoretical thinking and "Good is to be done and evil to be avoided" in practical thinking.

Also, this skeptical strategy of automatically questioning every premise of every argument is arbitrary, willful, and childish, as shown in the Reply to Objection 1. It can be done by a parrot.

Reply to Objection 3: (1) An open mind is a means, not an end. It is like an open door or an open mouth: its value depends on whether a friend or an enemy enters the door, or whether good food or poison enters the mouth.

(2) Progress is meaningless without a goal, and the goal of all intellectual progress is not the doubt of skepticism but the abolition of doubt in knowing the truth. Doubt is indeed an indispensable tool of intellectual progress, but a tool is only an instrument, and when we have used the tool of questioning to build the house of knowledge, we do not live in the tool, but in the house.

(3) Some errors consist in believing too much; others consist in believing too little. It is just as erroneous theoretically, and just as disastrous practically, to refuse to believe something that can and should be believed, as it is to believe something that should not.

Reply to Objection 4: Peace of mind is not the absolute end. "Woe to those who cry, Peace! Peace! when there is no peace." True peace of mind comes not by ignoring the mind's natural desire for truth but by satisfying it, just as true gastronomical fulfillment comes from real food, not from the unnatural suppression of all appetite.

Reply to Objection 5: Socrates was not a skeptic but a truth-seeker. Doubt is appropriate at the beginning of the process of learning, not at the end.

Reply to Objection 6: All these "moderate" forms of skepticism are just as logically suspect, since they are all subject to the same self-contradiction as simple skepticism. Is it only probable that all knowledge is only probable? Is it absolute that there are no absolutes? Is it universally true that there are no universal truths? Is it an objective truth that truth is only subjective, not objective? Et cetera.

Article 2: Whether truth is objective?

Objection 1: It seems that it is not, for people differ about what is truth, and that about which people differ is subjective. If truth were objective, there would be no disagreements and arguments. But ordinary discourse is full of continual disagreements, which have never been resolved. If there were objective truth, they would have been resolved. Therefore there is no objective truth.

Objection 2: Even granted that objective truth exists in science, for scientists do come to universal or nearly universal agreement, this is not the case in philosophy. For there is no philosophical teaching about which all philosophers agree. Therefore there is no objective truth in philosophy.

Objection 3: Even granted that objective truth exists in philosophy, it does not follow that we can know it. For if truth is objective, its existence does not depend on our knowing it, while if it is subjective, it exists only in our knowledge of it. Thus only if truth is subjective is it by definition knowable, while if it is objective it is independent of our knowledge and beyond it rather than in it, and this does us no good.

Objection 4: To claim that we *can* know objective truth is to assume that we *want to* know it, or *ought to* know it. But Nietzsche, in an unprecedented flight of boldness, questions even this "will to truth" when he asks: "Why truth? Why not rather untruth?"

On the contrary, if all truth were subjective, then *that truth* also would be subjective. But what is subjective is changeable and uncertain. Therefore if all truth were subjective, it would be changeable and uncertain, and thus *that "truth" also*—that all truth is changeable and uncertain—would be changeable and uncertain. But what is uncertain may be false, and what is changeable can be changed. Therefore the "truth" that all truth is subjective, is uncertain, and may be false; and it is changeable, and can be changed—and if changed, then changed to "truth is objective."

If it is only *subjectively* true that truth is subjective, or "true for you," then the fact that any supposed truth is "true for you," subjectively, does not entail that it is true for all, objectively, or that it is true for me. And therefore it has no rational authority over me and I have no reason to believe it. On the other hand, if it is objectively true that truth is subjective, we have an immediate self-contradiction.

I answer that what everyone means by truth is what Aristotle defined as "thinking and saying what is," i.e. the conformity of what is believed to what is, or of thinking to being. For all alternative definitions of truth (e.g. the pragmatic concept of truth, that "truth is what works," or the coherence theory of truth, that "truth is the coherence of ideas with each other," or the idealist theory of truth, that "truth is the conformity of what-is to thought") claim that *it is really the case* that truth is what works, or what coheres, or the conformity of thing to thought rather than thought to thing. In other words, in arguing that their philosophy is the true one, they argue that what they believe corresponds to what is, thus they presuppose the common concept of truth as Aristotle defines it. And this is what people mean by "objective truth."

What persuades people otherwise is always some confusion between two or more of the following five questions:

(1) Is this thing real?

(2) If so, do I, or do we, or can I, or can we, *know* that this thing is real?

(3) If so, is that knowledge certain rather than merely probable?

(4) If so, can I convince others of that certainty by rational argument?

(5) If so, does the argument use the scientific method?

A thing can be real without being known.

A thing can be known without being known with certainty.

A certainty can be private rather than demonstrable.

And proof or demonstration may use other methods than the scientific method.

Confusion between (1) and (2) produces philosophical idealism.

Confusion between (2) and (3) produces skepticism or probabilism.

Confusion between (3) and (4) produces subjectivism.

And confusion between (4) and (5) produces scientism.

Reply to Objection 1: All the premises of this argument are false. (1) People do not differ totally, but only partially, about what is truth. For if they differed totally, they could not argue, since all argument depends on *agreed* premises. (2) That about which people differ is not necessarily subjective, for two students may get different answers to a math problem, yet one is objectively correct and the other incorrect. (3) It is also not true that "if truth were objective, there would be no disagreements about it." In fact, *only* if truth is objective can there be disagreements about it. People do not argue about strictly subjective things. We never hear arguments like: "I feel sick!" "No! I feel well."

Reply to Objection 2: Universal agreement is neither the cause nor the criterion of truth. For it is possible that fools universally agree on something false. And as Socrates showed, those who do not admit the possibility that they are fools are the greatest of fools. But just as there are things fools agree on that are false, there are things that fools do not agree on that are true.

Reply to Objection 3: (1) The argument confuses two senses of the word "in" when it speaks of truth being "in" our knowledge: (a) as *received* into the order of our subjective knowing from without, i.e. from the order of objective being, and (b) as *generated by*, or at least dependent on, and not independent of, our subjective knowing. It is true that if truth is objective it *could* be unknown, while if it is subjective it is by definition known. But this does not prove that it *is* unknown.

(2) As skepticism denies that anyone can know they are right, subjectivism denies that anyone can be wrong. They are equally self-refuting.

Reply to Objection 4: To ask "*Why* truth? Why not rather untruth?" is to assume that all previous philosophers were wrong in not thus questioning the value of truth itself (i.e. were wrong in their trusting, unquestioning naiveté). And this is to assume that it is *true* that they were wrong. And this is to discriminate and prefer this truth to its opposite untruth. Thus we cannot *truly* prefer untruth to truth without committing intellectual suicide.

It is no accident that Nietzsche died insane, a martyr to his own philosophy, as well as a victim of syphilis.

Article 3: Whether we know things-in-themselves?

(This question is related to but not identical with the previous two questions. For there is another kind of skepticism in epistemology which maintains that knowing forms being rather than being forming knowing (this is the principle Kant called "the Copernican Revolution in philosophy"), and that therefore we should *not* be skeptical of our knowledge and fault it for failing in its task of knowing what is, or "things-in-themselves," not because it accomplishes that task but because its task lies not in conforming to, but in forming and structuring, all the objects of our consciousness, both sensory (space and time) and logical (the categories) and philosophical (ideas of God, self, and world). Objects conform to knowing rather than knowing conforming to objects. It is this Kantian epistemology which is refuted in this Article.)

Objection 1: It seems that we do not know things-in-themselves. For the Kantian epistemology, which maintains that we do not, is a reasonable mean between the unreasonable extremes of (1) empiricism, and the skepticism it naturally leads to (Hume) and (2) dogmatism, or dogmatic rationalism (Descartes, Spinoza, Leibniz, Wolff). Always, or nearly always, in the history of philosophy, the truth lies between two extremes. (For, as Chesterton notes, there are always at least two angles at which one can fall but only one at which one can stand upright.) Therefore it is most likely that this middle position is the true one.

Objection 2: The Kantian hypothesis accounts for all the data: both (1) the data of objectivity, i.e. the experience of "bumping up against" necessary limits in our knowledge, and (2) the data of subjectivity, i.e. the experience of the impossibility of climbing outside our mind's skin, so to speak, the impossibility of any absolute, unconditioned, non-perspectival point of view for human consciousness.

On the contrary, the Kantian epistemology attempts to draw a limit to all possible thought by denying that it can transcend phenomena (appearances) to know things-in-themselves. But as Wittgenstein said, "in order to draw a limit to thought it is necessary to think both sides of that limit." Thus Kantianism is self-contradictory.

I answer that if, as Kant claims, we cannot know things-in-themselves, i.e. objective facts independent of our minds, then we cannot know the objective facts about the real relation between knowledge and being, either. But the Kantian position that we cannot know things-in-themselves is just such a theory that claims to tell us about the real relation between knowledge and being. Therefore by its own standards it could not possibly be known. Nor can it be stated except by presupposing the opposite theory (epistemological realism, that the objects of knowledge are independently real things or facts about things), just as alternative theories of truth cannot be stated except by presupposing Aristotle's common-sense theory of truth, as was shown above.

There are also other, more specific, self-contradictions in Kant's epistemology. For instance, it accounts for knowledge by the mind *causing* its own *a priori* forms to be imposed upon experience, to structure it; but it also claims that causality is only a (transcendental) category, not a (transcendent) reality. Causality as a mere mental category could not *really cause* itself to be imposed upon phenomena.

Reply to Objection 1: (1) The principle that truth is found between two opposite errors is not a necessary principle, and therefore may have exceptions. For instance, Aristotle's application of it in ethics, that virtue is always a mean between two opposite extremes, is questionable, for some virtues have no limit, and his moderation and antipathy to extremes seems immoderate and extreme.

(2) Kantian idealism is not a mean between skepticism and dogmatism, for it is even more skeptical than Hume's skepticism, which allowed for at least a probable knowledge of at least empirical objects as they are in themselves.

Reply to Objection 2: (1) Two contradictory hypotheses, each of which is internally consistent, may often both account for all the data of experience, and yet at least one must be false. An example is materialism vs. spiritualism in metaphysics: see Question 2, Article 9.

(2) The Kantian hypothesis does not account for one aspect of "the data of objectivity," namely the experience of surprise and discovery of new categories as well as new data (e.g. Plato's "Cave" with its new "world of Forms," or a conversion from atheism to theism or from materialism to spiritualism or dualism).

(3) The "data of subjectivity" (i.e. the perspectival limits of all human knowledge) can be explained by the hypothesis of epistemological realism just as well, by the medieval principle that "whatever is received, is received into the mode of the receiver."

Article 4: Whether appearance coincides with reality?

Objection 1: It seems that it does, for to say that it does not is to adopt the Kantian dualism between appearances, which we immediately know, and reality, or things-in-themselves, which we do not. But this has already been refuted above.

Objection 2: Further, to deny their coincidence is to deny truth, or its knowability, which is precisely the coinciding of appearance with reality. But to deny truth is skepticism, which we have already refuted above.

Objection 3: To deny that appearance coincides with reality is to judge the one by the other. There are only two ways to do this: to judge reality by appearance, or to judge appearance by reality. But neither of these can be done. Reality cannot be judged by appearance, for "appearance" means "appearance *of reality*," and thus is relative to reality; and we cannot judge that to which a thing is relative by the relative thing itself. Neither can appearance be judged by reality, for reality must first appear in our consciousness in order for us to be able to know it and judge by it; but when it appears in our consciousness it becomes appearance, and not something different from the appearance it was supposed to judge. But a thing that is not different from another thing cannot be the judge of that other thing. Therefore appearance and reality cannot be judged not to coincide.

On the contrary, the first and archetypal philosopher, Socrates, assumed this distinction between appearance and reality in all his philosophizing. For he exposed the merely apparent truths in the opinions of his dialog partners by using logical reasoning to discover what is really true, or at least what is not. All subsequent philosophers depend on and use refinements of his method.

I answer that the distinction between appearance and reality is the origin of all questioning, whether commonsensical, philosophical, or scientific. No question can be raised, including the question of this Article, without assuming that distinction, and the consequent distinction between the true (in which appearances faithfully coincide with reality) and the false (in which appearances deceive because they fail thus to coincide with reality). To ask (1) what a thing is, (2) whether it is, or (3) why it is, is to express the will to know what is true; and this is to assume that there are both true and false, i.e. real and only apparent, answers to those questions, and thus that appearance and reality are not identical.

Reply to Objection 1: Distinguishing appearance and reality allows for questioning appearances by the standard of reality; and this is the opposite of Kantianism because it presupposes the ability to know reality beyond appearances. To distinguish appearance and reality is not to claim that we can know only the one but not the other. In fact, it is implicitly to claim that we can know both (Wittgenstein's refutation of Kant, above). We can distinguish dogs from cats because we know both, but we cannot distinguish dogs from Xs if we do not know what Xs are.

Reply to Objection 2: The distinction between appearance and reality is not skepticism but its opposite, for it assumes that we can know reality, not that we cannot. For if we do not know reality, we cannot judge appearances by it. In order to judge appearances, we must know something more than appearances. Truth is not the indistinguishability of appearance and reality, but their coincidence or conformity.

Reply to Objection 3: One thing may be different from another in authority, or in priority in being known, without being different in form. Such is the case whenever one thing is judged by another which is its standard or touchstone, e.g. when the fingerprint on a weapon is judged by the fingerprint in the police files, or when a $1000 bill is judged to be counterfeit or not by the original model of the $1000 bill in the U.S. Treasury, or when the shape of a key is judged to fit the shape of the lock. Such is the case when we judge anything apparent by its real touchstone—e.g. when we judge an apparently true story, which is told as part of the defendant's testimony in court, to be true or false by the ability or inability of the defendant to answer the prosecuting attorney's questions about what really happened; or when we judge an apparent death to be real or not depending on whether or not heart and brain waves are restored; or when we judge an apparently true scientific theory to be really true or false depending on whether the phenomena it predicts are observed or not.

Article 5: Whether all ordinary (natural) human knowledge begins with sense experience?

Objection 1: It seems that it does not, for this is empiricism, which leads to skepticism, as we see in David Hume. But skepticism has already been refuted.

Objection 2: This empiricism entails materialism, for only material things appear empirically.

Objection 3: We know that X=X, that 2+2=4, and that if it is true that X is, then it is false that X is not. But such things cannot be derived from sense experience. And this is ordinary knowledge, not extraordinary knowledge like mystical experience, mental telepathy, or near-death experiences. Therefore not all ordinary knowledge begins with sense experience.

Objection 4: Man innately knows God. But this is not empirical knowledge.

Objection 5: We cannot point to any piece of sense data that is unformed, uninterpreted, or undefined by reason. To have any sensory knowledge at all, it is necessary that rational categories be used to define and discriminate one sensed thing from another. Even "a patch of blue" includes six highly abstract, more-than-empirical notions, viz. (a) particularity ("a"), (b) vagueness and (c) geometrical shape ("patch"), (d) color in general and (e) specificity in color ("blue"), and (f) relativity of the color to the shape ("of").

On the contrary, common sense universally recognizes that we learn from experience, and scientific psychology confirms this.

I answer that (1) The blind have no innate idea of color, nor the deaf of sounds.

(2) We can verify in our own experience the fact that whenever we think of non-empirical entities (like "truth" or "human nature"), we use material analogies (like light, or a particular man or woman). We also explain general principles to ourselves and others by the use of concrete empirical examples.

(3) We are neither mere beasts nor angels but somewhere between them, and therefore our mode of knowing is neither wholly biological and bodily, nor wholly spiritual and immaterial. For our mode of knowing depends on our nature. Thus we rise from the empirical to the intellectual, and we interpret and understand the empirical by the intellectual.

Reply to Objection 1: The empiricism which leads to skepticism claims not merely that all knowledge begins with sense experience but that all knowledge is limited to it.

Reply to Objection 2: Again we must distinguish the claim that all our knowledge *begins* with sense experience from the claim that it is *limited* to it. From its beginnings in sense experience, by abstraction and reasoning, knowledge can rise to immaterial things.

Reply to Objection 3: (1) Such tautological truths are not *knowledge* properly speaking, for they are empty of all content.

(2) Such tautologies are indeed not *provable* by any set of particulars in sense experience; but we do not ever become aware of them unless we first experience some things through the senses and only then rise to such principles by abstraction and inductive reasoning. It is not infants but philosophers who formulate such tautologies.

Reply to Objection 4: We do not know God immediately and directly, but indirectly, from our knowledge of creatures and of ourselves and our own inadequacies and need for Him. But such knowledge of other creatures and of ourselves is empirical (dependent on experience).

Reply to Objection 5: (1) None of these six more-than-empirical notions is ever known without the relevant sense experience being present.

(2) To claim that empirical knowing is *prior* to non-empirical knowing is not necessarily to claim that there are two moments, one prior to the other in *time*. It is only to claim a *causal dependence* of trans-empirical knowing on empirical knowing. Some causes precede their effects, like one billiard ball bouncing off another; and some do not, like the iron ball making a concave depression in a pillow at the same time as the pillow is being concavely depressed. The causal dependence of non-empirical knowledge on empirical knowledge could be like either of these two cases.

Article 6: Whether there is *a priori* knowledge?

Objection 1: It seems that there is not, for we have just proved that all knowledge begins with sense experience, which is another way of saying that all knowledge is *a posteriori* knowledge, posterior to rather than prior to sense experience.

Objection 2: If there is a process of thinking that leads from *a posteriori* knowledge of sensed particulars to *a priori* knowledge of understood universals, it is invalid; for it is invalid to conclude to a universal merely from particulars. "All men are mortal" does not follow from "this man is mortal" or "these men are mortal" or "some men are mortal."

On the contrary, however we know them, it is evident that we do know such principles as "All men are mortal," "All men ought to do good and avoid evil," "The interior angles of all triangles add up to 180 degrees," and "Nothing can come into existence without a sufficient cause." But these are examples of *a priori* knowledge. Therefore there is *a priori* knowledge.

I answer that it is clear, from the authority of common sense, and admitted by everyone except a few philosophers and scientists, that man is different in species, or essence, from other animals. No other animal writes philosophy books. But how we know is part of our essence. Therefore we are essentially different from brute animals in how we know. But if we had no *a priori* knowledge, we would not in our knowledge be essentially different from animals in our knowing, but only different in degree of cleverness. Therefore we have *a priori* knowledge, knowledge of universals whose truth does not depend on the truth of any particulars met in experience.

Reply to Objection 1: There is no contradiction between saying that all our knowledge begins with sense experience and saying that from sense experience we can rise to knowledge that does not depend on sense experience, just as there is no contradiction between saying that we all begin on the earth and saying that there is a ladder which leads from the earth to a helicopter, which does not rest on the earth. The earth symbolizes sense experience and the *a posteriori* knowledge that it directly produces. The helicopter symbolizes *a priori* knowledge. The ladder symbolizes (1) the abstraction of universal form from particular matter; and (2) the intuitive intellectual understanding of the abstracted universal, in the "first act of the mind," or conception; and (3) induction from sensed particulars to cognized universals, in the "third act of the mind," or reasoning.

Reply to Objection 2: (1) Inductive reasoning can make it more probable, at least, that the universal conclusion is true, if the premises are numerous and representative. And probable knowledge is a kind of knowledge, though lacking in certainty.

(2) The process is not first of all one of inductive *reasoning* (the third act of the mind) but the *understanding* (the first act of the mind, "simple apprehension") of a universal which we find embedded in sensory particulars and which we abstract from those particulars. For instance, we meet Homer, Hester, and Harry in experience, then we understand and abstract universal human nature as we experience it

in these concrete particulars. We can distinguish necessary and essential features of human nature (e.g. mind and body) from contingent and accidental ones (e.g. race and gender), by abstracting the former from the latter. Examining this abstracted universal, we can perceive (with the intellect, not merely with the senses) that it necessarily includes an organic body, which in turn necessarily includes mutually dependent material organs which can decay, fall apart, and die. Thus our knowledge that all men are mortal is *a priori* knowledge, known with certainty even prior to observing everyone die, but it emerges only from abstraction from experience which is *a posteriori* and empirical.

Article 7: Whether ideas are the immediate objects of knowing?

Objection 1: It seems that they are, for Locke, a reliably common-sense philosopher, begins his entire epistemology by defining "idea" as "object of knowing."

Objection 2: Ordinary common-sense thought and language answers this question in the affirmative. For we often speak of "having an idea," and we think about our ideas whenever we question them or change them.

Objection 3: If ideas are not objects of thought, they cannot be criticized or changed. But they can be and often are criticized and changed. Therefore they are the objects of our thought rather than the acts of thinking themselves.

On the contrary, Aquinas argues, in *ST* I, 85, 2, that ideas (which he calls "intelligible species abstracted from phantasms," i.e. the essential natures of things abstracted from sense images of these things) are not the object (*quod*) of our thought but the means (*quo*) or instrument of thinking (this could mean the very act of thinking itself); and that the first, natural, and immediate object of thought (i.e. of the act of thinking) is reality, or real things. We can think of an idea as an *object* of thought only by reflecting on it by a second idea (act of thinking) after the first idea has first attained some real thing as its object. We know that we had an idea of a dog *after* we know the dog.

I answer that Aquinas gives two arguments for this epistemological realism (the claim that the direct object of human thinking is reality, not ideas).

The first is that sciences are specified according to their objects, and therefore if the objects of our thinking were ideas, all sciences would be subdivisions of psychology. (Perhaps some psychologists would *not* regard this as a *reductio ad absurdum.*)

The second argument is as follows. (1) We judge only about what we know. (2) Let us assume that we know only ideas. (3) In that case all judgments would be true, even judgments that contradict each other. (4) And this is logically impossible: it is literally meaningless to claim that contradictories can be simultaneously true. (For in that case, that very proposition is both true *and false.*) (5) Therefore the premise that we know only ideas must be false, by *reductio ad absurdum.*

Aquinas explains step (3) by an analogy with judgments we make about our sensations. If we know only sense images and not real material things, then contradictory judgments can be simultaneously true (which is logically absurd), for when something which tastes (appears) sweet to A tastes bitter to B, neither A nor B are wrong when they judge, respectively, "It is sweet" and "It is bitter," for they can mean by "is" only "appears."

In other words, two appearances can contradict each other, whether the appearances are sensory or intellectual (i.e. opinions), but no two realities can. Thus the currently popular, "nonjudgmental" idea that a statement about objective reality (such as "God exists"), like a judgment about subjective feelings, can be "true for you but not for me." The only coherent meaning this can possibly have is skepticism, the denial that anyone can know objective reality, but only their own subjective feelings and opinions. This may even entail solipsism as well as skepticism.

A third argument proceeds from analyzing the essential *meaning* of "opinion." An opinion is what the medievals calls a "sign" and what phenomenologists call "intentional"; i.e. it is an opinion *about* something real, and it can be either true or false depending on whether or not it corresponds to or accurately represents the reality that it is "about." If all we know are opinions, then we do not know which of them is ever true or false. We are like prisoners in window-less caves watching pictures and news reports of the outside world on TV. We have no way of knowing which of them are true of the world outside our caves (i.e. our minds and senses), so we must become skeptics. We cannot compare two contradictory pictures of, or two contradictory reports about, some person who lives outside our room, and judge which one is true, if we cannot get outside our room and meet that person directly.

Reply to Objection 1: No one is common sense incarnate, and common sense is not infallible, perfect wisdom. Locke is wrong, as is shown in this Article.

Reply to Objection 2: This objectification of ideas, like the objectification of the knowing subject or self, can be explained as a second, reflective or reflexive moment, always preceded by a first moment of knowing real things by means of these ideas. Common sense is reliable but not philosophically sophisticated, and we often are deceived by misinterpreting our own language, for instance assuming that every noun corresponds to a separately existing substance.

Reply to Objection 3: Ideas are indeed objects of secondary, reflective thought, but not of primary thought, as noted in the Reply to Objection 2 above. Indeed, ideas are criticized and changed only by the standard of real things, which must therefore first be known before being used as a standard to test ideas about them. This is implied in Aristotle's common-sense definition of truth as thinking and saying what really is.

Article 8: Whether certain knowledge is possible?

Objection 1: It seems that it is not, for no one would accept being tortured if any one of the ideas he claims to hold as certain were proved to be not certain at all. This shows that he is not really certain, as he claimed to be.

Objection 2: Whatever the purely theoretical arguments about probability and certainty, the belief that we know the truth only with probability, not with certainty, is (a) sufficient to guarantee our knowledge for all practical purposes, and (b) necessary in practice to prevent us from closed-mindedness and dogmatism, which are more serious and harmful errors than doubt.

Objection 3: Much harm has been done to philosophy by Descartes and his followers by the demand for certainty. For one thing, it has produced the reaction of skepticism, for the standards for knowledge were set too high. For another thing, it failed to correspond to all or nearly all of our existing knowledge, for even if some knowledge is certain, most is not. Finally, even those examples that Descartes regarded as certain (e.g. "I think, therefore I am") can be doubted and disputed, and have been, by other philosophers.

On the contrary, ordinary language distinguishes certain knowledge from opinion in many ways, e.g. "I know" vs. "I think," or "is" vs. "seems," or the very words "certain" vs. "probable." If the first set of expressions corresponded to nothing real, it would not be used so frequently and effectively.

I answer that (1) Probabilism, like simple skepticism, is self-contradictory. For either it is certain or only probable that all human knowledge is only probable and not certain. If that is certain, we have an immediate self-contradiction. If it is only probable, then it *may* be false. As with simple skepticism, where the skeptic forgets to be skeptical about his skepticism, the probabilist forgets to be probabilistic about his probabilism.

(2) In order to make the judgment that something is probable, one needs to know the standards of probability and how to apply them. But this knowledge must be more than merely probable. Thus, when statistical probabilities are given, they are accompanied by ranges of possible error. But these ranges of error are not also subject to statistical probabilities. "Possible error" is meaningful only in

contrast with "impossible error," and what is *impossible* is a kind of certainty.

(3) Self-evident first principles such as the law of non-contradiction, the principle of intelligibility (being is intelligible; nothing real is simply unintelligible), the principle of causality (whatever begins to be, has a cause), and the first principle of morality (do good, avoid evil) are known with certainty and indubitability.

Reply to Objection 1: The responses of a man threatened with torture are not a reliable index of truth. Many passions impair judgment. As pride can impair proper doubt, fear can impair proper certainty.

Reply to Objection 2: Probable knowledge is neither sufficient nor necessary, even in the practical order. (a) It is not *sufficient* because sometimes we need certainty, e.g. in matters of life or death. If a gun has 100 chambers, then 100 of them must be checked, yielding *certain* safety, and not just 99, unless you want to play "Russian roulette." (b) It is not *necessary* because dogmatism and closed-mindedness are combated most effectively not by the skepticism that refuses all certainty but by the contrast between what we aim for, viz. certainty, and what we do in fact achieve most of the time, viz. only probable and fallible knowledge. It is better to be humble and skeptical about our use of our minds, than about the mind itself. Indeed, skepticism, and the semi-skepticism that consists in probabilism, is often held quite dogmatically and closed-mindedly, as a secret known only to elitist intellectuals.

Reply to Objection 3: One need not be a Cartesian to distinguish certain knowledge and opinion. One need not ignore the vast parts of our knowledge that are only probable in order to assert that there is a small part that is certain.

Article 9: Whether the essential questions of philosophy are "mysteries"?

Objection 1: It seems that they are not. For if they were, then philosophy would not attain certainty, for mystery and certainty are opposites. But the previous Article argued for certainty. Therefore concerning philosophy's essential questions there is certainty, not mystery.

Objection 2: Mystery is the province of detective stories, occultism, or mystical experiences. Philosophy is the province of clear definitions and logically compelling arguments. The two can no more overlap than can darkness and light, or tar pits and algebra.

On the contrary, the questions everyone expects philosophy to deal with are mysteries like God, life after death, the foundations of morality, and free will and fate. But few people expect philosophy to transform these mysteries into totally clear certainties, but only to shed more useful light on them.

I answer that Marcel defines a "mystery," as distinct from a mere "problem," as "a problem that encroaches upon its own data," i.e. a question which so involves the very being and life of the questioner that it is impossible, and even undesirable and misleading, to have total detachment and objectivity, as is required in the sciences. Examples of such "mysteries" are the union of body and soul, why we fall in love, the "problem" of evil, and the intrinsic value of every human life. None of these "problems" has ever been or ever will be totally "solved" by man. Yet they are our most important questions. Indeed, it is *almost* true to say, paraphrasing Socrates, that whatever is most worth teaching cannot be taught (i.e. as "problems" rather than "mysteries" are taught) and whatever can be taught (proved, at least) is hardly worth teaching.

Reply to Objection 1: (1) The previous Article argued for certainty only in some small areas, not in the largest or most essential ones.

(2) Although there is indeed an opposition between most meanings of "mystery" and most meanings of "certainty," some meanings of the two concepts can overlap. For with regard to "mysteries" such as love, death, and God, we can attain a small spot of bright light surrounded by great darkness. We can also have intuitive or experiential certainties without being able to translate these into logical, demonstrable certainties. (Such is the case, perhaps, even with Descartes' "I think, therefore I am," which is personally, subjectively,

experientially, or existentially certain but not logically certain, since the predicate of "I am," viz. existence, does not logically belong to its subject, viz. any human self, necessarily and essentially but only contingently and accidentally.)

Reply to Objection 2: (1) Philosophical "mysteries," as understood according to Marcel's definition (see the "*I answer that*") are not like detective stories, which have simple, clear, and final solutions. Nor are they like occultism, which is not universal, and is both dangerous and forbidden. Nor are they like mystical experiences, which are unusual and inexpressible. On the other hand, definitions and arguments are merely two of the tools of philosophy, not its content or objects.

(2) Darkness and light not only can, but usually do, overlap in our experience, as black and white mingle in grey. And tar pits *are* subject to the laws of algebra.

Article 10: Whether we can have *knowledge* of mysteries such as God, freedom, immortality, morality, and the meaning (purpose) of life?

Objection 1: It seems that we can only have *opinion, belief,* or *faith* about mysteries like God, freedom, immortality, morality, and the meaning of life, but not *knowledge* because, while the existence of these things cannot be *dis*proved (and this allows us to believe in them), they cannot be proved either. And what cannot be proved does not constitute knowledge but only right *opinion* or true *belief.* For as Plato explained in the *Meno,* knowledge differs from right opinion by the addition of sufficient reason to logically justify the belief, whether this justification be a proof yielding certainty or perhaps an argument yielding only sufficient probability (however that may be defined).

Objection 2: It has already been admitted above that the most important philosophical questions are "mysteries" rather than "problems," since we cannot attain total detachment and objectivity regarding them; and this is why these "mysteries," unlike "problems," do not admit of final, definitive "solutions." Therefore these do not constitute knowledge.

Objection 3: The first of these five things mentioned, the knowledge of God, is personal knowledge (*kennen* or *connaitre* rather than *wissen* or *savoir*); and this is also the ultimate meaning of life (see *John* 17: 3). But this is not what most philosophers mean by "knowledge."

On the contrary, the massive authority of humanity contradicts a negative answer to this question. For most of the philosophical arguments and debates of mankind, both among philosophers and among ordinary people, concern these five things. If we can have no knowledge of them, then all of the most interesting and important debates in our history and our literature are hopeless, and the "wisdom" of all cultures, religions, and philosophies is composed of "gas."

I answer that (1) If we have no knowledge of these things, then human knowledge is trivial, for nothing is more important than these things.

(2) Furthermore, if we have no knowledge of these things, how do we know them well enough to know that we have no knowledge of them? For instance, how can we know God so well that we know we cannot know Him at all? Is not such skepticism, like all skepticism, ultimately both self-contradictory and arrogant?

Reply to Objection 1: (1) Religious *faith* is not the same as *opinion.* For faith, whether true or false, is a human response to a divine revelation, like light reflected in a faithful mirror, and thus its content is in itself most certain, even if not logically provable, for God can neither deceive nor be deceived; while mere opinion rests on the uncertainty of our human mind alone. Religious faith, being a *personal relationship* of trust, is also not the same as mere intellectual *belief,* though it includes belief.

(2) As is shown in various articles in this book, each of the five things mentioned in the first sentence of the Objection can in fact be proved to exist by good logical reasoning.

(3) Plato's definition of "knowledge" is too narrow, for there are some things we know, and even sometimes know with certainty,

which we cannot give adequate logical reasons for. See above, Article 2, "*I answer that.*"

Reply to Objection 2: The argument is an enthymeme with the questionable premise that whatever is not a "mystery," and thus admits of a final, definitive "solution," does not constitute "knowledge." But this is not true, for as the Apostle says, often "we know in part." (I *Corinthians* 13) Some knowledge is indeed "final and definitive" (e.g. mathematics), but other knowledge is not (e.g. the knowledge of God or of morality), for it is capable of continued growth, in content, in depth of understanding, in clarity, and in degree of certainty. Knowledge is a zero-sum thing only in mathematics.

Reply to Objection 3: So much the worse for most philosophers! Philosophers need to listen to ordinary people more than ordinary people need to listen to philosophers.

Question VII:
General Ethics

Article 1: Whether moral laws are objectively real?

Objection 1: *It seems that* they are not, for things that are objectively real are agreed to by everyone, eventually. But moral laws are not agreed to by everyone, but argued about, in all times and places. Therefore they are not objective. Disagreement proves subjectivity. If moral values were objective, there would be an objective way of determining them and settling moral arguments. But there is not.

Objection 2: Moral law is spiritual: it has no size, shape, weight, or color. Spirit exists in subjective consciousness, not in the objective universe, which is material, having size, shape, weight, and color. What exists in subjective consciousness is not objective. Therefore moral law is not objective.

Objection 3: Moral laws are values. Values are not facts, for they are about what ought to be, or about the obligations we have, not about what is. Therefore moral values are not facts. But what is objectively real consists only of facts. Therefore moral laws are not objectively real, because of the "fact-value distinction."

Objection 4: Let us analyze a moral situation. You witness a murder. You make the judgment that "that act was bad" or "that man is evil." But all that actually happens is that one man shoots another man dead. The value judgment of evil is not in the gun or the bullet or the trigger finger but in you the observer. "That act was bad" thus really means "I have bad feelings about that act."

Objection 5: Moral questions are a major part of philosophy's great classic questions. But it was already admitted (Question VI, Article 9) that philosophy's great questions are "mysteries" rather than "problems," and that "mysteries" were questions in which our subjective involvement made definitive, final solutions impossible. Therefore moral questions are not objective.

On the contrary, all men, in all times, places, and cultures, *argue* about whether certain acts, both in general and in particular, are morally right or wrong. But we argue only about objective truths, not about subjective feelings. Therefore, unless all men are wrong all the time in moral argumentation, moral rightness and wrongness are objective. But moral laws define and discriminate moral rightness and wrongness. Therefore moral laws are objective.

The very premise that the moral subjectivist uses most frequently to prove his conclusion, namely disagreement and continual argument about morality, proves the opposite. For we argue not about (1) purely subjective matters, like pains and pleasures, nor about (2) objective matters that are easy to resolve, like counting the pages of a book, but only about (3) objective matters that are not easy to resolve.

I answer that to call moral law "objective" is not to call it a *thing* or entity, like a cat, but to call it objectively true, like the laws of physics or mathematics. Just as different physical roads really lead to different physical destinations, so that it is impossible to get to the Pacific Ocean by walking east from Chicago, no matter how subjectively sincere and passionate you are; and just as it is impossible to get an odd number by adding up only even numbers, no matter how subjectively sincere and passionate you are, so it is impossible to get to moral goodness, or true happiness, or beatitude, by choosing evil and refusing good, no matter how subjectively sincere and passionate you are.

We *discover* moral truths rather than invent them, just as we discover physical, mathematical, or philosophical truths. This is immediately evident in ordinary human experience and needs no elaborate proof. "Conscience" is the usual word for the mental power by which we are aware of, and feel the obligation to obey, real moral laws. We discover or "bump into" the goodness and badness of human acts as we "bump into" curbs or colors, though not with our material senses. The act of experiencing or discovering a moral obligation is indeed subjective, but the object of the act is not. If it were, it would not be an *obligation* but only an "ideal" to us, i.e. a subjective desire. (*My* ideals need not be yours.)

Reply to Objection 1: (1) It is not true that objective things are always agreed about. On the contrary, it is only objective things that are argued about. No one argues about private, subjective feelings. No one responds to "I feel well" with "No, you feel sick."

(2) The argument assumes that what is not agreed to by everyone is not objective. This is also false. For instance, no discovery of science was agreed to by everyone before it was proved to be true (e.g. the roundness of the earth, or the origin of disease in germs); yet if it was a true discovery, it was an objective truth.

(3) Fundamental moral principles are one of the few things that are agreed to by everyone, or nearly everyone. No one believes that murder, theft, and adultery are morally right. People differ only about whether a certain war is an example of murder, a certain tax an example of theft, or a certain flirtation a case of adultery.

(4) Disagreement does not prove subjectivity. If it did, then a single person who did not agree that 2+2=4 would make that judgment subjective. The reason men disagree about moral values is two-fold: their own subjective ignorance and passions, and the objective nature of moral values, which are more complex and demanding than empirical or mathematical facts.

Reply to Objection 2: All judgments exist only in subjective consciousness, including judgments about material things like size, judgments about mathematical truths, *and* judgments about moral laws. But the *objects* of these judgments, unlike feelings, are objective. That is why we argue about them, while we do not argue about feelings.

Reply to Objection 3: If "facts" means "empirical facts only," then it is not true that what is objectively real consists only of facts, except according to materialism; for the existence of God, other minds, angels, and mathematical truths are all objectively real, but not empirical. If, on the other hand, "facts" means "whatever is objectively real," the argument begs the question in assuming that moral values are not facts. They are facts about what our real duties, laws, obligations, rights, and goods are. That is why we can err about them, and why we argue about them. The "fact-value distinction" is not absolute.

Reply to Objection 4: The analysis does not fit the situation, unless one is a materialist. An act of murder has a material quality, indeed, but it also has a moral quality. It is the act itself that we rightly judge to be evil, not our feelings. If it were our feelings, then "your act is evil" would really mean "my feelings are evil," which is absurd. We feel righteous, not wicked, when we meet a murderer.

Reply to Objection 5: "Mysteries" do not mean totally subjective questions but questions in which we are personally involved, though in themselves they are about objective and universal truths. Question VI, Article 10 refutes this misunderstanding of Question VI, Article 9.

Article 2: Whether there are any universal, exceptionless norms?

Objection 1: It seems that there are not, for every supposedly universal and exceptionless moral norm, law, or commandment has a reasonable exception. For instance, military defense, and private self-defense, are exceptions to "Thou shalt not kill"; seizing a madman's legally owned weapon is an exception to "Thou shalt not steal"; and spying, or deceiving an enemy about the location of his victims, are exceptions to "Thou shalt not bear false witness." Those who hid Jews from the Nazis did *right* to lie to them.

Objection 2: Subjective motives and infinitely varied and changing situations are two other factors in moral choices which alter the moral character of the choice. And neither of these two factors is objective, universal, and exceptionless.

Objection 3: Exceptionless norms are rigid, confining, and unyielding. But man, and his life, should not be rigid, confining, and unyielding.

Objection 4: Exceptions are part of life, and part of the rules of life. "The exception proves the rule."

On the contrary, a moral law has authority only if it is exceptionless, or unless the law itself makes the exception. For the agent to make an exception for himself is for him to set himself up above the moral law, as Kant showed in his first formulation of the "categorical imperative."

I answer that moral law, in order to distinguish good human acts from evil, must specify universal *kinds* of acts. (Thus consistent Nominalism, which denies real kinds, or universals, makes moral law impossible.) But a universal is by definition exceptionless.

Reply to Objection 1: (1) Whenever an exception is made to a moral law, there is always a more general moral law that justifies the exception. Thus there are other, more general, moral laws, such as the law of charity, that may justify exceptions being made to subordinate laws.

(2) But these are not really exceptions. For
  (a) The commandment forbids murder, not all killing. The attempted murderer forfeits his right to life by threatening other lives.
  (b) The commandment forbids theft, not all seizure. Seizing a madman's lethal weapon is not theft. The madman for feits his right to property when he uses it to threaten other lives.
  (c) The commandment forbids the evil of bearing false witness against innocent men, not protecting good men against evil men. The Nazis forfeited their right to know the truth when they sought for the Jews to kill them.

Reply to Objection 2: Motives and situations cannot make an act that is wrong in itself to be right. They can only make an act that is otherwise right to be wrong. As T.S. Eliot said in *Murder in the Cathedral* about motives, "The last temptation is the greatest treason:/ to do the right thing for the wrong reason." All three factors need to be right: the (moral) nature of the act itself, the motive, and the situation. Situations are not universal, but they *are*

objective. Motives are not objective, but their rightness and wrongness *is* universal. And the nature of the act itself is both universal
(exceptionless) and objective.

Reply to Objection 3: It is precisely the purpose of moral law to be
rigid, like a yardstick, so that it can measure men, acts, and lives that
are not rigid. It is precisely the purpose of moral law to be confining,
like a prison, so that it can confine and define evil. It is precisely the
purpose of moral law to be unyielding, so that it can judge men who
do yield to evil.

Reply to Objection 4: An exception (e.g. an I proposition like "some
lions are tame") *dis*proves a rule (e.g. an E proposition like "No lions
are tame"). What the cliché means to say is that an exception *presupposes* a rule. Some rules have exceptions and some do not. If *all* rules
have exceptions, what about *that* rule? It is self-contradictory.

Article 3: Whether 'ought' is a kind of 'is'?

Objection 1: It seems that it is not, for "is" and "ought" have meaning only in contrast to each other. But one of two contrasting terms
cannot be a subdivision of the other. Therefore what ought to be cannot be a kind of what is; and ethics, which is about what ought to be
cannot be a subdivision of metaphysics, which is about what is.

Objection 2: If ethics depended on, and was derived from, metaphysics, ethical arguments would be *non sequiturs*. For they would
contain more in their (ethical) conclusions, namely values, or oughts,
than was contained in their (metaphysical) premises. "Is" does not
logically entail "ought."

Objection 3: Premises can be said to "judge" a conclusion, and justify its truth, not vice versa. Such "judgment" is not a reciprocal relationship: the person or principle being judged or justified cannot at
the same time judge or justify that which judges. But values (or ideals,
or what ought to be) judge what is. Therefore what is cannot at the

same time judge what ought to be. And thus metaphysics, which is the study of what is, cannot judge or justify ethics, which is the study of what ought to be.

On the contrary, (1) It is common-sensical to argue that what you ought to be and do depends on what you are and on what is. For instance, "be a man" is meaningless if addressed to an animal, and "You ought to risk your life to save the drowning child in the lake" is meaningless unless there *is* a drowning child in the lake.

(2) We cannot but speak of values in metaphysical language, as when we say, "That *is* your obligation," or "That *is* good," or "This *is* evil."

I answer that (1) If ethics were not dependent on metaphysics, then ethical values would not be objectively real, but merely subjective. But we have already refuted that above, in Article 1.

(2) When we analyze how we disagree with an ethical argument, we find that there are two ways we do this. In the example given in the Reply to Objection 2 above, one could dispute the conclusion (e.g. that abortion is ethically wrong) by arguing against either the ethical premise (that all killing of innocent persons is morally wrong) or the metaphysical premise (that an unborn child is an innocent person). And since the conclusion follows only from both premises together, it depends on its metaphysical premise as well as on its ethical premise. Thus ethics depends on metaphysics.

Reply to Objection 1: "What is" is ambiguous. It can mean an empirical fact *as distinct from* a value (or a law, or an obligation), or it can mean, more broadly, any objective truth at all, including the truth that values are objective, and including truths about what these objective values are. Values have a certain kind of being, and therefore the study of values (ethics) can be called a certain kind of metaphysics.

At the very least, ethics must *depend on* metaphysics, for what *is* good and evil depends on what *is*. When we say that justice "is" good, we are not merely using a logical copula as in "a unicorn *is* a mythical beast," but we are asserting something about reality, about what really is.

Reply to Objection 2: Moral arguments have two premises, not one. One of them is about values and one about facts. Thus there is no *non sequitur.* E.g. "Killing an innocent person is morally wrong; abortion is killing an innocent person; therefore abortion is morally wrong" derives the specific ethical conclusion from a more general ethical premise combined with a metaphysical premise about the real nature of abortion and its object.

Reply to Objection 3: As seen in the example above (Reply to Objection 2), the conclusion of an ethical argument is justified only by the combination of an ethical premise and a metaphysical premise. Neither premise alone can justify the conclusion, as neither a man nor a woman alone can procreate a child, but only the two combined.

Article 4: Whether there is a natural law?

Objection 1: It seems that there is not, for a natural law, or law of nature, flows from, or is determined by, the nature of a thing. But those who speak of a natural moral law mean something that prescribes how man ought to act, by the proper use of his free will, rather than describing how he does act. Therefore there is an inherent contradiction in speaking of a law that is both natural and moral. (Cf. G.E. Moore, *Principia Ethica.*)

Objection 2: Natural laws are deterministic: they describe how things must act, by necessity of their nature. E.g. fire must heat, and matter must attract matter by gravity. But moral laws describe how man should act by free choice, not how he must act by natural necessity.

Objection 3: If there were a natural moral law flowing from universal human nature, it would be universally known, admitted, and followed, without exception, like the laws of physics or biology, or geometry. Matter *cannot* be immaterial, nor can an organism be inorganic, nor can triangles be non-triangular. But man can be inhuman. Individuals and societies are often ignorant of, dispute, and disobey moral laws. Therefore they are not natural laws.

Objection 4: God gave man commandments to guide his moral choices. Since these are from the will of God, they are not from human minds or wills. So there is no need for a natural law since man is under supernatural law. God's word, not man's reason, is the origin of moral law.

On the contrary, all cultures and religions, and all societies in history except modern Western post-Christian society, admit a natural law. (See *Romans* 2:14. and the Appendix to C.S. Lewis' *The Abolition of Man.*)

I answer that if there were no natural moral law, written in our very nature, then moral law could come to us only from without, from God's will or the will of men. But in that case it would be *a posteriori* rather than *a priori*; that is, it would be like the laws of the state, or of a language: a discovery of which we had no prior knowledge and which we learned only empirically, by experience. But this is not the case; for whenever we consider a moral law, such as justice or charity or the respect for life, we know *a priori* that it is right. This is not the case with any law from any alien will, such as civil laws passed by a government, or the grammatical laws of a foreign language. Anyone can discover the natural law simply by an honest attention to his conscience.

Reply to Objection 1: As ethics is not identical with but depends on anthropology and metaphysics, so the natural moral law, which prescribes what man ought to do, is not identical with but depends on laws of human nature which describe what man is, and on metaphysical laws, or laws of the nature of being.

Reply to Objection 2: (1) Since it is part of man's essential nature to have free choice of will, rather than to be determined unfreely, the natural law for man is a law that prescribes rather than describes, or which describes what man ought to do rather than what man necessarily does. Not all natural laws are deterministic. In fact it would not be a natural law *for man*, or a law of *human* nature, if it assumed determinism in man instead of free will.

(2) One may speak of moral laws as laws of a certain kind of

necessity too, even though they appeal to free choice, for they describe what *must* be done, or, as Kant put it, they are "categorical imperatives." Their necessity is of a different kind: moral, not physical.

Reply to Objection 3: Man alone, in the entire universe, can act contrary to his nature, because man alone has free will. And this is part of his nature.

Reply to Objection 4: God wrote His moral law within man's natural reason, which discerns good and evil, so that the natural law is, in Aquinas's language, man's "participation in" God's eternal law. This is why conscience is sacred and inviolable: because it is the reflection of the divine mind and will in us, like a prophet of God. The Ten Commandments are not the *origin* of moral law but an external divine reminder of the natural law already within us; that is why we recognize their rightness by our natural reason. So they are both from God's mind and will *and* recognized by our own; these are not exclusive alternatives, like fire vs. water or east vs. west.

Article 5: Whether evil is real?

Objection 1: It seems that it is not, for all that is real is either God or a creature created by God, and both of these are good. To say evil is a real thing alongside good is to be a Manichean.

Objection 2: It is possible to attain to a state of consciousness in which evil disappears. For "to the pure all things are pure." Thus evil is in the eye of the beholder; evil is an illusion of unenlightened consciousness.

Objection 3: The claim in Objection 2 is verifiable by experience. If we treat people as if they were good, they will respond by being good. If we love the things in nature that ordinarily annoy us, such as a mosquito or a snowstorm, they will reward us with pleasure rather than pain.

On the contrary, this view that evil is not real is contradicted by nearly all human cultures, by common sense, and by the repeated language about spiritual warfare against evil in the Bible as well as the Qur'an. It is also contradicted by the very existence of the word "evil" in all human languages. For all mankind does not invent a word that corresponds to no reality at all; words for unreal entities, like "unicorn," are specific to some cultures only.

I answer that if evil is unreal, then the fact that nearly all human beings believe it is real and fear it, makes our life needlessly painful, pessimistic, polemical, wasteful of time and energy, and ignorant. But in that case our life is even more evil than we think, rather than less, for then all our fear, pain, pessimism, spiritual war, waste, and ignorance are *needless.* Thus if there is evil, there is evil; and if there is no evil, there is also evil, viz. the evil that we believe that there is evil.

Reply to Objection 1: Everything is indeed ontologically good, but some human acts are not morally good. In saying that evil is "real" we are not saying it is a substance, as Manichean dualism says.

Reply to Objection 2: (1) This is not an argument at all. No proof is offered that this view is indeed "enlightened."

(2) The idea that evil is "an illusion of unenlightened consciousness" is self-contradictory, for illusion and lack of enlightenment is a certain kind of evil. If there is no real evil, our fear of it is not really evil. ("There is nothing to fear but fear itself" is *not* liberating.)

Reply to Objection 3: This is a very dangerous experiment to carry out on a rapist, a terrorist, or a man-eating tiger. It works only on things like mosquitoes and mild snowstorms.

Article 6: Whether evil is ignorance?

Objection 1: It seems that it is, for when one makes a moral choice between two acts, or between acting and not acting, one either knows or does not know that one choice (A) is good and the other (B) is evil.

If one knows that A is good and B evil, one will choose A rather than B because the will is related to the good as the mind is related to the true. Just as the mind never believes what appears to it to be false, so the will never chooses what appears to it to be evil. If, on the other hand, one does not know that A is good and B evil, one may choose the evil, but only because of this ignorance, which is the confusion between a misleading appearance and reality. Thus all evil is (due to) ignorance.

Objection 2: If it be said that one can know that B is morally evil and yet choose B because he prefers the good of the subjectively satisfying or pleasant, which can be found in B, to the moral good, which can be found in A (as the Reply to Objection 1 claims), then it can be replied that this is possible only if the mind is ignorant of the fact that the moral good is always, in the long run, more subjectively satisfying or pleasant, as Plato proves in the *Republic* ("justice is always more profitable than injustice"). And thus, again, the choice of evil is due to ignorance.

Objection 3: Continuing the above analysis, if it be said that the mind can know that B is evil and yet choose it because it is overcome by the passions, the same analysis holds. For either the mind knows or does not know that yielding to the passions is evil, and will even result in less *pleasure*. If it knows that, then it will not yield to evil, for no one will choose a greater pain over a lesser one. If it does *not* know that, then again the choice of evil is due to ignorance.

Objection 4: If the mind were not ignorant, it could never choose evil. For in the Beatific Vision, in which we share the very consciousness of God, we will never choose evil because we will see clearly the beauty and attractiveness of the good and the ugliness and utter unattractiveness of the evil. (This argument does not depend on the theological truth of the Beatific Vision, but the idea can be used simply as a thought experiment or a hypothesis, as a man can be contrasted with an angel even if one disbelieves in angels.) In this life, however, we do not have this clarity of vision, and therefore, like stupid fish, we can be tempted by the attractive worm on the fishhook of evil, only because of our ignorance.

On the contrary, everyone knows that evil is not ignorance, for if they believed that it was, they would not hold anyone responsible, since ignorance removes responsibility; and they would never punish, but only re-educate, evildoers.

I answer that Plato, who taught this doctrine, correctly perceived that ignorance is a necessary condition for evildoing, but confused it with a sufficient cause. He also thought it was the only cause, and the first cause, of evil, and he failed to see that the will often is a prior cause of the intellect's attention or inattention. In other words, he failed to see that the causal relationship between evil choices in the will and moral ignorance in the mind moves both ways: not only from mind to will but also from will to mind, when the will commands the mind not to consider the truth because it appears unpleasant or unwelcome. Thus evil is a cause of ignorance as much as ignorance is a cause of evil. The mind's ignorance can be caused by the will's *ignoring*. For the will can command the mind to think or not to think about a moral law.

Reply to Objection 1: The will can prefer a lesser good to a greater if the goods are of different kinds. Thus, although no one will choose to be whipped twice rather than once, some will choose to be whipped rather than dishonored, while others will choose to be dishonored rather than whipped. Thus one can prefer the pleasant good to the moral good, and commit immoral acts to gratify selfish desires, not because one is ignorant.

Reply to Objection 2: We all know, from experience, that we are capable of choosing evil (e.g. theft) even when clearly knowing that the good of the immediate pleasure desired (possessing the stolen object) is not only a lesser *kind* of good than the moral good that is our duty but even knowing that in the long run it will result in less pleasure and more pain (the pains of punishment, disgrace, regret, pangs of conscience, and/or lowered self-image). Whatever the psychological mechanism by which we do this, it is a fact that we do it. The difficulty in explaining how we can do this should not lead us (as it did Plato) to deny the data that we do it. The simplest explanation is that both the mind and the will are overcome by the passions.

Reply to Objection 3: (1) As with the previous objection, our data tell us that our passions do in fact often overcome our reason. However it is done, our inner captain (the will) is capable of willfully silencing or ignoring his navigator (the reason).

(2) The analysis commits "the fallacy of misplaced concreteness." For it is not the mind ("it") that chooses but the man ("he"), the whole person, and his will and passions are involved in the choice as well as the mind.

Reply to Objection 4: The argument proves that ignorance is a *necessary* cause of evil, for when we shall have no ignorance, we shall have no evil. But this does not prove that ignorance is the *sufficient*, the only, or the first cause of evil.

Article 7: Whether mankind is insane, to choose evil over good?

Objection 1: It seems that if mankind were insane, a man could not know it, for the insane no longer have the sanity of mind to discriminate between sanity and insanity.

Objection 2: This judgment is too severe. Intellectual and moral weakness is not necessarily insanity.

Objection 3: This judgment is harmful to our self-esteem, which is a necessary precondition to motivate us to improvement. Therefore it is counterproductive and should not be made.

On the contrary, all the prophets share this dark judgment on mankind, including Christ himself.

I answer that the prophets are clearly not mild psychologists dispensing mild psychological remedies, or "feelgood" preachers dispensing self-esteem, but radical, insulting, negative, shocking, doom-threatening firebrands. Even secular "prophets" like Socrates and Buddha begin by assuming that all mankind is in a "cave" of ignorance—

ignorance of the truest, best, and most important things—or in a state of unenlightened sleep except for one "Buddha," the "man who woke up." Although this is not the totality of their message, it is an essential first step, the "bad news" before the "good news."

If this judgment were not true and needed, then either the God who authorized and sent the prophets is wrong, or, if it is the prophets themselves who invented this message, then they are wrong, both about the content of the message and about its divine authority. But in that case they are not only bad psychologists and moralists but also false prophets, blasphemers, and usurpers of divine authority.

Reply to Objection 1: In two ways is this discrimination between sanity and insanity still possible for the insane: first, by receiving a revelation from without, from a wholly sane mind—and for the whole human race this would be the Mind of God—and second, by analogy and comparison. For the less insane can still know and judge the more insane, though not infallibly, clearly, or completely. And thus the more insane can know their insanity by a comparison with the less insane, and we can know our insanity by comparing ourselves with the saints.

Reply to Objection 2: When one is repeatedly given the opportunity for joy or misery and repeatedly chooses misery, it is not too severe to call this disorder insanity, as Einstein did when he defined insanity as "doing the same thing over and over again and expecting different results." But that is the human situation. For all moral evil causes deep misery, in the long run, while all moral good causes deep joy. And we know this by repeated experience, as well as by reason and by faith. And yet we repeatedly choose evil over good.

Reply to objection 3: (1) The question being argued is not whether it is harmful or helpful but whether it is true. It cannot be assumed that whatever ideas might be harmful must be false. It may be harmful to the victim that his murderer knows that the policeman is asleep, but it is still true.

(2) It is not harmful to tell a sick person that he is sick (whether the sickness is physical, moral, or mental), even though this causes

him pain. In fact, this painful knowledge is a necessary condition for his recovery, as a disturbing X-ray is needed before an operation.

Article 8: Whether there is more good than evil in man?

Objection 1: It seems that there is not, for we have just proved that man is so ignorant and evil as to deserve to be called insane.

Objection 2: The prophets more often condemn man's evils than praise man's goods.

Objection 3: A slight evil overpowers a great good, as *Ecclesiastes* notes: "dead flies spoil the perfumer's whole barrel." A few "rotten apples" rot out the good apples. One affair ruins a marriage; one tyrant can murder millions. Good is fragile; evil is not.

Objection 4: Whatever good is in man ends in death, the final evil, which destroys everything good.

On the contrary, Reverend Eli Jenkins, the preacher in Dylan Thomas's *Under Milk Wood*, prays: "We are not wholly bad or good/ Who live our lives under Milk Wood,/ And Thou, I know, will be the first/ To see our best side, not our worst." (It is fitting sometimes to quote lesser authorities rather than greater in order to connect with common wisdom.)

I answer that (1) Evil cannot be greater than good because evil is a corruption *of good* and can exist only in a subject that is good by nature. If it corrupted all the good, it would cease to exist, since it would have no subject to exist in, like a parasite who killed its host.

(2) Man always has, by his essential nature, and therefore cannot lose, the free will to choose good and to repent of evil. It is thus up to each man to choose how much good and how much evil there is in his life; it is not up to a philosopher who writes a book about it.

Reply to Objection 1: Even the insane can still have more good than evil in them. If they did not, we would not treat them with such care and compassion, but we would treat them like flies.

Reply to Objection 2: Men have more need to know unwelcome truths than welcome truths; that is why the prophets more often mention the unwelcome ones. The prophets do not measure and compare good and evil in man theoretically, as if they were quantities, but they give man the mental and moral medicines of which he has practical need.

Reply to Objection 3: Physical analogies are misleading. The perfume and the apple have no free will to resist evil influences, or to repent after succumbing, as man has.

Reply to Objection 4: Death is not the last word. Whatever is good in man does not end in death, but death ends in it. For it is demonstrable that souls are immortal (see Question 5, Article 8), and it is believable that bodies are resurrected.

Article 9: Whether virtue always brings happiness?

Objection 1: It seems that it obviously does not, for we see that virtuous people are often dour and unhappy, while the wicked laugh.

Objection 2: Happiness is the sum total of all our natural inclinations' satisfactions. But our natural inclinations are fallen, foolish, and fallible. To satisfy them is to patronize an addict and a tyrant. Furthermore, when they are all satisfied, we find that we are *not* happy but bored. So if happiness were the reward of virtue, this would not be a true reward at all.

Objection 3: "Virtue is its own reward." Doing good for the sake of doing good is true morality, whereas doing good in order to attain happiness is self-serving and mercenary and not truly moral. There is a popular saying, "A good conscience is your best pillow"; but moral virtue should not be pursued simply as a sleeping pill, or as means to the end of personal happiness, for that is egotism.

On the contrary, Plato states, at the beginning of Book 2 of the *Republic*, and proves, in the rest of the *Republic*, that virtue ("justice") is "profitable" both for itself *and* for happiness. It is the highest kind of good: good both for its own sake as an end and for the sake of its natural results as the means to happiness.

Christ summarized all our moral obligations to others in the command to "love your neighbor *as yourself*," thus using our natural self-love as a standard or index of virtue rather than an obstacle to it.

And anyone can verify in his own experience, by experiment, so to speak, the fact that practicing virtue, especially charity, always produces deep happiness, while sinning against the virtues, especially charity, always produces deep discontent and inquietude.

I answer that any being experiences a kind of natural joy when it attains its own proper perfection. Meaningful analogies of this "joy" can be found in animals, plants, and even minerals. For instance, bubbles are at peace when allowed to be round, but not when pushed into other shapes. And moral virtue is the proper perfection of man, of all the habits and acts of his soul. Therefore it must produce joy, by its own nature. As Boethius says, in *The Consolation of Philosophy*, "all things seek again their proper courses and rejoice when they return to them," like animals freed from cages.

Indeed, it is impossible for us, or *any* being, *not* to desire its own proper perfection. That is why God did not command us to neglect our own good, but instead united it both with the moral good and with the good of others, uniting it with the moral good by designing our nature to be happy only when virtuous, and uniting our natural self-love with love of others by creating us in a body, or a family, unlike the angels.

Reply to Objection 1: True virtue makes one joyful, not dour—so much so that joy, as one of the fruits of the Spirit, is one of the qualifications for canonization as a saint in the Catholic Church. And the laughs of the wicked do not manifest true happiness, for they do not last, do not express the deepest desires of the heart, and are doomed to end in misery and regret. They are brittle.

Reply to Objection 2: The objection assumes Kant's definition of happiness, which is not true, objective happiness (blessedness) but mere subjective satisfaction. This, indeed, can be found in successful egotists (temporarily, at least), but this is no more true happiness than it is the reward of true virtue.

Reply to Objection 3: (1) Happiness (blessedness) is virtue's *natural* fruit; it is to virtue what marriage is to courtship, victory to battle, or muscle strength to exercise. The reward for a life of virtue is not external and mercenary but the natural and inevitable consummation of that life itself: *that* happiness cannot be separated from virtue, as wages *can* be separated from work. God is not an unjust employer.

(2) It is not self-serving to desire one's own happiness, or the "good of delight" (the *bonum delictabile*) together with the good of moral virtue (the *bonum honestum*), because they are consummated together. Proper self-love is not wrong but right, and proper self-love and proper altruism should coincide: thus "love your neighbor *as yourself.*"

Article 10: Whether sanctity is the key to ontology?

Objection 1: It seems that this cannot be so, for sanctity is private, personal, individual, and subjective, while ontology is public, impersonal, universal, and objective. The two realms stand in sharpest contrast.

Objection 2: No philosopher in history has ever made such a strange suggestion. Yet both sanctity and ontology have been known for millennia. If one were really the key to the other, it would have been found by now.

On the contrary, Gabriel Marcel writes, in "On the Ontological Mystery," "the study of sanctity with all its concrete attributes seems to me to offer an immense speculative value; indeed, I am not far from saying that it is the true introduction to ontology."

I answer that this conclusion follows from two premises. One is Heidegger's new and radical idea, at the foundation of *Being and Time*, that the mode of be-ing which he called *Dasein* and which by others is usually called personhood or subjecthood, i.e. being an I rather than an It, is the key to being itself (*Sein*), and thus to ontology.

If we add to this premise the premise that the perfection of created personhood is sanctity, we get Marcel's conclusion.

This is most reasonable for a theist, who believes that personhood "goes all the way up" into ultimate reality, or God; and that charity, or self-giving, which is the essence of sanctity, is also the essence of the prime analogate and standard of all being, God, whose Trinitarian life, according to the central mystery of Christianity, consists in the total and eternal self-giving of each Person to the Others.

Reply to Objection 1: The two realms of the personal subject and the ontological object, or person and being, are joined in God, who is the standard for both, and for their relationship. Thus when He revealed His own true, eternal name as "I AM," He revealed the unity of personhood ("I") and being ("AM"). An indication of this comes from the mystics of all religions, who in diverse ways overcome the dualism between subject (person) and object (being) that is present in non-mystical consciousness.

Reply to Objection 2: As noted above, Marcel has made this connection, and Fr. Norris Clarke has laid bare its metaphysical foundations in *Person and Being*. It is not so surprising that this connection remained hidden from philosophy for centuries, since philosophers have not been notorious for either the practice of, the interest in, or the understanding of sanctity.

Question VIII:
Applied Ethics

Article 1: Whether there is
a moral obligation to worship God?

Objection 1: It seems that there is not, for if there were, it would be a universal moral duty, and in that case the public authorities should enforce it. But this use of public secular force to enforce religious obligations has in our history proved harmful and even disastrous, especially for religion itself.

Objection 2: As the Qur'an teaches, "there must be no compulsion in matters of religion." True worship must be freely chosen.

Objection 3: Obligations presuppose knowledge. But not everyone knows that God exists. Therefore not everyone has an obligation to worship Him. It would be absurd to expect an atheist to accept an obligation to worship a being he believed to be unreal.

On the contrary, St. Paul says of pagans without supernatural Jewish or Christian revelation that "what can be known about God is plain to them . . . clearly perceived in the things that have been made. So they are without excuse; for although they knew God they did not honor Him as God." He does not argue that they were wicked because they did not know the truth but that they did not know the truth because they were wicked: "who by their wickedness suppress the truth." (*Romans* 1:18–21) And St. John also diagnoses evil as the cause of ignorance rather than ignorance as the cause of evil when he says that "men loved darkness rather than light because their deeds were evil." (*John* 3:19) This obligation is known by nature, and binds.

I answer that justice obliges all of us to give to each person what is due to him. But worship and adoration is due to God, and God alone. Therefore justice obliges us to worship God.

This conclusion follows directly from what has been said above about the ability of natural reason to know that God exists. Even if in some men this universal natural knowledge of God is only implicit, or "deep down," it still brings an absolute obligation at least on that level. And on the explicit and conscious level, the agnostic and the atheist have the moral obligation to inquire honestly and assiduously into this momentous question, for no question makes a greater difference to his life even in this world, and infinitely more in the next. (See Pascal's *Pensées*, "Against Indifference.")

Reply to Objection 1: It is not true that the public authorities ought to enforce every universal moral obligation. There are many very serious universal moral obligations that are private rather than public, such as intellectual honesty, or care for one's own health; and there are many moral obligations which it would do more harm than good to enforce, e.g. the obligation to avoid drunkenness, sodomy, and fornication. The obligation to worship is of this nature. The state should *allow* it and even *encourage* it but not *enforce* it.

Reply to Objection 2: Obligation is not the same as compulsion. Moral obligation itself does not work by compulsion but by free conscience, as the Qur'anic quotation says. *Enforcing* a moral obligation by public and civil sanctions does add compulsion, and this is an argument for a separation of church and state, contrary to what Muslims practice, but it is not an argument for a denial of the moral obligation itself to worship God.

Reply to Objection 3: Of course atheists can have no direct and immediate obligation to worship God. But if God's existence and moral authority can and should be known by natural reason and conscience, then even atheists have an indirect and ultimate obligation to worship God—just as a person who does not know that a certain man is the king, and who therefore does not accept or obey his authority, is still under that authority, unless his ignorance of the king is wholly excusable and invincible. But if ignorance of God's existence is not invincible, it is not wholly excusable.

In fact, our moral knowledge of the natural law is prior to and clearer than our theological knowledge of God, and is not wholly dependent on it. This is why our inferences more naturally move from morality to God than from God to morality, and why the moral argument for God is convincing while the "divine command theory of morality" is not.

Article 2: Whether it is immoral to worship idols?

Objection 1: It seems that it is not, for this proscription comes from divine revelation, not from natural reason. Thus it is binding only on those who accept this revelation, and not morally binding on all by natural law.

Objection 2: The intention of the idol-worshipper is to do justice by giving to the gods the worship they deserve. Thus his moral intention is praiseworthy, even though his theological ignorance is not.

Objection 3: Those who take God's name in vain by flippant, impious, sacrilegious, or blasphemous reference to the holy things of any religion, are in one of two situations, neither of which deserves the title "morally evil." Either (1) they do not mean to dishonor God but are merely meaninglessly repeating socially accepted formulas, or (2) they mean to dishonor only a religion they do not believe in, in which case their intention is not immoral even if their disbelief may be erroneous.

On the contrary, the worship of idols and the vain use of holy names are condemned not only by the Commandment, but also by reason, by mankind's gradual but irrevocable realization of their wrongness.

I answer that just as the negative corollary of the positive law of identity ("X is X") is the law of non-contradiction ("X is not non-X"); and as the negative corollary of "Believe truth" is "Do not believe untruth"; and as the negative corollary of "Do good" is "Avoid evil"; and as the negative corollary of "Be faithful to your spouse" is "Do not be unfaithful and commit adultery"; so the corollary of "worship the one true God" is "Do not worship other, false gods," and the corollary of "Honor God's name" is "Do not dishonor it."

If God is the infinitely perfect Creator, then this corollary excludes the worship of any finite creature whatsoever, including abstract causes, ideas, or ideals, as well as concrete things and people, whether others or oneself—or one's pleasure, wealth, health, honor, comfort, intelligence, freedom, or virtue. And if one worships and honors God, an immediate corollary of this worship is not to *dishonor* God—which is what it means not to take His name in vain.

Reply to Objection 1: This command is not first created by divine revelation but only reinforced by it. It can also be derived from natural reason, either as a corollary of the previous Article, or as a part of justice ("Give each his due"), or as a deduction from the fundamental moral principle of conforming our lives and choices to knowable reality, not to falsehood, thus as part of the virtue and obligation of intellectual honesty. If reason can know God exists, it can easily derive this corollary.

Reply to Objection 2: (1) Intention is not the whole of morality. See above, Question 7, Article 2, Reply to Objection 2.

(2) The intention of idol-worshippers is usually not to give the gods their due but to use them for purposes of power and success in this world. No idol in history has ever been conceived as a God of perfect justice and charity, like the God of the Bible; and the worshipper of a god always conforms to and becomes more like the god he worships. (See *Psalms* 115:4–8)

(3) Even if theological ignorance of the one true God is the cause of the idolatry, this ignorance is both intellectually and morally blameworthy, as the previous Article demonstrated. And thus there is still an indirect obligation: first, to inquire into what is true, and then, if the inquiry succeeds in knowing the truth, to do the truth.

Reply to Objection 3: Dishonor of things that are supremely honorable does harm to all who hear it; for language, like music, is a powerful unconscious teacher. In case (1) in the objection, it is a fault to empty of meaning and value that which one knows or believes is in fact supremely meaningful and valuable by using it in a meaningless and disvalued way. In case (2), it dishonors other people by dishonoring their religious convictions.

Article 3: Whether leisure is as necessary for man as work?

Objection 1: It seems that it is not, for man can live without leisure but he cannot live without work.

Objection 2: Leisure is necessary for the sake of happier and more efficient work. But an end is more necessary and important than a means. Therefore work is more necessary and important than leisure.

Objection 3: Industriousness in work is a moral good or virtue (*bonum honestum*), while leisure is only a pleasant good (*bonum delictabile*). The moral good is more necessary than the pleasant good. Therefore industriousness is more necessary than pleasure, and work is more necessary than leisure.

On the contrary, history, religion, common sense, and the Bible all confirm the wisdom of the Sabbath commandment. (1) Higher civilizations appeared only among those peoples who cultivated leisure. (See Aristotle, *Metaphysics* I, 1.) (2) All the world's religions and wisdom traditions insist on it, usually in the form of one sacred day in each week. (3) It is a common-sense saying that "we work to live, we do not live to work." (4) And Christ praised Mary, who took the leisure to contemplate His words, more than Martha, who served Him by work. (*Luke* 10:38–42)

I answer that work is, by definition, a means to a further end: one always works *for* something. Leisure, on the other hand, is not a practical means to a further end but exists for its own sake, like play. And since the end is of higher value and more necessary than the means, leisure is of higher value and more necessary than work.

Without leisure and the contemplative freedom from work that it brings, it is difficult to remember God, to worship, and to contemplate one's origin, nature, and destiny. But these things are all more important than any other work.

Reply to Objection 1: Man can survive without leisure but he cannot truly live a human life without it.

Reply to Objection 2: The premise is false: leisure is not for the sake of work but work for the sake of leisure. For leisure is not merely the absence of work but the presence of the higher ends which work makes possible, such as the understanding of truth, the love of goodness, and the enjoyment of beauty. See Josef Pieper, *Leisure, the Basis of Culture.* Similarly, war is for the sake of peace, not peace for the sake of war, for peace is not merely the absence of war but the positive resting in and enjoying the end attained by efforts, including war.

Reply to Objection 3: Leisure is not itself a moral virtue, but giving it to others is, for leisure is the precondition for many higher goods.

Article 4: Whether family and ancestors must be revered?

Objection 1: It seems not, for reverence to ancestors and their traditions, while necessary in earlier, more primitive times as a transmitter of civilization, is an outdated concept in an age of progress, equality, freedom, and autonomy.

Objection 2: Reverence goes beyond reason and justice in preferring one's own family and ancestors not because their wisdom or virtues are superior to those of others but simply because they are one's own family and ancestors. What goes beyond reason and justice is not morally obligatory. Therefore reverence for one's family and ancestors is not morally obligatory.

I answer that honor to family and ancestors is morally obligatory because it is a debt of justice. In fact the debt of justice owed to one's parents and ancestors cannot possibly be adequately repaid, for our parents transmitted to us human life itself, as well as education and care, from the time we were helpless infants; and our ancestors invented almost all of the good things, physical and spiritual, that we inherit by entering the world they civilized. We cannot transmit life back to our parents, nor can we care for their infancy. And we cannot share our own civilizing inventions with our dead ancestors. Therefore justice demands that we pay our debt to them by gratitude and reverence, and carry on this transmission of life and culture by "paying it forward" to our children, who in turn will also revere "backward" and pay "forward." This is the wisdom in God's invention of the human family, both immediate and remote (ancestors).

Reply to Objection 1: The debt of reverence is not historically relative but in the nature of the human family itself, as is shown in the body of the Article. Any generation which absolutizes the values of progress, freedom, autonomy, and equality (which are real but not absolute values), and therefore denies a hierarchy of reverence to ancestors, who gave them all of the goods they inherited, mental and physical, breaks the great chain of giving and receiving, and of the gratitude consequent upon receiving. And without gratitude there is no wisdom.

Reply to Objection 2: (1) This going beyond justice and reason is called "love." It is not only a moral good but our *primary* moral good and the whole meaning of life.

(2) Even by the lesser standards of justice, reverence for one's own family and ancestors is demanded, even if they be no wiser or more virtuous than other people, because it is their gifts, more than those of others, that we inherit, first of all life itself, without which no other gifts at all could be received.

Article 5: Whether private property is a natural right?

Objection 1: It seems that it is not, for no natural right may be removed by human authority, but a person's property may rightly be taken by the state or its police if it threatens other citizens. Therefore private property is not a natural right.

Objection 2: The lower community should imitate the higher as far as possible. In the communion of saints in Heaven, and in the Church on earth, as described in the New Testament (*Acts* 2:44–45), and among the happiest families on earth, property is more communal than private. Therefore this should be the ideal of public society on earth. But no ideal takes away a natural right. Therefore private property is not a natural right.

Objection 3: It was not wrong for Jean Valjean, in *Les Miserables*, to steal bread from a rich baker to save his family from starvation. But that bread was the baker's private property. It is never right to deprive another of a natural right. Therefore private property is not a natural right.

On the contrary, the original version of the American Declaration of Independence spoke of three natural, "inalienable" rights: life, liberty *and property* (which was changed to "the pursuit of happiness" for rhetorical purposes).

I answer that stealing another's private property would not be wrong by nature if the possession of private property were not a right. Because private as well as public theft is a wrong, private as well as public property is a right.

The natural right to property follows from the natural right to life. Man cannot live on earth without using material goods. They become property when he seizes them and uses or consumes them for his own purposes. Each individual has a natural instinct to do this, because in the hierarchy of nature, lower beings are to be used for the good of higher beings: chemicals for plants; plants and chemicals for animals; animals, plants, and chemicals for man. Since man is the highest being on earth, other things are to be used for his true good. And because he alone among the animals has reason, he has the natural ability and right to creatively use these things as property for his life. And since his life on earth is both private and public, it follows that both private property and public property are natural rights of man.

Reply to Objection 1: If two natural rights conflict, because of unnatural human evil, the greater one must take precedence over the lesser. Life is greater than property. Therefore when life is threatened by property, the property may be taken.

Reply to Objection 2: There are also no policemen or soldiers in Heaven, or in the Church, or in happy families, but it does not follow that policemen and soldiers are not needed in public society on earth. What is a valid ideal for one order in human life is not necessarily a valid ideal for all of them.

Reply to Objection 3: What Jean Valjean did was not stealing, which is always wrong because it is a violation of the natural right to property. Stealing is the *unjust* seizure of another's property, but this was a just seizure. For others had the duty to save his life and the lives of his family, and when they failed in this duty, their lesser right to property yielded to his greater right to life. Similarly, a lethal attacker yields his right to life and bodily integrity by threatening the innocent life of another, and he may be defended against even by lethal force if necessary. He also forfeits his right to truth and may be deceived, to save lives.

Article 6: Whether it is ever right to kill?

Objection 1: It seems that it is not, for the Commandment says, "Thou shalt not kill."

Objection 2: Christ is the supreme moral example and authority. But one cannot imagine Christ killing another man for any reason. In fact, he sanctified martyrdom and told us to "resist not the one who is evil" (*Matthew* 5:29).

Objection 3: If one had the true vision to perceive the preciousness and sacredness of human life, which God made in His own image, one would no more destroy it than one would destroy the God in Whose image it is made. Thus the willingness to kill depends on a failure of vision.

On the contrary, John the Baptist, whom Christ called the greatest of all previous prophets (*Matthew* 11:11), did not tell soldiers to abandon their profession (*Luke* 3:14), which he would have done if all killing were wrong; for one cannot be a soldier without being prepared to kill.

I answer that man cannot attain his ultimate end except by making right choices. He cannot make choices if he does not have life.

Therefore he has a natural right to life. But we are animals, not angels, and therefore physically dependent on each other, and responsible for the protection of each other and each other's rights. The use of lethal force when necessary to protect innocent human life does not claim the authority to remove the natural right to life, but responds to the fact that the attacker has already done so. It is an exercise in stewardship, not dominion.

Reply to Objection 1: The Hebrew word misleadingly translated "kill" means not all forcible taking of human life, but only murder. In fact, though private vengeance was outlawed, the right of capital punishment was instituted, by the same Authority that gave this commandment.

Reply to Objection 2: (1) One's own human imagination is not the supreme moral authority.

(2) Christ's advice to "resist not the one who is evil" is a counsel for some, not a command for all; a maximal life of charity to which He invited us, not a minimal commandment of justice imposed on all. It is a good "beyond the call of duty." (This, by the way, refutes Kant's *identification* of morality with duty.) Not all are called to literal martyrdom.

(3) "Resist not the one who is evil" is addressed to individuals, not to public authorities. If public authorities did not resist evil men, many innocents would die.

Reply to Objection 3: It is precisely to protect the preciousness of that life that attacks on it must be repelled. When one person threatens the life of another, the only two choices are to let the right to life of the innocent person be violated or to protect it at the expense, if necessary, of the life of the attacker, who has forfeited his right to life by setting it in lethal opposition to that of his victim.

However, the intention in such a case must be the saving of life, not the taking of it (the principle of double effect[1] applies here), and non-lethal force should always be used if possible.

---

1   When an act has a lesser bad effect as well as a greater good one, and both are foreseen but only the good effect is intended, and the bad effect is not willed as a means to the good one but only reluctantly permitted as a necessary concession, the act is morally licit.

Article 7: Whether it is ever right to lie?

Objection 1: It seems that it is, for it is obviously right to fulfill one's promise to guard a secret, and if this secret can be guarded only by lying, the lying becomes not only right but obligatory. For instance, the Dutch who hid Jews from the Nazis had the obligation to lie to the Nazis about their whereabouts. No natural right can ever be violated; therefore, lying does not violate a natural right. Or, if it does, then the lesser right (in this case, the right to know the truth) must yield to the greater right (in this case, the right to life).

Objection 2: Social life would be impossible without "white lies" such as "the boss is not here." Sports would also be impossible without deliberate deception, such as a head fake in basketball. And no man could possibly have the moral obligation *not* to lie to a woman he loves when she asks him, "Am I fat?"

Objection 3: Since self-defense legitimates *killing* an attacker, it is *a fortiori* legitimate to defend ourselves or others by *lying*. For the lesser evil is to be preferred to the greater.

On the contrary, everyone recognizes, by common sense, that a "liar" is a morally wicked person.

I answer that there are three main reasons lying is wrong: one practical, one psychological, and one metaphysical.

(1) Without trust, especially trust in others to tell the truth and fulfill their promises, all human relationships break down. Lying breaks this trust. Therefore lying breaks down all human relationships, which is obviously a great evil.

(2) A lie is the deliberate contradiction between what one knows or believes and what one says to one who has a right to know the truth. Since knowing and speaking are both distinctively human powers,

lying sets two powers of our very nature against each other. This harms not only the hearer, who is deceived, but also the speaker.

(3) Man's rights depend on his essential human needs, which in turn depend on his essential nature. Man's distinctively human nature is rational (intellectual). And truth is the natural need of his rational nature. Truth is to the mind what food is to the body. Since this is a natural need, it is a natural right. Lying deliberately deprives others of this right. But it is not morally right to deprive others of their natural rights. Therefore lying is not morally right.

Reply to Objection 1: No universal natural law obligation can conflict with another. Just as seizure of a madman's weapon is not theft, and self-defense is not murder, so deliberately deceiving those who have no right to know is not lying. There is no universal right to know the truth about everything, even if tyrants, the paparazzi, and the media may assume they have such a right.

Reply to Objection 2: These are not lies but social conventions. For speech is not simply the relationship of a speaker with the truth, or with one other speaker only, but it is a set of complex interpersonal and culturally relative relationships.

Lying is bearing false *witness*; but not all speakers are in the position of giving witness, for a witness swears to tell "the truth, the whole truth, and nothing but the truth." Furthermore, lying is bearing false witness *against* your neighbor; thus lies always harm others. The social conventions above are for mutually agreed help, not for harm.

Reply to Objection 3: A good end does not justify an intrinsically evil means. One may not, e.g., commit murder, adultery, or blasphemy even to save oneself from death. Neither may one lie, for the same reason. But just as not all self-defense is murder, neither is all deception lying, such as the deceptions of the Dutch to the Nazis.

The lesser evil is always to be *tolerated* rather than the greater, but *no* evil ever ought to be *done*, or ever needs to be done. Moral commandments do not contradict each other. They are always possible to obey. If not, even Christ could not have been morally perfect. "Ought" implies "can."

Article 8: Whether sex is sacred and not to be adulterated?

Objection 1: It seems that it is not, for it is not necessary to see sex as sacred in order to see adultery as wrong, for adultery is simply another case of lying and of injustice against the Golden Rule.

Objection 2: To call sex sacred is to transfer it from the natural order of reason to the supernatural order of faith. But only natural law, not the values of any particular faith, obligates all men, of all faiths, by reason. Therefore if sex is sacred, its obligations bind only religious believers.

Objection 3: The sense of the sacred is *sui generis* and cannot be proved or derived from anything else. Therefore, it cannot be a conclusion of argument, but can only be a premise. Attempts to persuade those who lack this sense into accepting it is like attempting to persuade a blind person that color exists.

This is especially difficult today because no society in history before our own ever had a majority of citizens who were blind to the sacred.

Objection 4: Before the Sexual Revolution, when sex was seen as a sacred taboo, mankind lived in fear and superstition about sex. The Sexual Revolution, the essence of which was to detach sex from both the sense of sacredness and the fear of pregnancy, liberated mankind to orgies of enjoyment and heaps of happiness.

On the contrary, sex and death have always been the two primal sacred mysteries, for they are the doors through which we come into the world and exit it. This is why every society until ours has approached them with awe and reverence, surrounded them with taboos, proprieties, ceremonies, and laws, and taken great care not to adulterate them.

I answer that the sacredness of sex can be deduced from two premises: the sacredness of each individual person and the fact that sex is his origin. The first is admitted even by "Enlightenment" thinkers like Kant, who have elsewhere replaced religion with reason and sacredness with science. The second is simply a biological fact known by everyone in the world.

The same conclusion follows from two theological principles: that God is the creator of each human soul, which He makes in His own image; and that He does this upon the occasion of biological conception, which happens as the natural result of sexual intercourse. Thus sex is the sacred door by which God repeatedly enters the world to perform the greatest of miracles: the creation of human individuals each of which possesses immortality and intrinsic value. Compared to this miracle, the creation of the universe (the "Big Bang") was only a preliminary (for the cosmos is *not* immortal).

From the premise of this cosmic vision or "big picture," the practical conclusion "Thou shalt not commit adultery" and its corollaries follow with relative ease.

Reply to Objection 1: Adultery *is* all that, but it is different, and far worse, just as rape is far worse than other assault and battery. Lying by deed, to the most important person in one's life, against the most serious promise one ever made and about the most intimate and powerful use of one's body, is very different from lying by word, to a stranger, about something casual, accidental, and external.

Reply to Objection 2: Just as man himself is both natural *and* supernatural, both secular and sacred, so sex has both dimensions. Thus to call it sacred is not to deny its "secular" status in reason and nature. Furthermore, all men by nature sense something of its sacredness, for the sexual organs and acts are never treated in the same way as all the others. There is no contradiction in saying that there can be also a natural and secular knowledge of a supernatural and sacred thing.

Reply to Objection 3: This sense may be buried in many today, but it is not totally dead, for it is part of essential human nature. Thus it can still be appealed to, and restored. This can be seen in practice; for many of even the most uprooted souls, exposed to the sacred tradition for the first time, perceive its truth, goodness, and beauty. This would not be so if there were no innate potentiality to receive this perception.

Reply to Objection 4: These "heaps of happiness" are piled high with the torn remains of the souls and bodies of innocent children, both born and unborn: the living victims of the sexual revolution, and of divorce, and the dead victims of backup birth control, or abortion. Dozens of objective, scientific studies have demonstrated the results of the Sexual Revolution to be quite the opposite of happiness, especially for women and children.

Article 9: Whether lust is evil?

Objection 1: It seems that it is not, for it is natural to man, and nothing natural is evil.

Objection 2: Furthermore, lust is the natural origin of sexual intercourse, which is the natural origin of human beings. The previous Article argued that sexual intercourse is sacred because it is the origin of human beings, which are sacred. The implied premise of this argument is that the origin of a sacred thing must be itself sacred. But this premise entails the further conclusion that lust is sacred, since it is the natural origin of sexual intercourse, which is sacred. But nothing sacred is evil. Therefore lust is not evil.

Objection 3: Whatever directly causes evils, is evil. Condemning lust causes fear, guilt, a low self-image, and a lack of self-esteem, and these are evils. Therefore it is the condemnation of lust, rather than lust itself, that is evil.

On the contrary, everyone wants to be treated as an end, not as a means; that is, loved and esteemed for what he or she is, not for what he or she can do to another, whether this is the giving of sexual pleasure (which can be done by a prostitute as well as by a genuine lover) or the giving of menial labor (which can be done by a slave as well as by a free worker). But as everyone admits, we ought to treat others as we want others to treat us (the "Golden Rule"), and to act contrary to this is a moral evil. And lust acts contrary to this, for it uses the other as a means to one's own sexual pleasure. Therefore lust is a moral evil.

I answer that lust is an evil because it is the perversion of a good. Lust is not simply sexual desire, or even intense sexual desire, but disordered and selfish sexual desire. Whatever is disordered and selfish is a moral evil. Therefore lust is a moral evil.

Lust is disordered *because* it is selfish. It is selfish because instead of loving the other as such, for his or her own sake, it loves the experience of sexual pleasure in oneself that is given by the other. (And this could be true of psychological pleasure as well as physical pleasure.) The commonest opposite and enemy of love is not hate but *use*.

In concrete fact, unselfish love and selfish lust are often mixed, in various proportions. Most of our motives are mixed, unless we are very pure.

Reply to Objection 1: Man's present nature, as observed in action, is fallen and imperfect, and cannot be used as the standard for morality. It is also "natural" to man to be selfish and cowardly, but it does not follow that these are not evils.

What is truly "natural" to man, that is, as an expression of his fulfilled nature, is not lust but that of which lust is a perversion: honest, self-forgetful, self-giving love of the other for the other's sake in all aspects of life, including sex. Lust treats the other as an object, not a subject, and as a means to one's own sexual pleasure rather than as an intrinsically valuable end.

Reply to Objection 2: The previous Reply distinguished two senses of "natural": (1) typically observed activities of fallen man as he is, and (2) the expression and fruition of human nature as it ought to be. Lust is the "natural" origin of much sexual intercourse in the first sense; but love, i.e. the desire to give one's whole self to the other, is the "natural" origin of it in the second sense. Lust is evil precisely because it is a perversion of the kind of sexual desire that is very good.

Reply to Objection 3: The argument is clearly absurd, for the same argument may be made about any moral evil whatsoever, for instance rape or murder. The evil of a guilty conscience, which is caused by the condemnation of any moral evil, is not itself a *moral* evil, but only an emotional evil or suffering. Such emotional suffering is necessary to move us from evil to good, just as physical pain is necessary to move us from physical danger to safety.

If and only if lust were in fact not a moral evil, would it be true that the condemnation of this innocent thing, rather than the thing itself, is evil. But this is the objector's conclusion; he begs the question by assuming it as his premise.

Article 10: Whether greed is evil?

Objection 1: It seems that greed cannot be evil, for it is the foundation of our entire social order. If we desired and bought only what we truly needed, the entire world economic order would collapse and half the world would starve.

Objection 2: Greed is simply the old-fashioned, moralistic word for the profit motive. But the profit motive is good. Therefore greed is good. The profit motive is good because it is the necessary psychological fuel for an economy in which everyone becomes richer and happier.

On the contrary, "greedy" is universally employed as an insult. No one admires Scrooge in Charles Dickens's *A Christmas Carol*. Buddha calls greed or selfish desire (*tanha*) the origin of all suffering (*dukkha*), since suffering is the gap between selfish desire and satisfaction, and this gap is created by selfish desire itself. As the world's richest philosopher (Mick Jagger) laments, "I can't get no satisfaction," and "You can't always get what you want."

I answer that greed is usually applied to money and lust to sex, but the evil of both is the same: the perversion of a natural desire into selfishness. Just as lust respects neither the other person nor the nature of sex itself (since it typically fears the natural product of sex, namely children, since their existence imposes many obligations and inconveniences on their parents), but only the pleasure of sexual acts, so greed respects neither other people nor the product itself by taking a proper pride in the work itself, but only the acquisition of its monetary profits.

The desire to have, increase, and use property is natural, just as is sexual desire. But the natural desire for property is limited to natural needs for property and possible uses of it. Greed, by contrast, is disordered because it has no limit. Its primary object is money, or artificial wealth, the desire for which is unlimited, rather than natural wealth, the desire for which is limited by nature. No one can actually enjoy unlimited food, houses, or cars. Even lust, however addictive, has natural limits, but greed does not.

Reply to Objection 1: If this economic analysis is true, it does not prove that greed is good, but that the world economy is bad because it is dependent on something bad, viz. on disordered human desires, not on genuine human needs.

Reply to Objection 2: (1) The answer to Objection 1 could also be given to Objection 2.

(2) The profit motive can be distinguished from personal greed, since the object desired by the profit motive is not necessarily personal gain but can be the welfare of all through the profits of a business being reinvested in better products and services which improve general human happiness. This is clearly true of something like medical technology. (As with lust and love, these two motives, the selfish and the unselfish, are usually mixed in practice.)

(3) "Richer" does not entail "happier." Suicide, the most obvious index of unhappiness, is found much more among the rich than among the poor.

Question IX:
Political Philosophy

Article 1: Whether the state is natural to man?

Objection 1: It seems that it is not, for in the modern age, when political philosophy is taken more seriously and importantly, nearly all the important thinkers (Hobbes, Locke, Rousseau) teach that the state comes about by a free "social contract." This is a higher philosophy of the state than the pre-modern philosophy in which the state is natural, since freedom is a higher, more honorable, and more distinctively human origin than the necessities of nature.

Objection 2: Whether the state originated in a free contract is a question of fact, not theory. For we can empirically and historically observe the origin of diverse forms of government and see that they are indeed human contracts, simply by reading the founding documents of various states.

Objection 3: We observe a great diversity in governments. But nature produces uniformity in each thing. If the state were a natural thing, it would not manifest such diversity.

On the contrary, all pre-modern thinkers except the Sophists teach that the state is a natural institution. For instance Aristotle derives the state from the family, as follows: "There must be a union of those who cannot exist without each other, namely, of male and female, that the race may continue . . . when several families are united, and the association aims at something more than the supply of daily needs, the first society to be formed is the village. . . . When several villages are united in a single complete community, large enough to be nearly or quite self-sufficient, the state comes into existence. . . . If the earlier forms of society are natural, so is the state, for it is the end

189

of them, and the nature of a thing is its end. . . . Man is by nature a political animal." (*Politics* I, 2)

I answer that since the family is natural, and since the state is a natural outgrowth of the family, for the common good and the improvement of the life of all, therefore the state is natural.

Hobbes's theory (in *Leviathan*) that the state is artificial, that the origin of all law is the "social contract," and that in the "state of nature" before civil society there is no law and therefore no justice, no moral right or wrong, is a regression to the Sophists' position that natural moral law does not exist and that morality is man-made, artificial, and relative, which has been refuted above (Question 7, Articles 1–4)

Furthermore, there is no empirical evidence that such a "state of nature" ever existed. The earliest humans known to anthropologists lived in organized societies.

Reply to Objection 1: (1) The opinions of the moderns are no more authoritative than the opinions of the ancients.

(2) Taking a thing more seriously and importantly is no guarantee that the thinking will be *truer*, as is clear in the cases of idolatry and addictions. For any finite thing can be overvalued as well as undervalued.

(3) Since God is the author of nature while man is the author of human choices, the "natural origin" theory is actually higher than the "human free will" theory.

Reply to Objection 2: What we observe is a diversity in the various constitutions or forms of government, but not in the origin of government itself. We observe various constitutions empirically, but there is no observable constitution for the state as such.

Reply to Objection 3: Nature produces uniformity in essence but diversity in accidents. We observe that all men tend by nature to live in civil society as well as in families; and that these societies take on a diversity of accidental forms—exactly the two phenomena predicted by the hypothesis that the state is natural in origin.

Article 2: Whether a good state is "one that makes it easy to be good"?

Objection 1: It seems that it is not, for this definition, by Dorothy Day (from Peter Maurin) is far too simplistic and childish.

Objection 2: This definition commits the fallacy of circularity in using, as part of the definition, the very word to be defined ("good").

Objection 3: The definition is too individualistic, using the good life of the individual as the sole end of the state. This forgets or denies the priority of the common good over the private good, even for private citizens.

Objection 4: When it is easy to be good, one needs to expend less effort of will, thus making for *less* goodness.

On the contrary, the authority of common sense certifies this definition. For as soon as one hears it, one sees it as the naked truth underneath all more complex definitions, and responds with the same "of course" as the people in Hans Christian Andersen's fable "The Emperor's New Clothes." As C.S. Lewis says, paraphrasing Samuel Johnson, "The State exists simply to promote and to protect the ordinary happiness of human beings in this life. A husband and wife chatting over a fire, a couple of friends having a game of darts in a pub, a man reading a book in his own room or digging in his own garden—that is what the State is for. And unless they are helping to increase and prolong and protect such moments, all the laws, parliaments, armies, courts, police, economics, etc., are simply a waste of time." (*Mere Christianity*)

I answer that the state, like the Sabbath, was made for man, not man for it. The end of each man is blessedness, conceived as both subjective happiness, or joy, and objective goodness, or perfection. Therefore the state serves its natural end, and is good, insofar as it helps man to achieve his natural end, which is the good life, or blessedness. This definition does not define the *content* of the good life for man, or what *form* of state government best conduces to it, but the *relation* between the two.

Reply to Objection 1: A thing is not *simplistic* just because it is *simple*, or *childish* because it is *childlike*. In fact, simpler definitions are to be preferred, as are simpler hypotheses (Ockham's Razor).

Reply to Objection 2: It is not goodness as such that is being defined here but the goodness of the state, and the definition makes it relative to the goodness of the individual. This is not circular or redundant (tautological), as is shown by the fact that it is controversial and surprising to many.

Reply to Objection 3: It is true that individuals are obligated to sacrifice the private good for the common good when necessary (e.g. by paying taxes), as justice and charity demand. But it is not true that the state is its own end. Only individual human beings are intrinsic ends and must never be used merely as means, while there is no moral evil in treating the state in this way. For all states pass away, with everything else in the world; but all individuals have unending life.

(If one does not believe in individual immortality, it is natural for their philosophy to tend to totalitarianism, for states are much larger, last much longer, and are much more powerful than individuals.)

Reply to Objection 4: This is the Kantian error of making moral goodness proportionate to difficulty and inversely proportionate to inclinations. On the contrary, the better one is at anything, the easier it is. Thus the greatest saints have the most joy, for joy in virtue makes virtue more attractive and thus easier. Now if any good thing is made easier, more people will attain it, and therefore it is good to make goodness easier.

Article 3: Whether the state should have a substantive philosophy of the good life?

Objection 1: It seems that it should not, for especially in modern societies, which are "pluralistic" philosophically and religiously, different people have different religious and philosophical beliefs about the content of the good life, and even the *summum bonum*. If such a pluralistic society were to adopt one among many of these belief systems, it would disenfranchise and do injustice to those who did not adopt this belief, as, for instance, *shari'a* does to non-Muslims in a Muslim society. This is an injustice, therefore it should not be done. But it is done if the state has a substantive philosophy of the good life, or officially adopts one of many specific answers to the question of fundamental values, especially the *summum bonum*. Therefore the state should not have a substantive philosophy of the good life.

Objection 2: Throughout history, the closer the state has come to totalitarian claims, the more harm has been done—to individuals and also to religions and philosophies —when they are politicized. Because of man's lust for power and power's tendency to corrupt, the pretensions of government are worst when maximal and best when minimal. Therefore it should not be the state's business to pronounce upon the substantive philosophical questions of life, such as the ones in this book.

Objection 3: If democracy is the best form of government, individuals should be maximally free, for this is the specific virtue of democracy. As Supreme Court Justice Anthony Kennedy has written, one of the most basic of all freedoms is the freedom to determine for oneself the meaning of life and the mystery of existence.

On the contrary, the modern state in the West is the first in history that professes no substantive philosophy of life. Tradition and universal premodern precedent militate against a philosophically "neutral" state. And there is good reason for this tradition, for we must have an answer to the question of life's end(s) before we can reasonably judge about its political means, since the means are relative to the end.

I answer that if the state has no substantive philosophy of the good life, then the state cannot know what a good state is. For this depends on what a good human life is, which in turn depends on what man is, which in turn depends on what is, and on how we know it. And these are the four great philosophical questions of ethics, anthropology, metaphysics, and epistemology.

But if the state does not know even what a good state is, it cannot judge whether it is a good or a bad state in doing anything it does; and this would make active choice between alternative public policies impossible. Therefore the state must have some substantive philosophy of the good life.

For example, if human life is sacred, inviolable, and intrinsically valuable, then the state may not execute political dissidents, if they do not threaten the lives of others. And if "all men are created equal," then slavery and abortion are intolerable. Any state that refuses to pronounce on such questions is *not* "neutral" but chooses to allow rather than forbid political murder (killing political dissidents), or abortion, or slavery.

As Hegel wrote in his *Philosophy of History*, some states (despotisms) knew only that "one was free" (the despot); others, like Rome, knew that "some were free" (patricians); and some (enlightened democracies) knew that "all were free." No state *can* be neutral on such matters as this.

Reply to Objection 1: (1) The objection reduces philosophy to religion, reason to faith. A state with a substantive *philosophy* can still be *religiously* pluralistic, since it can be based not on a particular religious faith that is shared by only some but on a philosophy that is based on natural human reason that is shared by all. The American Declaration of Independence is a clear example of this, when it begins: "We hold these truths to be [rationally] *self-evident:* that all men are created equal; that they are endowed by their Creator [not by other men, or by the state] with certain unalienable rights; that among these rights are life, liberty, and the pursuit of happiness [originally, "property"]."

Thus it speaks of "nature and nature's God," like St. Paul in *Romans* 1, confining itself to what is knowable by natural reason.

(2) In some states, all, or nearly all, of the citizens may in fact believe one religion; and there is no reason why they should be denied the freedom to establish a state on that religious basis if they wish, as long as no natural human rights are violated. (However, those who believe other religions, or none, and do not wish to live subject to the laws of the state religion, should at least be free to emigrate.) Clearly it would be unjust to impose a typically Western secularism and a "separation of Church and State" on an Islamic state against the free choice of its citizens and against the teachings of their religion which do *not* agree with this separation.

Reply to Objection 2: The issue is not how much power the state should have but whether it should embrace a philosophy. Thus there are four possibilities, not just two. The state may have much power and no philosophy, much power and a substantive philosophy, limited power and no philosophy, or limited power and a substantive philosophy. Philosophy does not give one power (efficient causality) but meaning (formal causality) and purpose (final causality).

Reply to Objection 3: (1) The very statement that individuals are and/or should be maximally free is a philosophy, and not all states hold it.

(2) The famous "mystery passage" of Judge Kennedy really says to God, "Excuse me, You're sitting in my seat." For it confuses man's role (which is to *discover*, by reason, the meaning of life) with God's role (which is to design it). The philosophy of this "mystery" passage is postmodernist subjectivism and relativism, which is radically incompatible with the most fundamental philosophical principles of the documents the Judge is purportedly interpreting.

Article 4: Whether democracy is the best form of government?

Objection 1: It seems that it is, for the Declaration of Independence states that "governments are instituted among men, deriving their just powers from the consent of the governed." But this entails democracy.

Objection 2: Even Aristotle, as well as nearly all influential modern political philosophers, favored democracy. Aristotle also already noted, 2350 years ago, in his *Politics* that monarchy becomes rarer, and democracy more common, as humanity progresses through history. This would not be so if democracy were not superior; for mankind, like individuals, learns wisdom through experience.

Objection 3: There is no political question about which there is more consensus than this one. Nearly everyone in every democracy, past as well as present, agrees that democracy is the best form of government. Furthermore, most people presently living in regimes that are not democracies would prefer democracy; that is why so many want to come to America. But very few Americans want to live under any non-democratic regime. This constitutes a massive argument from common consent, based on actual experience.

Objection 4: Democracy gives more people more freedom than other forms of government, and this is what everyone desires.

On the contrary, Aristotle and Aquinas both teach that the best regime is a blend of aristocracy, monarchy, and democracy. This reflects the same kind of mature, inclusivist wisdom as their judgment that the best life is a blend of contemplation and action, the common good and the private good, and goods of body and goods of soul.

I answer that if democracy were the best form of government by nature, it would be best in all times and places, and therefore God would have established this best regime, a democracy, for His chosen people. But he did not. In fact, the only regime we know with certainty to be a good one, because it was established directly by God Himself, was *not* a democracy (ancient Israel).

The ideal structure of human political regimes is not a universal and unchanging absolute. For some peoples, especially in primitive conditions, are incapable of democracy; and others, even later in history, are happy and virtuous under enlightened and unselfish monarchies or aristocracies. As Aristotle said, the one universal and necessary principle that separates good from bad regimes is not the quantitative structure (rule by one, a few, or many) but the qualitative motive: that the rulers rule for the good of the ruled, not for themselves.

Nevertheless most of the reasons averred in the Objections are largely true, especially today, so that democracy is indeed the best form of government (1) for most states (2) in our time, and (3) for the most mature, wise, and educated citizens.

Reply to Objection 1: A citizen who is born into a just and legitimate monarchy but who does not agree with or consent to monarchy as a form of government is still subject to the laws of his state, unless and until he renounces his citizenship. Thus some legitimate governments do not derive their legitimacy from the consent of the governed. And even in a democracy, some citizens may *not* consent to democracy but prefer aristocracy or monarchy; yet they are subject to the laws of the democracy. Thus it is not a true premise that *every* government derives its legitimacy from the consent of the governed. And the premise of the need for consent, even if true, does not necessarily entail democracy as its necessary conclusion, for some consent to other regimes.

Reply to Objection 2: All four of the following propositions are only generally true, but not always: (1) that modern political philosophers prefer democracy, (2) that monarchy becomes rarer and democracy more common, (3) that humanity progresses rather than regresses, and (4) that mankind learns wisdom through experience. Thus the argument is only probable, not necessary.

Reply to Objection 3: This is largely true, but it does not prove that no non-democratic regime of the past was good or legitimate. Furthermore, there are a few regimes even in the present in which most of the citizens would *not* prefer a democracy and are satisfied with their present regime. To tell them that they are wrong and must change to democracy, against their will, contradicts the democratic values of tolerance, pluralism, and free choice.

Reply to Objection 4: This assumes that whatever government gives people the most of what they desire is the best one. But this is not true, because desires do not necessarily coincide with needs, since man is fallen, fallible, and foolish. The soundest justification for democracy is not that man is so wise and good that he should be given maximum freedom and power, but that man is so foolish and evil that no one should be given much of it, especially though central-ized control. To assume that power and freedom (which are almost correlative: see the next Article) do not corrupt is to assume that earth is already Heaven, where we will have freedoms and powers which, if we saw them now, we would call magical; for then alone can we be safely entrusted with them when we are perfected in wis-dom and charity.

Article 5: Whether freedom is an intrinsic good?[1]

Objection 1: It seems that it is, for it is naturally desired by all, and universally regarded as good.

Objection 2: Freedom is intrinsic to human nature, and cannot be taken from man, though it can be stifled in its exercise. What is intrinsic to human nature is an intrinsic good.

Objection 3: Slavery is the opposite of freedom. But slavery is by nature evil. Therefore freedom is by nature good.

On the contrary, freedom is equivalent to power, and in most of their forms the two are correlative; for instance imprisonment, slavery, paralysis, and poverty all remove both freedom and power from us. But as Lord Acton famously said, "all power tends to corrupt, and absolute power corrupts absolutely." No intrinsic good tends to cor-rupt, and no intrinsic good in its absolute form ever corrupts absolutely. Therefore freedom is not an intrinsic good, but an instru-mental and relative good.

Furthermore, freedom is not a moral good but a physical,

---

1 This article speaks mainly of *political* freedom. To distinguish and relate the different kinds of freedom, cf. Mortimer Adler's *The Idea of Freedom*.

psychological, and political good. For one does not automatically become more virtuous by becoming more free; and one can misuse freedom, but one cannot misuse true virtue. Since freedom is not a moral good and since only moral goods (morally good wills) are intrinsically good (as Kant argued at the beginning of his *Grounding for the Metaphysics of Morals*), freedom is not an intrinsic good.

I answer that freedom is a good but not an intrinsic good, for one cannot have too much of an intrinsic good, but one can have too much freedom, as one can have too much power. This is universally acknowledged by parents in raising children. But we never cease to be intellectual and moral children, for the defects of children are never wholly eradicated by adulthood, since none attains perfect virtue or wisdom in this life.

Reply to Objection 1: Not every good is an intrinsic good. Intrinsic goods should never be sacrificed. But wealth, power, and long life sometimes should be sacrificed, for they are not intrinsic goods, and this is evident from the fact that often they do more harm than good. Freedom is this type of good. For like wealth, power, and longevity, it is a means rather than an end in itself. Even if all desire these things, that does not mean that all are wise to do so, unless their desires are perfect.

Reply to Objection 2: (1) The freedom that is intrinsic to human nature and unalienable is free will, not political freedom.

(2) It is not true that all that is intrinsic to human nature as we find it today is an intrinsic good. Original Sin, and its observable effects in the universal tendency to selfishness, is intrinsic to human nature in its present, fallen form, but it is not an intrinsic good. Admitting intrinsic goods but not intrinsic evils is the Rousseauian one-sidedness, the opposite of the Hobbesian and Machiavellian one. When judging ourselves we must keep both our I's open.

Reply to Objection 3: Slavery, like poverty and impotence, is a physical evil when suffered, and a moral evil only when deliberately imposed on another. The argument proves only that freedom is an intrinsic physical good, like wealth and power, not an intrinsic moral good.

Article 6: Whether there is a double standard for good for states and individuals?

Objection 1: It seems that there is not, for Plato has shown, in his *Republic*, that the same four cardinal virtues of justice, wisdom, courage, and self-control constitute the definition or formal cause of the good of both the individual soul and the state by nature, and therefore always.

Objection 2: Lincoln defined good government as one "of the people, by the people, and for the people," since states are made *of* individuals as their material cause, *by* individuals, as their efficient cause, and *for* individuals as their final cause. It is reasonable to suppose that good states also must manifest the same *formal* cause as good individuals do. Now virtues perfect the form of individual souls, while vices are defects in that form. And therefore the same virtues must be the perfections of states, since they have the same essential form, while the same vices must be the defects of them.

Objection 3: A double standard would put the individual in an impossible moral quandary, for what is a vice for the individual could then be a virtue for the state, and vice versa; and in that case an individual would sin, either against his own soul or against the social order, no matter what he would do.

On the contrary, the common judgment of mankind praises individual martyrs who refuse to use force to defend themselves against unjust aggression, but blames states for doing exactly the same thing, for in defending themselves states are defending their own innocent citizens.

I answer that there are clear examples of an action being right for an individual but wrong for a state, or vice versa. For example, it is right for the state, and for a soldier who is acting in the name of the state, to attempt to kill an enemy soldier in a just war; but it is wrong for an individual, in the name of private vengeance, to attempt to kill another on his own authority, even if the other is deserving of death. And it is not wrong for an individual (especially one without a family) to let himself be killed as a martyr rather than killing another, even if killing the other would be just. In fact this is heroic. But a state would be seriously remiss in its duty to protect its innocent citizens if it practiced total pacifism and let itself be destroyed. For the state is like the father of a family: its self-defense is the defense of the lives of others, not just of itself.

It is also obviously right for a state, but not for an individual, to levy taxes, to make laws for all citizens, and to draft soldiers; and right for individuals, but not states, to marry other individuals, to write books, and to insist their children eat healthy foods.

Reply to Objection 1: This is true of essential virtues such as the four cardinal virtues, as Plato showed, and also of honesty, and charity, but not of accidental virtues which may pertain only to one order and not the other. For instance, ready wit is a minor virtue for individuals, but not for states; and the desire to perpetually increase wealth is a vice (greed, or avarice) for individuals, since their end is by nature egotistic, but it is a virtue for the state, since the state's end in increasing wealth is by nature altruistic, for it is the increase of economic ease and welfare for its citizens.

Reply to Objection 2: As noted in the reply to Objection 1, this is true for essential virtues, especially the four cardinal virtues, but not for accidental ones.

Reply to Objection 3: Precisely because there is a double standard, for states and for individuals, no individual is ever in this situation. See, e.g., the examples in the *I answer that.*

Article 7: Whether wars are ever just?

*Objection 1: It seems that t*hey are not, for war is the attempt to solve disputes by killing people. This is so contrary to reason and charity that our descendants will see us as barbarians, and war as insanity.

Objection 2: It is impossible to imagine Christ shooting a machine gun at an enemy soldier. But Christ is the ideal man and should be our standard.

Objection 3: Christ both taught and practiced nonviolence. He waged spiritual warfare against evil, not physical warfare against men. And His apostle told us that "we wrestle not against flesh and blood but against principalities and powers of wickedness in high places," i.e. evil spirits (*Ephesians* 6:12).

Objection 4: Fighting a war for the sake of peace is indeed better than fighting a war for the sake of war, but it is still an evil because a good end does not justify an evil means. If war is evil, it cannot be justly opposed by war, for evil does not eradicate evil, only good eradicates evil.

On the contrary, the main-line tradition of all three Western religions, as well as common sense, teach a "just war" theory rather than pacifism.

I answer that if no wars are just, then it is not just to fight even a defensive war to protect the innocent citizens of a country for whose public welfare the rulers are responsible; and in that case, it is also not just for the father of a family to use lethal force if necessary to protect the lives of his children against lethal threats from unjust aggressors. But even Gandhi, the most famous of pacifists, said that he would do that. Therefore some wars are just.

The concept of "a just war" should be called instead the concept of a just *warring*, for the first condition of a just war is that it be defensive, not aggressive. Even the Qur'an says that "Allah hates the aggressor." The judgment on war as an insane and barbaric invention is not incompatible with waging a just defensive war; for that is like building a backfire to extinguish a forest fire.

Once a great evil is unleashed upon the world, extreme measures are sometimes necessary to extinguish it; but since a good end does not justify an evil intention, even in cases of dire necessity a right intention is necessary. The proper intention of war is peace, not war. In other words, one of the qualifications that is needed to make a warring just is that the object hated by the warring is the war, not the persons waging it.

Reply to Objection 1: This may be true, but it does not prove that it is always unjust to go to war, especially to end or prevent this "barbarian" "insanity." The aim of war is peace, not war.

Reply to Objection 2: Christ may be our standard, but our imagination is not. It is also impossible to imagine Christ pregnant, or gambling, or cheering for the Red Sox, but these are not evils. The imagination is limited to particulars and cannot judge universals.

Reply to Objection 3: (1) When Christ taught nonviolence He was addressing individuals, not states, and taught this as a counsel of perfection, not a universal command of justice.

(2) All are called to wage spiritual warfare (*jihad*) but only some are called to wage physical warfare.

Reply to Objection 4: (1) It is true that evil cannot justly be opposed by evil. But defensive war is not intrinsically evil, while aggressive war is.

(2) Defensive war is justified by the principle of double effect. The moral end of defense is not to destroy human lives but to end the war and protect the lives that are threatened by aggression, by disabling the aggressors. Although the destroying of enemy lives is a *foreseen* effect, it is not the *desired* effect. And it is unavoidable.

Article 8: Whether human law should be superior to human wills?

Objection 1: It seems that human laws are created by human wills. It is contrary to the ontological order that a creator should submit to his creature. Therefore law should not be superior to human wills.

Objection 2: Laws, being made by contingent and changing entities, that is, fallible persons with changing wills, and made at changing times *for* changing times, should be changeable, not binding, if they are to reflect the nature of their makers. In order to serve persons, whose opinions are changeable, and for situations which are changing, laws must be flexible, not rigid.

On the contrary, Aristotle says that the difference between a good regime and a bad one, in any form of government, is whether it is a rule of law or a rule of will. And history shows many malign examples of the rule of will, especially dictatorships, including the dictatorship of majorities, such as Rousseau's supposedly infallible "general will."

I answer that the human will is weak and foolish and needs time, deliberation, and experience to correct itself. It tends to be arbitrary and irrational, especially when empowered immediately. But law does not tend to be arbitrary, since laws are usually made after long and deliberate consideration by those who are chosen for their wisdom and moderation. And since the rule of reason is better than the rule of arbitrariness, the rule of law is better than the rule of will.

Also, the rule of law over human wills is a good thing in itself, for law curbs and disciplines wills, and thereby educates wills in self-control, which is one of the most difficult and necessary virtues for states as well as for individuals.

Reply to Objection 1: A law is like a promise: its whole intent is to bind one's will. Thus the intention of its creator is honored if and only if it does bind. And this is what is meant by the law being superior to human wills.

"The laws of the Medes and the Persians" were irrevocable, even by the King. Therefore they were decided only after two days of deliberation. On one day, everyone was sober, and on the other day, everyone was drunk. If both days did not produce the same result, the law was not enacted.

Reply to Objection 2: Human laws are indeed changeable, and this makes them flexible, not absolute and unchangeable, like the natural law. But they are not *easily or immediately* changeable, otherwise they would not be binding. This double character of human laws makes them faithful to the double intention of their makers; for one of those intentions is precisely that the laws be binding while they last, and the other intention is that they be changeable, after due consideration, unlike the natural law.

Article 9: Whether the principle of subsidiarity is true?

Objection 1: It seems that it is not, for this principle states that whenever feasible, what can better be done by smaller and more local levels of government should not be done by larger ones. This assumes a hierarchy of (1) first individuals, (2) then families, (3) then extended families, (4) then neighborhoods, (5) then local communities (cities and towns), (6) then states, (7) then national governments. But this principle is a mere tautology, for it is equally tautological that whenever feasible, what can be done better by larger levels of government should not be done by smaller ones. Since the principle does not define "feasible" or "better," it can work either way.

Objection 2: The principle leads to the absurd conclusion that local militias are preferable to national armies, that local tax collectors are preferable to federal ones, and that each community should construct its own local part of an interstate highway.

Objection 3: There are many human rights possessed by all as a matter of natural law, such as life, liberty, and property. These must be guaranteed to all by all and enforced by all, not relegated to diverse local authorities. But these are the most important rights and principles. Therefore the central government, whose task is to enforce them, is more important than local governments, whose task is to deal with lesser things.

Objection 4: The principle of subsidiarity calls for the most decentralized state that is feasible. But a centralized state is more efficient. It is also better for the poor, for they are more in need of social services than the rich or the middle class. So a "preferential option for the poor" would call for a more socialized state, with, e.g., socialized medicine, where health care is free for all rather than being dependent on ability to pay, which unjustly favors the rich.

On the contrary, Augustine describes government as a "necessary evil" due to sin. But necessary evils should be decreased as much as is feasible, not increased. Therefore government should be decreased and localized as much as is feasible. ("Small is beautiful.") This is what subsidiarity does. And the Constitution of the United States, after listing the powers of the federal government, explicitly states that all other powers not mentioned there are relegated to the states, or to individuals.

I answer that the principle of subsidiarity states that no higher organization should do work that a lower, subsidiary organization can do, for the higher exists to empower and perfect the lower, not to absorb or replace it, as grace perfects nature. If this were not so, then the rights that nature gives to individuals and families would be pointless. The duty of the nation-state is to help individuals, families, voluntary associations, and local communities to flourish, and to intervene only when necessary for the common good (such as a military draft) or when they fail to regulate themselves (as happened with big business under early capitalism).

Also, decentralization allows more variety in experimenting with different solutions to common social problems; a federal government can learn from the successes and failures of its diverse states.

Reply to Objection 1: The principle is not tautological, for it privileges the smaller rather than the larger unit as the "fallback" or "default" position. It says that it is always more feasible and better for a smaller or more local level of government to perform a service if it can be done by either the smaller or the larger. (Obviously, sometimes there is no choice; for instance only individuals, not governments, can get pregnant; and only governments, not individuals, can make laws binding on all citizens.)

Reply to Objection 2: These absurd conclusions are not entailed by the principle, for they are examples of the few services which obviously local communities cannot do as well as the nation as a whole.

But it is regarding the vaster number of services which can be performed by either local or national agents, such as health care, day care, and censorship of art, if any, that the principle asserts local control to be preferable. The principle is not absolute but favors decentralization only when feasible.

Reply to Objection 3: The objection is quite true, but it is perfectly compatible with the principle of subsidiarity. And the objection does *not* entail the conclusion that the central government is also more important than the local in enforcing these many "lesser things" outside natural law.

Reply to Objection 4: According to polling results, it is the rich who oppose, and the poor and middle class who favor, decentralization and subsidiarity in principle—though of course the poor welcome free government services and welfare. For it is the poor who tend to think and act locally, while the rich tend to think and act globally. (Who reads the local neighborhood newspapers? Who reads *The New York Times?*)

Social services, charity or "safety nets" for the poor, and health care, are usually more personally effective, more prompt, and more economically efficient when given and administered locally. (Compare Canada's or England's system of socialized medicine with America's system of more privatized medicine.) For centralization always multiplies bureaucracies and "middlemen," whose salaries necessarily take both money and power away from both the givers and the receivers of such services.

Article 10: Whether there should be a world organization of states?

Objection 1: It seems that there should not be, for the principle of subsidiarity, which we have already established, favors decentralization whenever possible; but a world organization of states such as the United Nations tempts the world to maximal centralization and eventually a single world state. This, in turn, would be the most dangerous of all forms of government, for the same reason that monarchy is more dangerous than aristocracy or democracy: because it centralizes power, and thus the power to corrupt.

Objection 2: States would have to yield at least some of their sovereignties to such an organization. But this would mean that there were no longer any *sovereign* states.

Objection 3: Either an international organization has sovereignty over individual nations, or not. If they do, this leads toward a single World State. If they do not, they have no power over nations. This is why the League of Nations failed to prevent World War I and the United Nations failed to prevent many smaller wars.

On the contrary, world opinion massively supports the existence of the United Nations or some better version of it.

I answer that as Aristotle said, the village and the state are the natural outgrowths of the family. The next step in this progression is a world organization of states, which should do the same to nations as nations should do to smaller communities, smaller communities to families, and families to individuals, namely protect, foster, and perfect rather than rival and absorb them. We live in a "global village" with a global economy and a global military fragility where war in any one place always threatens to spread to others and spark another world war. Under these conditions, an international organization is morally necessary.

In an age of advanced technology, especially nuclear weapons, the absence of any world organization of nations would strongly tempt rogue nations to commit mass murder and nuclear aggression that would threaten the entire human race. And even lesser threats to human welfare, such as "ethnic cleansing," need to be prevented by international sanctions. For human nature being what it is, nations, like individuals, will always include some dangerous "black sheep."

Reply to Objection 1: A world organization of states must be distinguished from a world state, and need not have the authority of a state, just as a meeting or treaty between diplomats from two states does not constitute a third state and does not have the authority of a state.

Reply to Objection 2: National sovereignty, unlike divine sovereignty, is *not* absolute. It is relative to human welfare and natural law. If these two goods call for some such world organization, then national sovereignties must yield somewhat to it—but not wholly, for the elimination of plural national sovereignties would eliminate the many goods brought about by this pluralism.

Reply to Objection 3: (1) If an international organization is morally necessary, as proved below, then the failure of early forms of it do not invalidate the need to find more workable forms.

(2) An international organization will have to have some sovereignty over nations, as the state took over some sovereignty from formerly independent villages and the village from formerly independent families. But this necessary transfer of sovereignty should and can be limited and defined by both natural law and consensual agreement.

Internal sovereignty can and should be preserved in each state, but external sovereignty must be limited; otherwise, if it is not, eventually a nuclear disaster is very likely.

Question X:
Aesthetics

Article 1: Whether beauty is an objective reality?

Objection 1: It seems that it is not, for it is well known that "beauty is in the eye of the beholder" and that "love (of beauty) is blind." To Dante, Beatrice was a goddess; to others, she was quite plain.

Objection 2: Objective realities are verifiable by reason. Beauty is not. Therefore beauty is not an objective reality.

Objection 3: People disagree about beauty, more than about almost anything else. What everyone disagrees about is subjective, like the pleasures in the tastes of different foods.

On the contrary, the immediate experience of every artist, in every art, is the awareness and love of some beauty that is an *object* of that awareness and love. The *love* of beauty can also be studied, and made the object of a second, reflective act, but not until the first, non-reflective act has occurred, which is the awareness of beauty as an object — just as our acts of knowing can be known, reflectively, but not until first some real thing has first been known, and that primary act reflected upon by the second act. (See Question VI, Article 3 and *ST* I, 85, 2.)

I answer that (1) If we conceive both "art" and "beauty" broadly, we may define art as the love of beauty (and a "work of art" as the product and expression of that love). Any human act, or act of a human subject, is by definition subjective, and its object objective. Now if art is the love of (objective) beauty, it is not the love of the (subjective) love of beauty. For nothing can be both subjective and objective at the same time and in the same respect.

(2) If beauty were subjective, then the love of beauty would be

egotistic: it would be only the love of *my* beauty, or of my experience of beauty, or of my love of beauty. But the love of beauty is not egotistic, for it is ec-static, drawing the lover out of himself in self-forgetful admiration. Nothing can be both egotistic and ec-static, for the object of all egotistic desires is the desiring self, while the object of all ec-static desires is something other.

(3) If beauty were subjective, then the love of beauty would really be the love of the love, or subjective experience, of beauty, so that what appeared to be objective would really be subjective. But if that were so, then the object of *that* act-of-loving-the-love-of-beauty would, *a fortiori*, be subjective, so the-love-of-beauty would really be the-love-of-the-love-of beauty; and the-love-of-the-love-of-beauty would really be the-love-of-the-love-of-the-love-of-beauty. But this is absurd, for it entails an infinite regress in which the original object loved diminishes and disappears, like light in an infinitely long hall of mirrors.

Reply to Objection 1: The cliché is false, whether taken literally or not. Taken literally, it would mean that when Dante exclaims to Beatrice, "Your eyes are beautiful," it is Dante's eyes that are beautiful, not Beatrice's. Even if not taken literally, it is false, for it means that beauty is a subjective sense or feeling, not a judgment of fact. No lover of beauty agrees with this. Dante, e.g., insists that true love opens the eyes rather than blinds them. If love is blind, then God is blind, for God is love. (See *The Figure of Beatrice* by Charles Williams and *The Theology of Romantic Love* by Mary McDermott Sheideler.)

Reply to Objection 2: Not all objective realities are verifiable by ordinary reason. For instance, the love of God to man is an objective reality but is not verifiable by ordinary reason, but by faith. If objective reality is only that which is verifiable by ordinary human reason, then objective reality is very small indeed!

Reply to Objection 3: (1) Disagreement does not prove subjectivity. If everyone disagreed about the correct answer to a complex mathematical equation, or about the location of a hidden treasure, that disagreement would not make the truth of the matter subjective.

(2) Disagreement in aesthetics is caused by the great variety of aesthetic receptors of beauty, not by the lack of an object to receive.

And this variety is not a defect, as it would be in the sciences, but a glory, as it is in friendships, each of which is a unique appreciation of a unique set of personal qualities in the friend.

(3) Disagreement is not total. Many significant and nearly unanimous agreements about what is and is not beautiful emerge from the passage of time, both individually (from childhood to maturity) and historically (over the centuries). There is a canon of classics in each of the arts, through the canons are "soft" rather than "hard."

Article 2: Whether beauty consists in harmony?

Objection 1: It seems that it does not, for as Plotinus points out in the *Ennead* "On Beauty," simple colors are beautiful, but they are not harmonies.

Objection 2: This definition is too artistically limited, for it is taken from music rather than the other arts. And even there, dissonances are often more beautiful than consonances.

Objection 3: This definition is also too culturally and geographically limited. It does not account for the beauty of disharmonies such as the deliberate irregularities in Northern European, Romantic, or Victorian architecture as distinct from Southern European, Classical, or Mediterranean architecture; or for the beauty of darkness, horror, and ugliness in tales of terror.

Objection 4: This definition does not account for the beauty of the infinite, which is not a proportion and therefore not a harmony. And thus, by this definition God would not be beautiful—truly a *reductio ad absurdum*.

On the contrary, nearly all premodern authorities (Plato, Aristotle, Augustine, Cassiodorus, Aquinas) define beauty as a harmony.

I answer that the greatest of all works of art, other than persons, is the cosmos itself. But the cosmos is held together by physical and mathematical harmony among the multitude of diverse entities, forces, and exceedingly complex laws in the cosmos. This is even more evident in modern physics than in ancient cosmology. And the greatest beauty in persons is love, which is the harmony of persons and their wills and goods with each other. Truth is the harmony between what is thought and what is. Virtue is the harmony between what is willed and what is good. Thus all the things that are beautiful are harmonies: art, the cosmos, persons, truth, and virtue.

Reply to Objection 1: Colors are *not* simple or absolute but complex and relative. So they too can be harmonious.

Reply to Objection 2: (1) The analogy is taken from music but it is applicable to all the arts because all forms of physical energy occur in waves and rhythms.

(2) Furthermore, music may be the primal and privileged art and the primal language, the language in which the cosmos was created, as ancient sages say. (See Article 10.)

(3) Harmony is not limited to consonances. The harmony of dissonances *with* consonances is part of music's higher harmonies, as colors are harmonious blends of light with darkness. The dissonances frame, reveal, and augment the beauty of the consonances as darkness does to light, absence to presence, and pains to pleasures.

Reply to Objection 3: These irregularities are like the dissonances spoken of in the above Reply.

Reply to Objection 4: Even in the infinite God, there is a perfect harmony among the three Persons of the Trinity, and also among the divine attributes such as mercy and justice, gentleness and strength, and transcendence and immanence.

Article 3: Whether beauty is the object of love?

Objection 1: It seems that it is not, for often we rightly love what appears *less* beautiful, when the love of something more beautiful would be harmful, such as exciting physical dangers or pleasant immoral indulgences.

Objection 2: If beauty were always the object of love, as Plato taught in the *Symposium*, there would be no sin, as Plato also taught ("evil is only ignorance"). Since this consequent is false, so is the antecedent that entails it.

The entailment is explained as follows. The only reason we sin is the lure of something that is loved because it is attractive, i.e. beautiful, in the sin. When we resist sin, therefore, we resist the lure of beauty and love moral goodness instead. In such a case there is a conflict between the good and the beautiful. Now since the object of love is always the apparent good, if that object were also always perceived as beautiful, there would never be such a conflict in this life between the good and the beautiful, as there will not be in Heaven. Since there is such a conflict, it follows that the object of love is not always beauty.

Objection 3: We often love things that are not beautiful, even in appearance, such as our own unjust advantage, revenge, or the destruction of something beautiful. Sometimes we love an evil thing simply because it is evil, like the forbidden fruit in Eden; for the mere forbidding of something makes it attractive to us.

Objection 4: Sometimes we are bored by beauty and prefer ugliness; for instance, we are soon bored with a beautiful flower show and yearn for a horror movie—the uglier, the better. In such a case we do not love beauty, but ugliness.

On the contrary, Plato observes in the *Symposium* that we love only what is beautiful, and experience confirms this by many examples.

I answer that if the terms are conceived broadly enough, beauty can be defined as *id quod videtur placet,* "that which, being seen, pleases." Whatever (*id quod*) is apparently (*videtur*) pleasing (*placet*) and satisfying is the object of our desire, for desire always seeks its own satisfaction. And whatever is desired, is loved. Therefore beauty is the object of love.

Reply to Objection 1: In such cases we rightly love the higher beauty of the good more than the lower beauty of the tempting evil. Goodness is not other than beauty but is by its very goodness beautiful.

Reply to Objection 2: When we resist sin, we are aware (at least by faith) of the higher beauty of virtue, and our attraction to its beauty overpowers our temptation to prefer lower beauties. It is only when sin clouds our vision that we experience an apparent conflict between the good and the beautiful. When we resist sin, we perceive their ultimate harmony.

There is never truly, but only apparently, a conflict between goodness and beauty, since the highest beauty is the beauty of goodness, and the higher the goodness, the greater the beauty. Thus God is the maximum and archetypal standard of both goodness and of beauty; and the most beautiful thing in this world is a perfected saint.

Reply to Objection 3: As Augustine discovered in reflecting, in the *Confessions*, on his adolescent theft of forbidden pears for no apparent reason, no one can love evil as such, but only when some apparent good is attached to it, such as friendly association with other evil men, or the divine prerogative of being above the law. Evils such as injustice, revenge, or destruction gratify an evil desire in us, and the gratification of any desire is pleasant, and thus psychologically beautiful, at least in appearance.

Reply to Objection 4: We do this only when the ugliness appears somehow beautiful to us (e.g. because it is exciting) and the beauty somehow ugly (e.g. because it is boring). We never love ugliness *qua* ugliness but only *qua* beauty; thus the formal object of our love is always beauty even if the material object is not.

Article 4: Whether beauty moves us more than truth?

Objection 1: It seems that it does not, for it is psychologically impossible for us to believe what we know to be untrue, no matter how beautiful that would be. Thus we are all "tough-minded" and honest enough to disbelieve in fairies and Santa Claus simply because they are not true, even though a world that contained them would appear more beautiful to us.

Objection 2: Judgments of truth are much more universal than judgments of beauty; and the demand to know truth rather than to be in ignorance is more universal than the demand to see beauty. What is more universal is also stronger in man. Therefore we are more strongly moved by truth than by beauty. We can endure not seeing beauty but we cannot endure not knowing truth. We prefer ugliness to ignorance.

On the contrary, there are far more poems in praise of beauty than in praise of truth. Poems may not be a reliable index of objective truth, but they are a reliable index of what moves human love.

I answer that the beauty of a place, a religion, or a person will "sell" it more effectively than anything else, even its truth, goodness, or utility. Thus we see people prefer to live in more expensive and harsher places such as the stormy seashore or the high and dangerous mountains, rather than in duller and more economically efficient places; and they are attracted to more mysterious religions that are full of ritual and art rather than ones that are plain and Puritan, even if the latter seem more moral and more rational; and men are more attracted to women who are beautiful in face and figure than those who are better for them in any and every other way.

This is also true of spiritual beauty, for nothing is more attractive and irresistible than a saint. This is how the Christian religion won the world: not through its mysterious and apparently irrational theology, or its difficult, uncompromising and unflattering morality, but by the spiritual beauty of its saints. (This is also the reason for the power of a beautiful liturgy.)

Reply to Objection 1: Even though we do not believe, with our minds, in fairies or Santa Claus, our desires and imaginations are often moved more by such fantasies than by the apparently less beautiful realities that replace them in our minds, such as germs or taxes.

Thus, while our minds believe in the limitations of physical laws, our desires and imaginations prefer stories about magic.

Reply to Objection 2: This conclusion is simply a false observation. Lack of truth (ignorance) causes us less unhappiness, at least immediately and in itself, than lack of beauty, even though the eventual consequences of ignorance may be more severe. We cannot be happy without some kind of beauty, for it is the object of our love, as has been shown above. And since love is the central power of the soul, the satisfaction of love is the primary cause of happiness.

Although judgments of beauty are less universal than judgments of truth, and forms of beauty more diverse than kinds of truth, still the need for some form of beauty is as great and as universal as the need for truth.

Article 5: Whether beauty moves us more than goodness?

Objection 1: It seems that it does not, for it has been demonstrated above (Article 3, Objection and Reply 2) that beauty and goodness are not separate and therefore cannot be contrasted. For beauty is simply the attractiveness of something that is (at least apparently) good.

Objection 2: Beauty is a property of, and is relative to, goodness, being its effulgence or appearance or attractiveness, But a property cannot be stronger than that of which it is a property, nor can the relative be stronger than that to which it is relative. Therefore beauty cannot be stronger than goodness.

On the contrary, when someone speaks of love, the hearers always first think of beauty, and they think of goodness only later, if at all. Thus beauty moves us more than goodness.

I answer that (1) If beauty did not move us more than goodness, temptation would be impossible, for temptation uses the attractiveness, or apparent beauty, of something that is evil to lure us to prefer it to what is good.

(2) We observe very commonly that men are more attracted to beauty than to goodness in their choice of women, cars, and lifestyles. Whether or not this also applies equally to women, must be decided by a woman, not a man.

Reply to Objection 1: When we must choose between (1) a thing that seems more beautiful but less good in some other way (especially good morally, or good physically) and (2) a thing that seems more good in this other way but less beautiful, we *do* compare the two things by contrasting these two standards. For instance, we choose to risk or to forego interesting physical dangers, or we choose to indulge or resist temptations to forbidden pleasures.

Reply to Objection 2: This is true objectively but not subjectively. What is in itself greater may move us less, and what is in itself relative may move us more than that which is absolute. For we respond to appearances first, and often do not penetrate very deeply beyond them into the realities of which they are the appearances.

Article 6: Whether souls are more beautiful than bodies?

Objection 1: It seems that they are not, for we are more powerfully attracted to bodily things than to spiritual things. Thus we do not need to be reminded to turn our attention to physical beauties and goods, but to spiritual ones. But we are more attracted to the greater beauties, for the greater the beauty, the more the power of attraction. Thus bodies must be more beautiful than souls, not souls more beautiful than bodies.

Objection 2: As Plotinus says at the beginning of his treatise "On Beauty," beauty is primarily visual and physical. Only analogically can souls be said to be beautiful. But the literal is greater than the analogical. Therefore the beauty of bodies is greater than that of souls.

On the contrary, the pagan sages (Plato, Plotinus, Buddha) as well as the saints (David, Solomon, Christ, Paul) teach that souls can be far more beautiful (or more ugly) than bodies.

I answer that (1) Just as our souls can understand more by reason than our bodies can know by sensation, and just as souls can conceive more by reason than bodies can perceive by sensory imagination, and just as souls can suffer or enjoy many more pains and pleasures than bodies can, so souls can manifest greater beauties, and greater ugliness, than bodies can. This is because souls are less limited than bodies. For by reason we can rise to a knowledge of universals, among which are goodness and beauty; and an infinity of particulars can be chosen to exemplify these universals. But bodies are limited to concrete particulars, one at a time.

(2) Souls, unlike bodies, can know and love God, not just His works. But God is infinite beauty, while His works have only finite beauty. Knowing and loving beauty makes the knower and lover more beautiful, for the perfections of the objects known and loved come to reside, to an extent, in the souls that know and love them. Therefore souls, which can know and love God, can participate in God's infinite beauty, as bodies cannot.

Reply to Objection 1: Due to the spiritual blindness caused by sin and selfishness, it is *not* true that we are always more attracted to the greater beauties.

Reply to Objection 2: (1) The priority of physical beauty is temporal, not ontological.

(2) Since physical things are expressions of, and caused by, divine thoughts and intentions (although *our* thoughts and intentions are expressions of, and caused by, these physical things), therefore physical beauty is an expression of spiritual beauty rather than vice versa, as our bodies are expressions and manifestations of our souls rather than souls expressions of bodies. Thus we speak of "body language."

Article 7: Whether persons are the most beautiful things in the world?

Objection 1: It seems that they are not, for persons are the subjects who perceive and judge beauty, and they can be perceived and judged only by a second, reflective judgment, as was shown above (Article 1). But secondary and reflective objects cannot be greater than primary ones. Therefore the objective beauty known *by* persons is greater than the beauty *of* the human subjects or persons.

Objection 2: Persons alone are defiled by sin, while everything else in the creation is pure and perfect. Our being alone is divided: as Sartre puts it, our "being-for-itself," or subjective existence, does not coincide with, and indeed is alienated from, our "being-in-itself," or our human nature. Thus while everything else in the universe is ontologically beautiful, we alone, i.e. persons, can be called ontologically ugly.

On the contrary, Aquinas says that the person is "that which is most perfect in all nature." (*ST* I, 29, 3). And what is most perfect is most good and most beautiful. Therefore the person is the most beautiful thing in all nature.

I answer that among all creatures only persons are subjects because they alone are created in the image and likeness of God, who is "I AM." What is created in God's image is by nature more Godlike than what is not. What is most Godlike by nature is most beautiful, for God is the archetype and standard of beauty. Therefore persons are most beautiful.

Reply to Objection 1: That the objective beauty known is greater than the subective beauty of the knower is true *theologically* insofar as the beauty known by human persons is the divine beauty, or points to divine beauty. It is also true *psychologically*, in that beautiful and good persons do not perceive their own beauty, but are self-forgetful. But it is not true *ontologically*, for only human persons are created in God's image, and thus possess greater ontological goodness, and therefore also greater ontological beauty, than anything else in the universe. (Thus it is not *always* true that reflective objects cannot be greater than primary objects.)

Reply to Objection 2: Even if true, this does not entail the conclusion that persons are not the most beautiful things in the universe. For if "the corruption of the best (and the most beautiful) are the worst (and ugliest)," then the worst, and ugliest, are corruptions of the best, and the most beautiful.

Article 8: Whether all persons are beautiful?

Objection 1: It seems that they are not, for some persons are great evildoers. Since the corruption of the best is the worst, these persons are the ugliest and least beautiful of all things in nature. Hitler is uglier than a hyena.

Objection 2: Ontological beauty, which persists even in evildoers, is not as important as moral and spiritual beauty; for the former exists, in man, as a potency for the latter. But men *lack* moral and spiritual beauty, for all are sinners, as the saints are the first to admit, and some are notorious sinners, and thus notoriously *un*-beautiful.

On the contrary, the most important of all moral obligations is to have love and goodwill for all persons. But we are not to love evil, only good. And whatever is good, is also beautiful. Therefore all persons are beautiful.

I answer that the two causes of the beauty of persons are the ontological beauty of what they are, as made by God and nature, and the moral beauty of what they make of themselves and their lives by their choices and their loves. In all persons, no matter how evil, ontological goodness remains, as explained above, and even some moral goodness. For if no moral goodness remained at all, they would cease to be human entirely. The processes by which even a monster like Hitler became more and more evil throughout his life are traceable and reversible in principle, as long as free will remains.

If not all persons, but only the good, were beautiful, then it would not be good or praiseworthy to love, help, reform, convert, and save the wicked, especially at the expense of great sacrifice, for there would be nothing in them worth loving, helping reforming, converting, saving, or sacrificing for.

Reply to Objection 1: Great evildoers are ugly only because they have defaced the image of God, their personhood, which is the most beautiful of all things in nature. But this image remains even when defaced, like a great painting beneath layers of dirt. Great evildoers are morally ugly only because they are ontologically beautiful.

Reply to Objection 2: This is true, but the conclusion does not necessarily follow that their ontological and spiritual beauty is not also the greatest in nature. An actor's performance may contain great defects and few glories, yet its perfection is far greater than that of even the best scenery.

Article 9: Whether God is beautiful?

Objection 1: It seems that He is not, for beauty consists of harmony (see Article 2), and harmony is a relationship between different parts of a whole. Whatever has parts is finite, for one part of the finite limits another. But God has no parts, since He is infinite. Therefore God is not beautiful, but beyond beauty.

Objection 2: God is Being ("I AM"), Truth ("Logos"), and Goodness (love), which are ascribed to the three divine Persons. There is no room for an equal Fourth, Beauty.

Objection 3: God is "that than which nothing greater can be conceived" (St. Anselm). But a God who is beyond beauty is greater than a God who is beautiful. Therefore God is not beautiful, but beyond beauty.

On the contrary, Psalms 27:4 says: "One thing I have asked of the Lord,/ That will I seek after:/ That I may dwell in the house of the Lord/ All the days of my life,/ To behold the beauty of the Lord."

I answer that (1) Whatever is true and good is beautiful, for beauty is a property that flows from truth and goodness. But God is supremely true and good. Therefore God is supremely beautiful.

(2) If God were not beautiful, we would not be attracted to Him

and long to contemplate Him; for beauty is that by which truth and goodness attract us.

(3) Furthermore, if God were not beautiful, then either there would be no perfect archetype of beauty, which would render true judgments of relative beauties impossible, or this absolute would be something other than God, which is idolatrous.

(4) God is the summit of beauty because He is the summit of love, and love is the most beautiful of all acts.

Reply to Objection 1: As explained above (Article 2, Objection and Reply 4), God is not only one but also a harmony of three divine persons, and this harmony is love. God has no *parts*, being supremely one; but God is three *Persons*. If God were only one Person, He could be a *lover* but not complete love itself; and He would need creatures in order to love anyone but Himself with altruistic love. But God cannot need creatures. Therefore He is more than only one Person, and these can be in harmony, and thus beautiful.

Reply to Objection 2: Beauty is the eternal child of the eternal spiritual intercourse between truth and goodness, as Truth is the eternal child ("Son") of Being, and the Goodness of love is Their eternal relationship with each other.

Reply to Objection 3: "Beyond beauty" is meaningless and self-contradictory, like "beyond being," unless beauty is misunderstood as something only finite and imperfect. Similarly, some philosophers ("essentialists") speak of God as "beyond being" because they misconceive being as finite essence rather than infinite existence.

Article 10: Whether music is the primal art and language?

Objection 1: It seems that music is not the primal language, for music is a decoration of speech, and added to it. But what is added cannot be primal or prior.

Objection 2: No scientific research into early languages by anthropologists finds any language that is primarily musical. Nor do we find, among preserved languages, a progression from the more to the less musical.

Objection 3: Music is the most primitive art, rather than the highest one, for it is the only human art whose beauty can be appreciated, in part, even by some brute animals.

Objection 4: Music is the least rational of the arts. But it is reason that raises man up above the beasts. Therefore music is not the highest of the arts.

On the contrary, everyone senses that there are profound meanings in some music that transcend the ability of any other art, or of language, to express. This is evidence that music is the highest art. And very young, very old, and very ill people can be observed to respond to music even when incapable of speech. This is evidence that music is the primal language.

I answer that music is the primary art because everything in the universe is held together by harmonious musical waves of energy/matter, and God is the highest music of all, which is the harmony of love. Music has the ability, more than any other art, to ravish us into out-of-body experiences, or transcendence of self-consciousness.

Music is the original language, the universal language spoken before Babel and in Eden, and is still universally "understood." For it is a natural language, not an artificial language, like all others. Adam and Eve lived in harmony in Eden because they lived in music.

Reply to Objection 1: (1) What is added later temporally can sometimes be primal and prior ontologically, as one can add a relationship with God to one's life if it had been lacking before.

(2) Not everything earlier is less, and not everything greater is more; for God is earlier than the universe.

(3) Music is not evolved and ornamented poetry, and poetry is not evolved and ornamented prose; prose is fallen and devolved poetry, and poetry is fallen and devolved music. In music the universe was made.

Reply to Objection 2: Scientific research cannot explore as far back as the origin of mankind and language. One would not expect to find traces of a 100,000-year-old language, any more than one would expect to find traces of apples, snakes, or loincloths from the Garden of Eden.

Great music sometimes preserves some echoes of Eden, through the deep racial memory of something like the collective unconscious; that is why we are irresistibly drawn to it, as Ulysses and E.T. are drawn to their home.

Reply to Objection 3: What is the highest can also descend into what is lowest, by its ontological universality or by its moral humility.

Reply to Objection 4: There is a higher reason that transcends ordinary reason, and this is seen in mystical experience. Music transcends ordinary reason, not by being inferior to it, like pleasure and pain, but by being superior to it, like mystical experience.

Question XI:
Sample Questions in Ten Extensions of Philosophy

Sample Question 1. Philosophy of religion: Whether organized religion has done more harm than good?

Objection 1: It seems that it has not, for war is the most destructive of human enterprises and most wars have originated in religious quarrels.

Objection 2: Religion has elicited more loyalty and passion, throughout history, than any other human enterprise. This is shown by the fact that more people are willing to sacrifice their lives for religion than for anything else. What elicits the most passion does so either for unity and harmony or for disunity and conflict. But religion does so for disunity and conflict, since each religion teaches that it alone is totally true and all others in error about something very important. Thus religion divides mankind more than anything else.

Objection 3: Religion tends to hypocrisy, for all men fail but no one wants to admit failure in things they deem supremely important, and religion is deemed supremely important by its believers.

Objection 4: Religion makes man maximally unhappy, for religion's impossibly high ideals naturally induce guilt, and few things make man more unhappy than guilt. Religion teaches man that he is a sinner, and this impairs self-esteem and self-acceptance, which is a precondition of both happiness and good behavior.

Objection 5: Religions have always been patriarchal, thus perpetrating many injustices against half the human race, women.

On the contrary, the images of the world's religions are typically images of peace, not of war. Religions typically exalt the victims of violence (the martyrs), not the perpetrators of it.

I answer that in all times and places, those who have practiced the teachings of their religion, rather than violated them, have typically worked for peace, not for war, and have bound up the wounds of war and violence rather than causing them. Because the corruption of the best things are the worst things, some of the most terrible wars have also been fought for reasons that seemed religious to their participants.

Even religions that arose in primitive and violent conditions, like Islam and Judaism, mitigated that violence by demanding much stricter moral criteria for war, such as justice instead of personal vengeance.

Reply to Objection 1: (1) Many wars have been religious simply because most people have been religious.

(2) All religions teach the evil of selfishness, envy, hate, and aggression, which are always the real origin of war.

(3) Eastern religions tend to pacifism, and Western religions teach that only just wars may be fought, and that only wars that are necessary, moral, and defensive are just.

(4) There were thirty-two major wars in the 20th century. Only two of them had anything to do with religion.

Reply to Objection 2: Religion's practical and moral components are more important to most people than its theoretical and theological components. Even if religions divide theologically, they unite morally, for all religions teach essentially the same high morality of unselfishness, altruism, and compassion: nothing less radical than the displacement of the ego. Rarely in human history has any non-religious morality risen this high.

Reply to Objection 3: All religions teach the need for humility and honesty, and condemn hypocrisy. Religions also offer and command mercy and forgiveness.

Reply to Objection 4: (1) Guilt, like pain, is necessity if it is true and accurate. (2) Religion vastly *raises* self-esteem by calling us to higher goals. (3) Western religions also teach man not only that he is a sinner but that he is precious to God, loved and forgiven, and must forgive. Eastern religions teach man not only that he is foolish, unenlightened and asleep, but that he is also full of unacknowledged light.

(4) Religion has made men happier. This is empirically provable by actuarial statistics. Atheistic psychiatrists frequently encourage religion to their patients because they see its happy effects in their lives.

(5) Religion makes us happier by opposing war and selfishness.

Reply to Objection 5: In primitive times injustices to women abounded everywhere. In these conditions even patriarchal religions like primitive Judaism and Islam mitigated rather than increased injustice against women by giving them more rights than they had before, not fewer, though by the standards of later and more mature developments these were still inadequate.

Sample Question 2. Philosophy of history: Whether history is a meaningful story rather than a series of accidents?

Objection 1: It seems that it is not, for as even Hegel admits in his *Philosophy of History*, history appears as "the slaughter-bench at which the happiness of peoples, the wisdom of States, and the virtue of individuals have been victimized."

Objection 2: If history were meaningful, there could be a science of it. But there is no science of history, for science requires predictability, but history is random and unpredictable.

Objection 3: Belief that history is a meaningful story presupposes the existence of a divine storyteller, a divine providence. But this is a matter of faith, not reason. The meaningfulness of history does not appear to our reason. If it did, it would not require faith.

On the contrary, ever since the Pentateuch, Herodotus, and Thucydides, men have written history as a meaningful story. This could not be done with something that is totally random, like flipping a coin. Therefore history is not random but meaningful.

I answer that if history is meaningless, so are the parts of which it is made. But those parts are the lives of all men and women. Therefore if history is meaningless, so are all human lives in it. But pronouncements about the meaninglessness of human life are part of human life. Therefore if all human life and history are meaningless, so are pronouncements about that fact, which are thus shown to be self-contradictory.

Furthermore, we *complain* about the apparent meaninglessness of history and individual lives, thus judging them by a meaningful *standard* of meaning, as we judge evil by good, falsehoods by truth, and darkness by light. But we could not judge by this standard unless we knew it, and we could not know it if it was not in any way real.

Reply to Objection 1: Hegel goes on to add that appearances do not exhaust reality, and to note that "the question involuntarily arises to what principle, to what final aim these enormous sacrifices have been offered." These sacrifices, while often tragically unnecessary, were not meaningless. People do in fact die for causes. If these tragedies were really meaningless, they could not be the subjects of great stories.

Reply to Objection 2: There is no exact science of history for the same reason there is no exact science of an individual life. Unpredictability does not logically entail meaninglessness. History is unpredictable because of human free will, which is not meaningless but the precondition for human and moral meaning. Free will follows from reason, and reason is the *opposite* of randomness.

Reply to Objection 3: Faith in the meaningfulness of history is neither wholly rational nor wholly irrational but *partly* rational. "For now we see [with our reason] through a glass, darkly"—but we do see something, some clues, at least, like the loose threads on the back side of history's tapestry. (See *The Bridge of San Luis Rey* by Thornton Wilder, which shows how these meaningful clues do not necessarily *presuppose* God but can be *reasons for* belief in God.)

Sample Question 3. Philosophy of science: Whether science and technology do humanity more harm than good?

Objection 1: It seems that they do, for science and technology augment the powers of mind and body that man already possesses. But man is foolish, selfish, and evil. Therefore science and technology augment human evil.

Objection 2: Good is more fragile than evil. As *Ecclesiastes* says, one dead fly can ruin an entire barrel of the perfumer's ointment. One madman can murder dozens of innocent people. One finger on a nuclear button can destroy billions of lives. One affair can ruin a marriage. Therefore even if the augmentation of human powers by science and technology do much good, they do much more evil, since it takes only a little evil to ruin much good.

Objection 3: When people are allowed to choose where to live, by possession of money and leisure (e.g. when they take their vacations), they choose the least technologically developed places. All men choose what makes them happy. Therefore technology has made us unhappy, and its absence makes us happier.

Objection 4: The rich, the smart, and the powerful are more unhappy than the poor, the simple-minded, and the meek and humble. This is made evident by comparing their suicide rates. But science and technology make us all richer, smarter, and more powerful. Therefore they also make us unhappier.

Objection 5: Man is blessed by having leisure time and close personal relationships. But science and technology have made these things rarer, not more abundant. Even though all of technology is a series of time-saving devices, each generation has *less* leisure time, more responsibilities, more worries, and more complaints than the previous generation. Also, relations between the generations become looser, not tighter, the more technology becomes abundant in their lives. Each generation of parents has less time for and less contact with their children as technology increases.

On the contrary, if men believe a thing is helpful to their happiness, they embrace it, and if they believe it is harmful to their happiness, they shun it. But man embraces rather than shuns science and technology. That is why we expend so much time, energy, money, and thought upon it. Therefore it must be more helpful than harmful, unless man is such a total fool that he deliberately cultivates the source of his misery.

I answer that scientific knowledge and technological power are ontological goods (though not moral goods). Man is made happy by knowledge and unhappy by ignorance. And he is made unhappy by weakness and frustration of his desires, and happy by the power to satisfy them.

Even though success in these two enterprises typically results in much harm and misery, because of human folly and sin, this corruption is a corruption of something that is by nature good. Cain's rock and Babel's tower were examples of technology, but so were Noah's ark and Solomon's temple.

Reply to Objection 1: Man is a mixture of wisdom and folly, selfishness and unselfishness, good and evil. ("There's a little good in the worst of us and a little bad in the best of us.") Whatever powers are given to him will augment both his good and his evil. Which will be greater cannot be foreseen or proved because it depends on his free choice. So these powers *can* work for good rather than evil, if we choose wisely.

Reply to Objection 2: The fragility of human good is offset by its resiliency and by man's power to learn from his mistakes. His instinct for good must be stronger than his penchant for evil because it is inherent in his nature, as his "default" position. Good is to the will as a magnet is to iron, truth to the mind, or light to the eye.

Reply to Objection 3: Even though some prefer wilderness to cities for vacations, most prefer cities to wilderness to live in. And no one wants to live in a time or place without medical technology, especially anesthetics!

Man is not happiest in places totally untouched by technology, for when he goes to such places he brings his technology with him (e.g. camping equipment). He is happy when technology serves him rather than dominates him. The ugliness and excesses of technology which he seeks to escape are misuses, and misuse does not take away proper use.

Reply to Objection 4: If the premise were true simply, men would seek to burn their money, destroy their intelligence, and deliberately cripple their powers. These things are ontologically good, not evil, and by nature contribute to our happiness, though any ontological good can also be misused for evil and unhappiness. Other things that increase wealth, such as effective economic policies, or that increase intelligence, such as education, or that increase power, such as exercise, are universally regarded as good by nature; and so science and technology should be regarded also.

Reply to Objection 5: This loss of time is another perversion and misuse, and is not inevitable. It is due not to the nature of technology itself but to man's unconscious sense of dread, fear, and guilt, which he seeks hide from himself by busyness, as Pascal explains in the *Pensées* (on "diversion"). Technology gives him opportunities to increase *or* decrease this busyness. For example, some use computers to simplify, and others to complicate, their lives.

Sample Question 4. Philosophy of education: Whether virtue can be taught?

Objection 1: It seems that it cannot, for as Plato points out in the *Meno*, if there are no teachers of a thing, it cannot be taught; and there are no teachers of virtue.

Objection 2: If virtue can be taught, there must be a method of teaching it. But there is no such method, for if there were, it would be universally used.

Objection 3: The greatest teachers of virtue (Jesus, Socrates, Buddha, Aristotle) always had disciples who did not learn virtue from them (Judas, Socrates' sons, Alexander the Great); therefore their teaching was unsuccessful. If even the greatest teachers of virtue were not successful in teaching virtue, no one can be.

On the contrary, all the greatest teachers in history have taught virtue: Moses, Solomon, Socrates, Plato, Aristotle, Lao Tzu, Confucius, Buddha, Jesus, Paul, Augustine, Zoroaster, Muhammad, Maimonides, Aquinas.

I answer that insofar as virtue depends on wisdom, it can be taught, for wisdom can be taught. It can also be self-taught, by experience and practice, leading to the cultivation of good habits (which are what virtues are). When we think of "teaching," we usually think of teaching *institutions,* but virtue is most effectively taught by personal example, for only the most wicked can resist the winsomeness of true virtue when actually practiced rather than just preached, especially the virtues of honesty, humility, wisdom, and charity.

Reply to Objection 1: There *are* teachers of virtue. They are called "parents." That is why most children are not the barbarians and sociopaths at twenty-two, that they are at two.

Reply to Objection 2: The method of teaching virtue is by example. Virtue, like vice, is contagious. The reason why this method of teaching is not used more successfully is because it is so demanding, not because it does not exist or is not known. There is indeed no impersonal, guaranteed, objective, and detached method for teaching virtue, as there is for teaching most other subjects. For virtue is not impersonal, guaranteed, objective, and detached but personal, freely chosen, and subjectively involved.

Reply to Objection 3: As pointed out above, this teaching's success is not automatic, impersonal, and guaranteed, but takes its effect only by free choice on the part of the student. Jesus, Socrates, and Buddha *were* successful, for if you were to subtract these three men from history, you would have a radically less wise and virtuous world.

Sample Question 5. Philosophy of language: Whether there is an ideal language?

Objection 1: It seems that there is not, for there is no historical or empirical evidence whatever of such a thing.

Objection 2: Language is a utilitarian human artifact, an invention. Such things do not exist in single ideal versions.

Objection 3: The idea of an ideal language is repudiated by the vast majority of philosophers, anthropologists, linguists, and historians today.

On the contrary, many ancient traditions speak of such a single ideal language: e.g. *Genesis* 11 and Plato's *Cratylus*.

I answer that (1) Language is not merely human but also divine: God "speaks." But whatever is divine is ideal. Therefore there is a language that is ideal.

(2) All will understand each other in Heaven. But this can be done only by a single language, or a single meta-language, as at Pentecost. Since nothing will be imperfect in Heaven, this will be a perfect language.

(3) Even now there is empirical evidence, though not proof, of such a single ideal language, in the fact that we recognize "that's the right word" for proper names, as in Tolkien. To judge that one word is more proper than another is to judge by a linguistic standard or ideal which must be known at least unconsciously.

(4) Moreover, the only work God gave man in paradise was to name things. If that is so, there must be a perfect language.

Reply to Objection 1: (1) That there is no empirical evidence for something so ancient does not prove that it never existed.

(2) The idea that there "is" such a language does not necessarily mean that it exists as a historical and empirically observable entity. It may be a Platonic Ideal.

(3) It may also have been an actual language spoken in Eden, or before Babel, but forgotten, or one that will be spoken in Heaven. None of these possibilities is refuted by lack of empirical evidence.

Reply to Objection 2: Language is more than a utilitarian artifact invented by man; language *makes* man man. As Heidegger says, "Words and language are not mere tools for the commerce of those who write and speak. Rather, it is in words and language that things first come into being and are." (*Introduction to Metaphysics*, ch. 1) "In the beginning was the Word." (*John* 1:1)

Reply to Objection 3: Modern scholars are not infallible, though some would like to think they are. They tend to practice a kind of common in-house authoritarianism. And as the more rational and critical thinkers of the Middle Ages knew, "the argument from (human) authority is the weakest of arguments."

Sample Questions 6. Philosophy of culture: Whether there is a "culture war"?*

Objection 1: It seems that there is not, for this term is used almost exclusively by "conservatives" to *create* a "culture war" and to divide the culture, while "liberals," who seek unity and peace, eschew needless talk of "war" which becomes a self-fulfilling prophecy. No liberal is ever called a "culture warrior."

---

*   (Note: In using "conservative" categories to defend the "conservative" answer to this question, I do not necessarily refer to *political* conservatism but to social and cultural, and especially moral, "conservatism" or traditionalism. The unusually polemical nature of this Article reflects the fact that the "culture war" is a *war*, literally a matter of life or death, not a safe, detached, polite, theoretical discussion.)

Objection 2: There is a culture war, but it is not specific to today. There have been many culture wars, e.g. the *Kulturkampf* under Bismarck, the French Revolution, the Bolshevik Revolution, and the Spanish Civil War. "Culture war" is the normal condition. The bland social peace and bourgeois consensus of the '40s and '50s in America was the exception, and should not be used as a standard. What conservatives call our "culture war," historians call normalcy.

On the contrary, ever since the term was coined in the early '90s by James Davison Hunter's book by that title, it has circulated like real, not counterfeit, coinage. People do not constantly and fruitfully use a term that designates a thing that does not exist.

I answer that when one segment of the population is permissive toward abortion, euthanasia, assisted suicide, the farming and utilization of human embryonic body parts, divorce, "recreational" but not procreational sex, and lethal homosexual activity (AIDS is fatal), and scorns the traditional "family values" of the other segment of the population that opposes all these things, we have a "culture war" that can fairly be called a war between a "culture of death," which denies the intrinsic value and inviolable sanctity of every human life, and a "culture of life" that affirms it.

Reply to Objection 1: (1) Society used to have a "conservative," i.e. traditional, consensus, especially in morality. It is "liberals" who have created division and a "culture war" by repudiating this consensus.

(2) Conservatives did not create the culture war. They just exposed it, like the little boy in "The Emperor's New Clothes." They are the prophets who say, "Woe to those who say 'Peace! Peace!' when there is no peace." (*Jeremiah* 6:14)

(3) The liberal attack on conservative "divisiveness" is an attack on the very "pluralism" and "dialog" liberals claim to favor. The claim is hypocritical. How many conservatives are there at Ivy League universities?

(4) The liberal demand for "consensus" is a demand for a consensus around liberal, not conservative, ideas. It is a demand for *surrender.*

Reply to Objection 2: Whether or not culture wars are the normal condition, there is still a culture war. And a single one. For at the heart of all four of the examples given of modern "culture wars" is the conflict between "Enlightenment" atheism, agnosticism, or secularism and traditional religion, especially Roman Catholicism. This "culture war" is indeed the normal condition in Western civilization, but only for the past 250 years. Before the "Enlightenment," there was a larger and longer "normalcy" and "consensus" in Western civilization called "Christendom."

In fact, for almost 4000 years, ever since God intervened "counterculturally" with Abraham, there has been a culture war. The Christian and Muslim versions of it are the continuations of the Jewish one.

Sample Question 7. Philosophy of sexuality: Whether sexuality is spiritual?*

Objection 1: It seems that it is not, for God and the angels are not biological beings, therefore they are not sexual beings. If sex were spiritual, it would exist not only in the human spirit but also in the divine and angelic spirits. But it does not.

Objection 2: If sex were spiritual, it would follow that souls as well as bodies were masculine or feminine, which is absurd. Only bodies, by nature, and social roles, by artifice, are masculine or feminine.

Objection 3: The idea that souls are masculine or feminine is simplistic monosexual stereotyping.

Objection 4: The idea that sex is spiritual and extends even into God, and the idea that God is "He" rather than "She," are correlative to each other. But this idea is the foundation for male chauvinism. As Mary Daly argues, "If God is male, then male is God."

---

*   See also Q. V, A 4.

On the contrary, all the mystics use sexual imagery, more than any other, for the most spiritual experience in human life.

I answer that the reason sex and religion are mankind's two most passionate relationships is that the one is an icon of the other. God created sex to image in the body the spiritual love of the Trinity and the love between Himself and mankind.

This is why sexual desires are so powerful: because we are designed not just for any kind of love but for ecstasy (*ek-stasis,* "standing-outside-oneself"), and if we do not achieve this supernaturally, its natural image is the closest approximation to it that we can find. As Aquinas says, "No man can live without joy. . . . That is why one deprived of spiritual joy goes over to carnal pleasures." (*ST* II-II, 35, 4 ad 2)

Reply to Objection 1: (1) The argument begs the question in assuming that sex is only biological, not spiritual, when it says that God and the angels are "not biological beings, *therefore not sexual* beings."

(2) Sex is not irrelevant to God, for He is always referred to as "He" and never as "She" throughout Jewish, Christian, and Muslim scriptures and history.

(3) In Christian theology, God is a Trinity of divine persons in an eternal love-relationship. Sex is the icon or image of this. But whatever is in an image pre-exists in a more eminent way in its original.

Reply to Objection 2: (1) The idea of masculine and feminine souls is not absurd, for it logically follows from the two premises of (a) the sexuality of the body, by nature, and (b) the psychosomatic unity, by which every pervasive, inherent, natural feature of the body has some equivalent, echo, or image in the soul and vice versa.

(2) If there were no such thing as masculine or feminine souls, there would be no such thing as people who feel like "a woman ('s soul) trapped in a man's body" or vice versa.

Reply to Objection 3: It is not simplistically monosexual because just as bodies, though masculine or feminine, possess secondary sexual characteristics of the other gender (e.g. both hormones), so with souls: in all souls there is "anima" (femininity) *and* "animus" (masculinity) in different mixtures. And it is not a (social, artificial) *stereotype* but a (natural, universal) *archetype*.

Reply to Objection 4: If anything it is *female* chauvinism, for all souls are feminine to God. He "impregnates" our spirit; we do not impregnate Him. And Mary Daly's "argument" is the fallacious conversion of an A proposition.

Sample Question 8. Philosophy of death:
Whether death is a friend?

Objection 1: It *seems that* everyone sees death as an enemy, and the Bible calls it our "last enemy" (*I Corinthians* 15:26). But an enemy is not a friend. Therefore death is not a friend.

Objection 2: Death is a friend only if it helps us. It helps us only if we survive it and live after death. Therefore for those who doubt life after death, death cannot be not a friend.

Objection 3: If death is a friend, we should cultivate it and invite it to come, for that is what we do to friends. But this would justify suicide.

On the contrary, St. Francis of Assisi speaks of "sister death." And Sheldon Vanauken speaks of it as "A Severe Mercy" in his remarkable autobiography by that title.

I answer that "A friend is the other half of myself" (Aristotle), and "A friend is a person with whom I may be sincere" (Emerson). Death is the other half of myself, for it is I myself who die, just as it is I myself who live. And death elicits the greatest sincerity and honesty, for few people are so foolish as to lie to themselves or to God, or even to others, as they are dying. Therefore death is a friend, though it is also an enemy, for it takes away what is most precious to us: life.

Reply to Objection 1: An enemy can also be a friend, e.g. a sparring partner or an opponent in chess. Death can be many different things to us, and we may choose different relationships to it, e.g. enemy, stranger, friend, mother, lover. (See the author's *Love Is Stronger than Death.*)

Reply to Objection 2: Even prescinding from life after death, death is a friend in giving us a frame for our life. Without it—e.g. if we discovered the secret of artificial immortality through genetic engineering—we would lose our identity, like a painting overflowing all frames and borders and becoming everything, and therefore nothing in particular.

Reply to Objection 3: The conclusion does not follow. Some friends are friends only if they come at the right time, e.g. matchmakers, menstrual periods, rainstorms, and undertakers.

Sample Question 9. Philosophy of law: Whether reform and deterrence should be the only motives for punishment?

Objection 1: It seems that they should be, for reforming the criminal and deterring others from doing criminal harm are both acts of charity that stem from goodwill and the desire to help others, the first toward the guilty and the second toward the innocent. The alternative to reform or deterrence as a motive for punishment is retribution. But retribution is vengeance and stems from hatred, ill will, and the desire to harm the criminal.

Objection 2: Justice is higher than injustice, but mercy and forgiveness are higher than justice. Reform and deterrence are motivated by mercy and forgiveness, while retribution is motivated by justice, at best, if not vengeance. Therefore reform and deterrence are higher motives for punishment than retribution.

Objection 3: Personal guilt or innocence is often uncertain and merely probable. Many trials are mistrials. It is better to forego punishing the guilty than to risk punishing the innocent. A concern for justice, which is the justification for retribution, is less important than a concern for persons and their welfare. Justice is made for man, not man for justice.

On the contrary, the roles of reform and deterrence are less clear and more variable than the role of justice in human law. The one universal consensus of all human law is that "the punishment must fit the crime." And this is the definition of just retribution.

I answer that (1) Reform and deterrence are future possibilities that are not guaranteed but only hoped for, while justice can be enacted with certainty in the present. Therefore it must come first.

(2) Reform is rarely accomplished by punishment, especially incarceration. But justice always is, if the punishment is just. And this can be known, as reform cannot.

(3) Deterrence is accomplished even more effectively by terror than by just punishment. The only reason terror is not preferable is that it is unjust. Thus we all recognize, implicitly, that justice, not deterrence, must be the justification for punishment.

(4) Punishing for deterrence assumes a knowledge of the future that we do not have, except very imperfectly. It is "playing God." And if it is the only motive, it is also an example of "the end justifies the means."

Reply to Objection 1: Retribution is not the same thing as vengeance. Vengeance is personal ill will, while retribution is impersonal justice.

Reply to Objection 2: When punishment is motivated by the desire for justice, there is no reason it cannot also be motivated by the desire for reform and deterrence. But when it is motivated by the desire for reform or deterrence only, without justice, then this is not superior to justice but inferior, for justice is the necessary minimum, or beginning, as a foundation is the necessary beginning of a building without which the higher stories do not stand. As shown below, punishment is grossly immoral, no matter what motivates it, if it is not justly deserved.

Reply to Objection 3: (1) The percentage of cases in which guilt or innocence is wrongly decided is a very small minority of cases. If this were not so, the argument given would be an argument for abandoning the justice system entirely.

(2) Assuming that we can, in some analogical way, quantify injustices, it could be argued that even if the injustice of punishing one innocent person is greater than that of not punishing one guilty person, the injustice of not punishing 100 who are *certainly* guilty is greater than that of punishing one who *may* be innocent.

(3) The logical conclusion of the objector's argument is not that reform or deterrence should motivate punishment, but that no punishment should ever be given at all.

(4) Human welfare is *not* served by foregoing deserved punishment, because criminals will then be free to harm the innocent again. It is true that justice is made for man, not man for justice, but in order to serve man, justice must be served.

Sample Question 10. Philosophy of humor: Whether human life is a great joke?

Objection 1: It *seems that* all the great philosophies of life are serious. To call life a joke is to trivialize it. This is especially insulting to God, for all of life is part of Divine Providence.

Objection 2: To call life a joke is to insult the memory of all those who have suffered, for instance the victims of the Holocaust.

On the contrary, the two wisest peoples in the world are also the world's greatest comedians: the Jews and the Irish. They are also people who cannot get rid of the divine haunting, try as they may. And they are also the people who have suffered the most, so they have the most right to laugh.

I answer that human life has been described under various images: a bowl of cherries, a war, a bitch, a beach, a beautiful thing, Alice's Restaurant, a handbasket to Hell, and a narrow road to Heaven.

None of these images communicates the irony and the mystery as well as the image of a joke.

Furthermore, if there is a joke, there is a jokester. This image thus is not impious but pious, for it leads the mind immediately to God and divine providence.

To call divine providence a joke is not to deny that it is serious. Many jokes are very serious indeed, such as sex. (Not just jokes *about* sex but *sex*!)

God created the ostrich, the platypus, and the gooney bird. They did not happen simply by accident, for nothing does. To deny that God is the greatest of all comedians is an insult to the divine imagination.

The greatest joke of all time is the Incarnation. Only the devil did not laugh with glee at this, as the angels did. Which will you side with?

To deny that God makes jokes with creation is to reveal one's own boorish thick-headedness. For jokes "take" only when people "get" them. Thus they are tests, and laughter passes God's test.

Reply to Objection 1: Seriousness and humor are not exclusive. At the height of both, they converge, as in the Creation and the Incarnation, both of which had the angels singing with awe and laughter forever. The reverberations of their laughter are what makes all the waves of energy in the universe. That is why the Theory of Everything has never been found: it has neglected the angels. (The fact that the reader is unsure whether the writer is serious or not here is evidence that seriousness and humor are not exclusive.)

If divine providence is both humorous and serious, then it is not insulting to God to laugh at Divine Providence as well as taking it seriously; rather, it is to appreciate His work and His intent completely.

Reply to Objection 2: It was humor that enabled the Jews to survive the Holocaust. And it is humor that enables parents to survive children, women to survive men, citizens to survive governments, and philosophy students to survive philosophy professors.

Appendix:
Fifteen Recommended Philosophical Classics

These books are fifteen deep and useful pools to practice philosophical swimming in. They all argue both clearly and profoundly. They are not all good and true, but most of them are, and they are all beautiful.

1. Plato, *Republic* (also *Gorgias*)
2. Aristotle, *Nicomachean Ethics* (also *Metaphysics*)
3. Augustine, *Confessions* (Sheed translation)
4. Boethius, *The Consolation of Philosophy* (Green translation)
5. Anselm, *Proslogion*
6. Aquinas, *Summa Theologiae* (also *Summa Contra Gentiles*)
7. Descartes, *Meditations* (also *Discourse on Method*)
8. Pascal, *Pensées*
9. Hume, *Enquiry Concerning Human Understanding*
10. Kant, *Groundwork for the Metaphysics of Morals*
11. Kierkegaard, *A Kierkegaard Anthology* (ed. by Robert Bretall)
12. Sartre, *Existentialism and Human Emotions*
13. Heidegger, *Introduction to Metaphysics*, especially ch. 1, "The Fundamental Question"
14. G.K. Chesterton, *Orthodoxy* (an utterly unorthodox, unclassifiable book)
15. Kierkegaard, *Concluding Unscientific Postscript*

Meta-Philosophical Evaluation of All the Above

straw

Index

Index of Biblical Citations